Inflection Journal
Volume 11 - Regeneration
December 2024

Inflection Journal is published annually by the Melbourne School of Design at the University of Melbourne and Melbourne Books.

Editors: Abbey O'Regan, Alexandra Khomenko and Jarel Cheah.

Deputy Editors: Anna Kilpatrick, Rhea Nagi, Mingxun (Gary) Ma, Hallie Vermeend and Dana Jepsen.

Academic Advisor: Dr. AnnMarie Brennan

Academic Advisory Board: Dr. AnnMarie Brennan.

Inflection acknowledges the Traditional Custodians of the land on which we work and are published, the Wurundjeri People of the Kulin Nation. We pay our respects to their Elders past, present and emerging, and acknowledge First Nations people as our first storytellers and regenerators of Country.

The editors would like to thank all those involved in the production of this journal for their generous assistance and support.

Special thanks are due to AnnMarie Brennan, whose continual support, guidance and encouragement has been invaluable.

For editorial enquiries contact:
editorial@inflectionjournal.com

For sales enquiries contact:
info@melbournebooks.com.au

inflectionjournal.com
facebook.com/inflectionjournal
instagram.com/inflectionjournal

ISSN 2199-8094

ISBN 9781922779342

Melbourne Books
Level 9, 100 Collins Street,
Melbourne, VIC 3000,
Australia
www.melbournebooks.com.au
info@melbournebooks.com.au

Cover image:
Rock of Ages #1 Active Section, E.L. Smith Quarry, Barre, Vermont, USA © Edward Burtynsky, courtesy Flowers Gallery, Hong Kong / Sundaram Tagore Galleries, Singapore, 1991. https://www.edwardburtynsky.com/

Inside cover:
The Quarry © Ivan Masic / These Are The Projects We Do Together, 2023.

MELBOURNE BOOKS

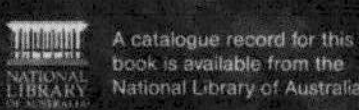

CONTRIBUTORS

Andre Bonnice

Andre is an architect and director of Simulaa, a Naarm-based architecture practice and Lecturer and Creative Practitioner at the Melbourne School of Design at the University of Melbourne.

Andrea Crudeli

Andrea obtained a Ph.D. in Architectural Composition at the University of Pisa, where he currently teaches. Formerly a Visiting Scholar at the Canadian Centre for Architecture in Montréal, he is a member of the Polit(t)ico Research Lab group at the University of Pisa. Having grown professionally in Paris, Tokyo, and Seattle, he is a founding partner of the *Dedalo Building Lab*, an architecture studio based in Florence.

Anna Jankovic

Anna Jankovic is an architect and director of Simulaa, a Naarm-based architecture practice and Associate Lecturer at RMIT Architecture.

Architect Brew Koch

Architect Brew Koch was first founded in 2004 by Dr Peter Brew and Simone Koch. They recognise that the value in architecture is not in the final form but as a catalyst for realising the success of the place or community. It would be better understood as an armature for local relationships to thrive. It might not be noticed at all. For them, architecture is not a singular vision and is never static but is always available.

Ariani Anwar

Ariani is a Melbourne-based architect and a founding editor of *Inflection* journal. She is an Associate at Australian architecture firm, Wardle and a design educator at the University of Melbourne. She was recently a Property Council of Australia Future Leader Finalist, and her Master of Architecture Thesis received a Graduate Prize awarded annually by Victorian Chapter of the Australian Intitute of Architects. She has an interest in how design can benefit communities and has extensive experience in the design and delivery of cultural and educational buildings.

atelier local

atelier local is an architecture studio founded by João Paupério and Maria Rebelo in Valongon, Portugal. Between 2014 and 2018 they have worked together for BAUKUNST, in Brussels. Maria has worked for Atelier da Bouça (Tiago Correia & Filipa Guerreiro, arquitetos) between 2019 and 2021. Since 2020, João is a Ph.D. candidate and researcher at the Centre for Studies in Architecture and Urbanism (CEAU-FAUP).

Claire Miller

Claire completed her Master of Architecture and a Ph.D. in urban studies at the University of Melbourne, focusing on controlling security measures in public space; and has extensive experience teaching history and theory of architecture, urbanism and planning. Claire is a heritage consultant with 10 years' experience at Trethowan Architecture working with a wide range of historic places and precincts across Victoria. She is interested in the role of historic places in creating shared urban and social identities.

Clara Reutter

Clara is an architect with a Master of Architecture from the Pontifical Catholic University of Chile. She developed landscape design studies focusing on recovering industrial landscapes at RMIT University and the University of Melbourne.

Claudio Torres

Claudio is an architect graduate from the Pontifical Catholic University of Chile. He obtained his Master of Environment in 2022 from the University of Melbourne. From 2013-2018, he collaborated in architectural design studios such as Teodoro Fernandez, Smiljan Radic, and Sean Godsell. He is currently involved in collective housing design workshops at the University of Melbourne, where he is starting his doctoral studies.

Dylan Newell

Dylan is a Ph.D. candidate at the Melbourne School of Design at the University of Melbourne, who is passionate about tackling the environmental emergency through an equitable transition. His PhD is critically testing a method of architectural creative practice that uses a framework of degrowth to examine the potential for transformative adaption of local built environments through care, repair, re-use, and maintenance, with a particular focus on the 2022 Maribyrnong River floods.

Emile Straub

Emile is an architect who graduated from the Pontifical Catholic University of Chile in 2016. He collaborated in Cecilia Puga's studio in Santiago, Chile, from 2013 to 2016. Since then, he has been working as an independent architect and photographer.

Eva Prats

Eva Prats is an architect and principal of Flores & Prats, an office based in Barcelona dedicated to the confrontation of theory and academic practice with design and construction activity. Eva is Full Professor at the Accademia di Architettura di Mendrisio and Associate Professor at Escola Tècnica Superior d'Arquitectura in Barcelona, and has been Guest Professor at ETH Zurich from 2019-2021.

Francesco Stassi

Francesco is a Lecturer and Creative Practitioner in the Faculty of Architecture, Building and Planning at the University of Melbourne and a registered architect in Italy and Rwanda, with extensive experience in socially engaged architecture in East Africa. He is the Director and Partner of the architectural firm ASA Studio - Active Social Architecture.

Georg Hubmann

Georg is a researcher and project coordinator at Bauhaus Earth, focusing on circularity in architecture and urban design. His work addresses climate change, socio-environmental configurations, and regenerative construction practices. Georg works in the fields of urban political ecology, urban metabolism, and transformation research. He is currently leading the ReBuilt project, which aims to demonstrate how the novel concept of a regenerative built environment can be put into practice.

Harriet Mena Hill
Harriet is an artist who has lived and worked in Walworth, South-London since 1984. Her art practice has been highly informed by her community education and outreach work she has undertaken in the area where she lives, teaching in schools, youth clubs and community centers for the past 20 years.

Isabella Chow
Isabella holds a Bachelor of Environments (Architecture) and a Master of Urban and Cultural Heritage from the University of Melbourne. She currently works as a heritage consultant at Trethowan Architecture and has a strong interest in the role of the historic built environment in our transition to more environmentally and socially sustainable forms of designing and building.

Jack Rogers
Jack is a graduate of architecture, finishing his postgraduate studies in 2022 at the University of Sydney. During his time at University, he honed his interest in the development of high-density housing in Australia over the last century, with particular focus on its evolution in Sydney. He has a keen interest in how the urban intersects with the financial world, and in how this is reflected in policy and built forms alike. He currently works in large practice, mostly in the multi-residential sphere.

Janice Yeung
Janice holds a Master of Architecture and a Master of Urban and Cultural Heritage. Currently specialising as a heritage consultant at Trethowan Architecture, she is interested in issues surrounding East Asian architectural history, post-colonial architecture, migrant heritage, and cultural relativism.

Jarrod Haberfield
Jarrod is an architect, educator and scholar with an abiding interest in the relationship between architecture and museology. The potency of this relationship is at the heart of his doctoral research into art collectors' houses, and the emergence of the house-museum as a hybrid architectural type, which he is completing at the University of Melbourne.

Katie Skillington
Katie is an architect and Lecturer in Architectural Design in the Faculty of Architecture, Building and Planning at the University of Melbourne. Her research lies at the nexus of architectural design and sustainability, with a specific focus on the environmental consequences of dematerialisation, circularity, and retrofit. Driven by her passion for improving the sustainability of our built environment and interest in Japan, in 2017 she completed a Master of Sustainability Science at the University of Tokyo, Japan as a Monbukagakusho (MEXT) scholar.

Matthew Mindrup
Matthew is a Sydney-based architect and architectural-historian at the University of Sydney whose research explores the role of materials and physical models for the conception and construction of architecture. In 2007 he completed a Ph.D. on the physical and metaphysical coalition of two models created by amateur Merz architect Kurt Schwitters during the 1920s. He lectures broadly and publicly on this subject and those of his other published works.

Nancy Yao Ji
Nancy is a Lecturer in Architectural Design in the Faculty of Architecture, Building and Planning at the University of Melbourne, from where she graduated with a Master of Architecture. After working for architecture firms in Melbourne and Tokyo, Nancy moved to Japan for doctoral studies at Keio University on a Monbukagakusho (MEXT) scholarship where she conducted fieldwork on architectural renovation and rural revitalisation. She continues to research contemporary design practices in the Asia-Pacific region and community engagement through architectural design.

Dr Olivier Cotsaftis
Olivier is a post-disciplinary researcher-practitioner exploring pathways towards regenerative and more-than-human urban futures. At RMIT University, his work focuses on unlocking practical and scalable potentials for sustainable urban development, specifically in the areas of biomaterials and climate adaptation of the public place. He was a design lead at *Fjord Design and Innovation* and the founder of future ensemble studio. Ollie is also an editorial board member for *Research Methods: Biotechnology Design.*

Open Studio
Open Studio is a Melbourne-based architectural practice established by Britta Klingspohn and Heribert Alucha in 2005. Many Open Studio projects are located in heritage sensitive areas or fragile natural environments where a considered analysis of the context and site is critical. Some key themes permeate the work. These include simplicity, natural light, a sense of place and materiality, in pursuit of a quiet and understated architecture that creates an ideal backdrop for the rituals of everyday life.

Paul Walker
Paul is a Professor of Architecture at the University of Melbourne where he teaches architectural history, theory and design. He has written widely about modern and contemporary architecture in Australia and New Zealand. He is the editor and lead author of *John Andrews: Architect of Uncommon Sense* (Harvard Design Press, 2023). His work has appeared in the *Journal of Architecture, Fabrications, CLOG, Architecture Australia,* and *Volume.*

Rafael Luna
Rafael is the co-founder of the architecture firm PRAUD, a Senior Lecturer at the University of Technology Sydney, and the director of the Infra-Architecture Lab. He received a Master of Architecture from the Massachusetts Institute of Technology in 2010 and his Ph.D. in Architecture, which he completed in 2022, focused on Infra-architectural typologies as urban models from L'Accademia di architettura dell'Università della Svizzera italiana, Mendrisio, Switzerland.

Ricardo Flores
Ricardo is an architect from the University of Buenos Aires and has a Master in Urban Design and Doctor of Architecture. He established Flores & Prats Architects with Eva Prats in 1998. The practice has worked throughout Europe on projects of adaptive reuse, social housing and urban public spaces. Flores & Prats won the Grand Award at the Royal Academy of Arts in 2009 and has been invited to the previous five editions of La Biennale di Venezia.

Secil Taskoparan Stassi
Secil is an architect, educator and a Ph.D. candidate in the Department of Architecture and Urban Design at Monash University. Her academic and professional career spans six countries, including Turkey, the US, Rwanda, and Finland, where she practised and taught architecture. Her practice-based doctoral research explores the socio-spatial connections in modified riverfronts of Indonesia and Malaysia through various use of drawing and ethnographic methods.

Tino Imsirovic
Tino is an urban and regional designer and researcher at Bauhaus Earth, working in the fields of climate-oriented urbanisation processes and participative planning approaches. He is currently researching value chains of nature-based building materials and regenerative transformation pathways of Bhutan's construction sector.

Yuji Harada
Yuji graduated in Architecture in 2008 from Yokohama National University; he obtained his Master's in Architecture in 2011 from the same university. He worked in Smiljan Radic's studio in Santiago, Chile, from 2012-2017.

CONTENTS

FROM THE GROUND UP

EDITORIAL

Abbey O'Regan, Alexandra Khomenko and Jarel Cheah

Inflection acknowledges the Traditional Custodians of the land on which we work and are published, the Wurundjeri People of the Kulin Nation. We pay our respects to their Elders past, present and emerging, and acknowledge First Nations people as our first storytellers and regenerators of Country.

Our cities and built environment exist within a narrative of growth. But they also exist within a narrative that is constantly rewriting itself in a context of economic changes, resource shortages and ongoing consequences of the climate crisis. The construction industry consumes half of all raw materials extracted annually by humans.[1] Moreover, the sector accounts for nearly 40% of the global CO_2 footprint.[2] Statistics like these are well-cited and widely circulated, and whilst there is strong incentive to explore alternative futures, such proposals are quickly dismissed for being too utopian, too naïve, or simply unrealistic.

The concept of sustainable development has emerged as the universal consensus on how to improve quality of life whilst reducing our environmental impact, yet it has been criticised for continuing to address these concerns within the parameters of economic growth.[3] Simultaneously, there is growing scepticism for the shallow or cynical deployment of faux-ecological imagery and practice, finding its definition in rhetoric through the term greenwashing.[4] Our discourse is beginning to get comfortable with calling in to question the dominant perspectives of growth and the existing frameworks which hinder sustainable authenticity. *Inflection* positions Vol. 11 as a collection of pragmatic discussions as to what that questioning could look like, focusing on architectural regeneration thoroughly and carefully, beyond mere speculation, from the ground up.

In biological terms, regeneration denotes the ability to renew, restore, or grow tissues in organisms and ecosystems in harmony with natural fluctuations. Applied to architecture, it necessitates similar reciprocities that address the renewal of space, function, and resources. Understandably, as a concept that straddles the ecological world and the built environment, there is no singular approach to regenerative architecture. Rather, it emerges as a whole-scale practice, a framework, an overarching model. One that does not operate in isolation. The diverse paradigms that arise from this field, including but not limited to, biocentric design, regenerative building strategies, and (re)construction processes, must also delve into deeper regenerative concepts of place that consider the cultural, social and historical aspects of a given context and the tectonic implications of this approach. All while being mindful of the more sinister tendency to conflate 'regeneration' with projects of large-scale development that undermine a wider discourse that appeals for us to produce (and do) less.

Our cover features a photograph of an active quarry in Vermont, USA. It pieces together the lineage of the construction industry's extractive processes by taking us to the material source. What is at first glance a scarred landscape becomes poetic evidence of resources spent; nature transformed as well as realised. In Victoria, Australia, legislation states that rehabilitation is the final stage of quarrying works.[5] Typically, such sites are remediated to a 'rehabilitated' state through either flooding or filling. But the return of extensive disturbed land to a stable, productive and self-sustaining condition takes a long period in time.[6] Moreover, this conventional approach adopts a tabula rasa condition that can erase a site's complex history of occupation; an underlying social and cultural lens that should be firmly acknowledged as part of the regenerative process.

Flipping between the front cover and its internal counterpart reveals another layer to the regenerative story. We are left to fill in the gaps where human and the machine retreat, and the slow process of regeneration can finally begin. Since 2016, Melbourne-based research practice *These Are The Projects We Do Together*, who's work leans towards the self-confessed 'problematic' site, have been working on this post-extractive landscape as a project of care. The disused Arkose Sandstone quarry in Victoria's Otway Ranges, within the traditional lands of the Gadubanud People, establishes itself for a range of creative regenerative practices. Here, rehabilitation is treated not as an end goal but rather an ongoing process of learning. The photograph is best read across both the front to the back internal covers; doing so begins to reveal the sheer sense of scale of the 86,000 square metres undergoing rehabilitation.

A small white shed is perched at the ridge of the quarry. Exhibition materials from the National Gallery of Victoria's many installations are stockpiled on the site, where they find new use as a material bank for the campgrounds that are being built to accommodate the quarry's research and education communities.[7] In a similar acknowledgement of the necessities of replenishment, it is an ongoing project that leverages a context fuelled by the fundamentals of maintenance and care, to further investigate regenerative processes on the construction level. With reference to the quarry's long history of providing crushed sandstone for road and rail building, there is scope here to consider material applications in a post-extractive and ecologically conscious context.

Much like how the imagery of the quarries draw reference to a number of regenerative approaches, the pieces that follow similarly glide between these many interpretations of the term regeneration. Rather than operating in isolation, they piece together to reveal a variety of approaches that exist within the gaps of existing policy, infrastructure, and traditional approaches. It is at these critical junctures, we can begin to reframe the discussion from one of binaries of the natural and the built, to one of overlapping interests.

Background image: The Quarry © Ivan Masic /These Are The Projects We Do Together, 2019.

01 BIO Intelligence Service "Service Contract on Management of Construction and Demolition Waste - SR1: Final Report Task 2," *European Commission*, February 2011.

02 Ibid.

03 "The 17 Goals," United Nations Department of Economic and Social Affairs: Sustainable Development, effective 1 January 2016, https://sdgs. un.org/goals. See also Benjamin Wells, "An Architecture of Degrowth," originally published on *Arc-space*, February 2018, https://benjaminwells.eu/an-architecture-of-degrowth.

04 Bobby Jewell, "Architecture is drowning in greenwash," *Architect's Journal*, 15 July 2022, https://www.architectsjournal.co.uk/news/opinion/architecture-is-drowning-in-greenwash.

05 Mineral Resources (Sustainable Development) Act 1990 (Victoria) Part 7C S.

06 J.C. Hannan, *A Handbook for the Coal Mining Industry* (New South Wales Coal Association, 1984).

07 *These Are The Projects We Do Together*, in conversation with the authors, 2 August 2024.

TIME-BASED ARCHITECTURE: WHAT HAPPENS TO THE SOIL THAT WASHES AWAY?

Andre Bonnice and Anna Jankovic

Levi Walter Yaggy, *Geological Chart*, Published by C.F, 1893.

In the context of the schemes, programs, agreements and 'pledges' that have been established in an effort to reduce our reliance on high-carbon materials and construction processes and to shift the prevailing paradigms of the build-environment the discipline of architecture needs to reckon with the critical path of transitioning from traditional linear building models to *circular* modes of practise.

Despite the good intentions behind initiatives to be 'carbon neutral,' 'net-zero' and the many measurement schemes, standards and codes that have (and haven't) been put in place to steer current practises, the building and construction industry still generates around one-third of the 67 million tonnes of waste generated in Australia each year and accounts for 37% of anthropogenic energy and process-related $C0_2$ emissions.[1] Nothing within the industry can be claimed to be neutral (with respect to carbon) or indeed regenerative.

Alternative materials and methods of production that sit outside of the current standards of our industry are often met with risk-averse decision-making and equally normative short-termist economic thinking. Risk is often misassigned to the viability and implementation of 'non-standard' practices, even in cases where these have been effectively applied in other contexts. Similarly, cost-benefit analysis methods consistently fall short on evaluating and accounting for long-term benefits which can be difficult to define (intangible), and are omitted altogether from consideration. The built environment that has resulted from this paradigm, is a one-way entropic flow of energy and materials; from production, to consumption, to waste; along a timeline that is becoming increasingly foreshortened. This downturn into short-termist and 'wasteful' thinking is impacting our contemporary society in numerous ways — consequently with increasing harm to our own health and our relationship to the biosphere.

How might we shift our thinking, practises and behaviours to embrace a regenerative long-term perspective? Could redefining our relationship to time by becoming a 'time-literate' society, provide meaningful change to design thinking and to the broader built environment sector?

Above: University of Melbourne Dookie Campus, Drone Photography, 2024, Dookie. Photography by Andre Bonnice & Lachlan Welsh.

Below: Murray to Mountain Rail Trail, 2023, North Eastern Victoria. Photography by Tope Adesina.

Outside a few specialised disciplines most of us do not consider our relationship to vast timescales to be of much significance. Simultaneously, our lives are ever more increasingly defined by smaller and smaller fractions of time. In a world reliant on growth and increasing productivity, our time is measured and organised to the second to maximise our day and ensure things run 'on time.' For geologists, the study of Earth's history spanning billions of years allows them to understand planetary-scale behaviours.

By examining processes that operate over vast timescales, such as plate tectonics, erosion and climate change, they gain tangible insights into how Earth's systems have evolved and how to predict change in the future. A long-term perspective helps contextualise short-term fluctuations and events, providing a more comprehensive understanding of Earth's dynamics.

In her book *Timefulness*, geologist Marcia Bjornerud describes the Earth as a 4.5 billion-year-old closed-loop regenerative system and that life on Earth developed a circular logic quite early on.[2]

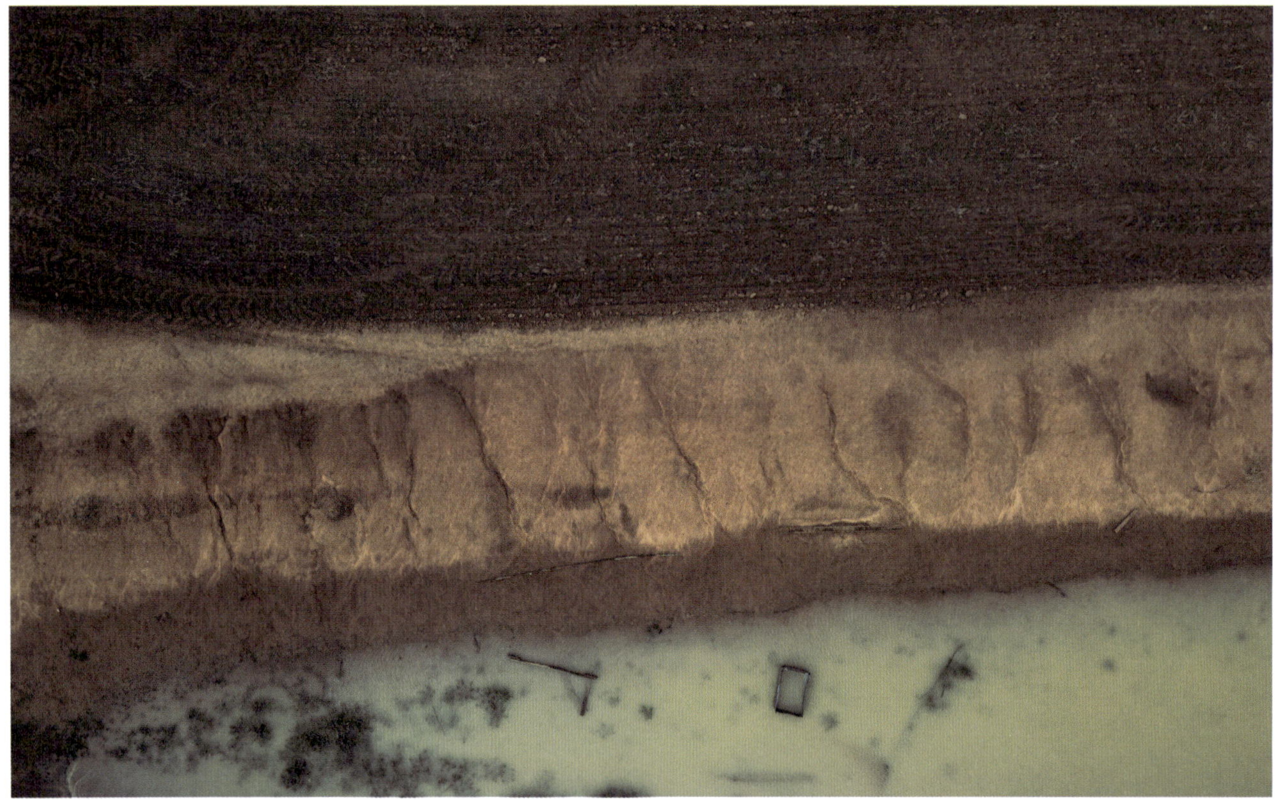

Bjornerud explains that the Earth has not acquired any significant new mass since it formed 4.5 billion years ago and yet the median age of continental crust is only about 500 million years, the oldest ocean crust is 170 million years old and ocean water is refreshed every few millennia. Over billions of years “everything on the planet is incessantly recycled, reforged, and restocked.”[3] Despite this slow constantly moving cycle, we commonly perceive the Earth's geomorphology as a stable unchanging landmass.

In 1788, Scottish physician, farmer and naturalist John Hutton published his *Theory of the Earth*, positing that the Earth was not static, or young, but ‘infinitely’ old and that geological processes operated in a continuous cycle of uplift, subduction and erosion, over immense timescales. This realisation came about from 25 years of work, following Hutton’s concern for the large amounts of soil washing away from his fields into the ocean each year. From these observations he hypothesised that sometime in the future all land mass would be eroded to sea-level resulting in an uninhabitable planet. Consequently he actively sought to find evidence of some compensatory process of rejuvenation, which he fortuitously encountered at Siccar Point, on Scotland's East coast. There Hutton observed two sequences of rocks; one older, nearly vertical strata, overlaid by another, younger almost horizontal strata. He interpreted this as evidence of an ancient mountain belt eroded to sea level, with new rocks deposited over the top. This led Hutton to conclude that the Earth had undergone countless cycles of uplift and erosion, envisioning an old and continuously regenerating Earth and verifying his concept of a vast and sublime geological time.[4]

Above: University of Melbourne Dookie Campus, Drone Photography, 2024, Dookie. Photography by Andre Bonnice & Lachlan Welsh.

Above: University of Melbourne Dookie Campus, Drone Photography, 2024, Dookie. Photography by Andre Bonnice & Lachlan Welsh.

Below: University of Melbourne Dookie Campus, Drone Photography, 2024, Dookie. Photography by Andre Bonnice & Lachlan Welsh.

Although lost from the collective consciousness; an understanding and appreciation of these vast and slow forces can begin at the small scale. Bioregionalism, a re-emergent eco-philosophy originating in the 1970s, was founded on a critique that governments are too big, too centralised and too unresponsive to act on ecological issues.[5] In response, a Bioregional approach prioritises intensive observation of small-scale environments to reveal broader ecological and systemic patterns as a way of identifying with a place and weaving oneself into a region through careful observation of and responsibility to the local ecosystem. A Bioregional view recognises the material reality that precedes humans and considers the complex interconnected relations between ecological actors. Viewing our context through this lens becomes an important way to understand the forces and timescales we operate within.

Critical to this thinking, is the recognition that bioregions are defined through natural features such as landforms, watersheds, soil types, climate zones and the regions of flora and fauna. These natural divisions often do not align with municipal borders, which arbitrarily divide ecosystems and bioregions. Early Bioregional advocate Peter Berg stated that "When people ask where I'm from I say that I am from the confluence of the Sacramento River and San Joaquin River and San Francisco Bay, of the Shasta bioregion, of the North Pacific Rim of the Pacific Basin of the Planet Earth," a decidedly interconnected relational view which highlights how our current language and conventions of place are detached from the natural and geological systems that make up our environment.[6]

As architects and designers, we can start by evaluating the places where we work, through geological and climate conditions; flora and fauna; culture and social histories; and existing and latent local industries. The practice of Atelier LUMA, established in 2017 by *LUMA Arles,* located within the Parc des Ateliers campus, offers a blueprint for how a Bioregional focus can lead to new forms of design practise. The programs and activities of Atelier LUMA are centred in the Camargue bioregion- the unruly marshes between the city of Arles and the Mediterranean Sea. As Jan Boelen, artistic director of Atelier LUMA explains, "We began Atelier LUMA by mapping the territory of Arles and the Camargue, identifying layers of resources and imagining ways they could be reassembled or reconfigured to contribute to its adaptation to changing environmental and social conditions."[7] To identify underutilised and undervalued resources, the first phase of the project involved meticulous research, through immersion in the cultural and environmental ecosystems of the region.

Their approach centres on developing natural, non-extractivist and renewable resources and materials from agricultural byproducts, algae and industrial waste. Algae is abundant in the Camargue region and can be processed into various products, such as bioplastics, textiles and building materials, offering a biodegradable and regenerative alternative to conventional petrochemical plastics. A survey of existing agricultural processes within the region revealed by-products, such as sunflower stems, that Atelier Luma have subsequently utilised to create composite biomaterials for items such as acoustic panelling.

Time-Based Architecture: What happens to the soil that washes away?

Opposite: University of Melbourne Dookie Campus, Drone Photography, 2024, Dookie. Photography by Andre Bonnice & Lachlan Welsh.

Above: Tarrawingee Station, Murray to Mountain Rail Trail, 2023, North Eastern Victoria.

This localised approach reduces dependency on distant supply chains, fostering sufficiency and direct relationships between production and consumption that enable transparency and accountability.

As artist and writer Jenny Odell argues, Bioregionalism practises offer opportunities for reimagining social and economic systems in ways that are more attuned to ecological principles.[8] By focusing on a region's unique ecological features and resources, individuals and communities can foster a deeper appreciation and stewardship of their local environment. In biomaterial production, each material and its processes become a new set of relationships that help foster communities. Through local production and exchange, Bioregional approaches can help reduce reliance on global networks and minimise environmental impacts. Odell emphasises ecological and cultural connections within bioregions that can forge viable long-term outcomes.

In contrast, current material paradigms and anthropocentric thinking prioritises the places we live over the unknown and distant places that support our livelihoods. Australian philosopher Val Plumwood described these as *shadow places* that “provide our material and ecological support, most of which, in a global market, are likely to elude our knowledge and and responsibility."[9] Whilst bioregional principles would feasibly reduce our reliance on *shadow places* for the built environment, there are other technologies and infrastructures we rely on that make it difficult to altogether break from global networks.

To enable the transition to renewables and the electrification of our energy supply and grid, there will be an ever-increasing reliance on the storage of energy (utilising lithium-batteries) to help mediate the intermittency of wind and solar energy generation. But the extraction processes for mining lithium, often results in water and soil contamination and damaging ecosystems. This by-and-large disproportionately impacts vulnerable communities in developing nations. It is undeniable that there will be growing demand for minerals and other resources that enable the implementation of renewable energy production (wind and solar), highlighting the pertinent question of how industrial actors and governance frameworks can (if at all) adequately manage the extraction and distribution of these resources, with collective benefit and a long-term view at the forefront of decision making?

As Plumwood argues, if we are to perceive a ‘separation’ from these places of production and consumption, it means that the environmental degradation and social injustices occurring in these areas remain largely invisible and outside the realm of our personal and collective responsibility. It is this detachment that allows for the continued exploitation and neglect of these regions, perpetuating unsustainable practices and failing to address the broader ecological impacts of our behaviours of consumption. For the building and construction industry, this demands new forms of material production that are not reliant on global networks of untethered extraction and exploitation.

Driven by an inherently singular linear concept of time, the building and construction industry places little value on a material's capacity to be recycled and reforged. Instead, materials are argued for on the basis of their ‘longevity,’ typically between 40 - 60 years which, in the context of Earth’s history, is still incredibly short. Building codes and standards put in place to protect users from hazards such as fire often regulate the use of toxic fire-retardant chemicals that can pose serious health risks.[10] These same petrochemicals utilised in achieving ‘safe’ standards often eliminate the capacity of materials to be reused, or to break down naturally. In contrast, natural materials are considered ‘combustible’ and therefore unsuitable for many building applications even if they achieve successful fire testing. The industry places very little value on a material's cyclical capacity over time.

Above: Nature Kit Map, Yackandandah Station, Murray to Mountain Rail Trail, 2023, North Eastern Victoria.

Opposite: Yackandandah Station, Murray to Mountain Rail Trail, Murray to Mountain Rail Trail, 2023, North Eastern Victoria.

In our practice, we have been exploring ways to implement a Bioregional lens across two recent projects. One is centred on a systems-based analysis of the University of Melbourne's agricultural campus in Dookie, Victoria; a 2,440-hectare landholding for the Faculty of Science and Agriculture that hosts students, researchers, teaching staff, merino sheep, an orchard, a robotic dairy farm, a winery, GM research and a bush reserve. With Atelier LUMA's practice as a guide–through a series of Architecture design studios at the Melbourne School of Design, we have begun to survey and analyse the existing landholding, livestock, production and waste streams to propose possible opportunities for creating on-campus material systems, mapping ways to transform existing resources on campus and the surrounding region into low-carbon building products.

The campus is a confluence of agricultural production, research and conservation, making it a particularly interesting test case at a manageable scale.

Situated within the campus is a vast array of demolition material and soft plastics waste from temporary agricultural storage, alongside by-products like organic wheat husks, grape stems, threshing waste and cow manure, that all have the potential to be repurposed into low-carbon building material. Currently, fava beans are used as a cover crop due to their high nitrogen-fixing rate and large deep roots that help break up heavy compacted soil. Hemp (cannabis sativa) also replenishes soil health and when used as a cover crop produces vast amounts of excess stalk and hurd that can be used in many different material applications. The entire plant can be utilised; the exterior bark (or bast) of the main stalk can be harvested for fibre, the interior woody shiv (or hurd) can be used in combination with lime and water to make hemp-blocks and hemp-crete and the seeds can be crushed to extract oils.[10] At their end of life, these products can either be broken up and reformed, or used as mulch to naturally decompose.

Similarly, our project situated along a 110km bike trail, that follows a series of former rail lines in North Eastern Victoria on the lands of the Yorta Yorta, Wiradjuri and Waveroo Peoples, demanded a rethinking of time and materials. The project incorporated a series of 'rest stops' along this vast stretch and by virtue of its scale, demanded a re-reading of boundaries from one of 'hard-edged' property lines, to overlapping and interconnected networks of bioregions, watersheds and geological conditions. To grasp the scale of the project and the different ecologies it traverses, more detailed mapping was required, alongside a survey of undervalued materials and resources. The seven rest stops situated along the trail were each designed and curated to reveal, enhance, or capture a particular aspect of the local industry, ecology and geology. Landscape is regenerated with flora that are endemic to bioregions. Rocks specific to each site's geology are repurposed as elements of infrastructure – to support a bench seat, or to hold up a solar-cell–alongside ubiquitous industrial materials that are redeployed as building elements. At one rest stop, a nearby abandoned quarry becomes the source of salvaged stone that forms a new amenities block. Far from a comprehensive demonstration of Bioregional practises, the project is a modest attempt at re-establishing connections to the local landscape, its cycles and timescales while enhancing rather than exhausting local resources.

As the architecture and construction industry reckons with its pivotal role in the global transition towards 'net-zero', a paradigm shift to circular and regenerative models becomes crucial. The urgent need to redefine methods and approaches to material production is underscored by the significant environmental impact of current practices reliant on high-carbon, energy-intensive processes. This shift challenges existing regulations and supply chains and demands a fundamental change in the valuing and sourcing of materials. Practices such as Atelier LUMA demonstrate that through considered research and local engagement, it is possible to create alternate, low-impact solutions that challenge conventional risk-averse and short-termist thinking. By embracing Bioregional principles we can foster a deeper engagement with local ecosystems, informing design practise. This involves a holistic understanding of local ecologies, cultures and materials, fostering resilience and adaptability within the built environment. Despite challenges in implementing biomaterials within existing standards, recalibrating economic models to respect natural limits is crucial for this transformation. By reimagining our practises through a time-based and bioregional lens, we can pave the way for a future where architecture can recognise the broader ecological systems upon which we depend.

Opposite: Murray to Mountain Rail Trail, 2023, North Eastern Victoria. Photography by Tope Adesina (1).

Above: Nature Kit Map, Yackandandah Station, Murray to Mountain Rail Trail, 2023, North Eastern Victoria.

01 Peter Berg, *The Biosphere and the Bioregion: Essential Writings of Peter Berg*, edited by Cheryll Glotfelty and Eve Quesnel (New York: Routledge, 2014). Mrinmayee Bhoot, "A bioregional approach to refurbishment informs Atelier LUMA's new workspaces," STIRworld, 2023, https://www.stirworld.com/see-features-a-bioregional-approach-to-refurbishment-informs-atelier-luma-s-new-workspaces.

02 Marcia Bjornerud, *Timefulness: How Thinking Like a Geologist Can Help Save the World.* (Princeton, NJ: Princeton University Press, 2020).

03 Oliver Gordon, "Building and Construction Emissions Hit All-Time High in 2021 - UNEP." *Energy Monitor*, 2022. https://www.energymonitor.ai/built-environment/building-and-construction-emissions-hit-all-time-high-in-2021-unep/.

04 Melanija Grozdanoska, "Is My House Trying to Kill Me?" *Canadian Centre for Architecture*, 2024. https://www.cca.qc.ca/en/articles/issues/32/keep-safe/94839/is-my-house-trying-to-kill-me.

05 Paul Lewis, Marc Tsurumaki, and David J. Lewis, *Manual of Biogenic House Sections* (ORO Editions, 2022).

06 Justin McGuirk, "Islands of Coherence." *Future Observatory Journal* 1, no. 1 (April 2024).

07 Yara Murray, "Australians Create 67 Million Tonnes of Rubbish Each Year. Here's Where It All Ends Up," *ABC News*, 2019. https://www.abc.net.au/news/2019-12-27/where-does-all-australias-waste-go/11755424.

08 Jenny Odell, *How to Do Nothing: Resisting the Attention Economy* (Melbourne: Black Inc., 2019).

09 Val Plumwood, "Shadow Places and the Politics of Dwelling," *Australian Humanities Review*, no. 44 (March 2008): 139-150.

10 Francisco J. Toro, "Stateless Environmentalism: The Criticism of State by Eco-Anarchist Perspectives," *ACME: An International Journal for Critical Geographies* 20, no. 2 (March 2021): 189-205.

REGENERATIVE CONSTRUCTION PRACTICES FOR THE CLIMATE EMERGENCY

Georg Hubmann and Tino Imsirovic

How to produce architecture at a moment when the construction industry is biting its own tail? The current construction practices significantly contribute to climate change, which in turn heavily impacts the health of communities, economies and ecosystems worldwide. The built environment accounts for 37% of annual energy-related CO_2, including embodied and operational emissions.[1] Projected new construction will double the global building stock in size by 2060.[2] If realised using conventional materials and methods, this would lead to drastically increased negative climate impacts.[3] To achieve the emission targets for aligning the global economy with net zero by 2050, the construction sector would require an annual emission reduction rate of 8%, equivalent to the reduced emissions during each year of the COVID-19 pandemic.[4] Thus, from a global standpoint, construction remains the most environmentally damaging sector, with no apparent change in sight.

Efforts to merely decarbonise the current urban building material palette are unlikely to reverse the building sector's impact on our climate. For instance, simply improving the efficiency of steel and concrete will not considerably reduce greenhouse gas emissions. Regarding the production of architecture and its resource use, we argue that a systemic overhaul of the sector must replace a significant portion of the required carbon-intensive materials with regenerative materials, added by circular building practices.

To effectively meet housing and infrastructure needs, along with retrofitting demands, in a less environmentally harmful way than current practices, we need to move beyond 'sustainability' ambitions towards 'regenerative development.' Surpassing current sustainability approaches and their alleged ineffectiveness, the idea of regeneration offers novel conceptual pathways for construction that go beyond mere mitigation. This approach aims to store CO_2 in the building stock, thereby contributing to ease the climate emergency. By incorporating principles of systems thinking, nature integration, circular economy and just transition, construction can be transformed into a force for positive environmental and societal impact.

This article navigates three scales; local, regional and global — and their relevance in transitioning towards a regenerative built environment. At the local scale, we analyse site-specific implementation practices. The regional scale encompasses landscapes and cities with a specific focus on supply chains for construction.

Meanwhile, the global scale, with its concerning statistics provides an important perspective on environmental impact. By exploring these three scales, we address the central question: How can we shift from extractive to regenerative construction practices? Before delving into the ProtoPotsdam case study; an experimental pavilion that challenges conventional construction materials, we present the concept of a regenerative built environment and review related literature. By analysing the case through various scales, we highlight the importance of interlinkages between resource availability, implementation practices and global climate change. Therefore, we access the pavilion's material value chains, technical details of its building components and environmental impact through the Life Cycle Assessment (LCA) methodology.

This underscores our argument that architecture, to be more climate-friendly, must be more closely entangled with its regional resource base. This may disrupt existing value chains, necessitate new engineering and construction skills and influence aesthetic considerations and maintenance cycles. Additionally, we introduce the element of value chains as a crucial element connecting various spatial scales. This provides a new analytical perspective for understanding a regenerative built environment and a lever to fulfil its promises.

Integrating Socio-Cultural and Ecological Systems

Development paradigms have evolved significantly over the decades. Contemporary sustainable development, although still anthropocentric, aims to balance ecosystems through ecosystem services, human well-being and engagement. This approach often goes hand in hand with the extractive use of resources in construction. By default, the construction of buildings involves extractive processes that can have partly devastating impacts on natural resources and societies, often in remote locations.[5] An advancement of the notion of sustainability is regenerative development, which not only maintains but also regenerates ecosystems by integrating socio-ecological systems holistically.[6]

It focuses on building the capacity of these systems to thrive, going beyond harm reduction, to actively replenish natural ecosystems.[7] Regenerative fields have primarily developed from ecological or living systems perspectives, enabling a rethinking of human roles within ecological, technological, economic and social systems.[8] This paradigm seeks to dissolve the divide between humanity and nature, as well as between urban and rural environments, promoting their reintegration and co-evolution in a symbiotic relationship.[9] The core message of regenerative development is to create systems; such as buildings, cities, energy or water supply, that not only minimise environmental impact but actively restore and regenerate natural systems. In other words, "this paradigm attempts to address the dysfunctional human-nature relationship by entering into a co-creative partnership with nature."[10] By doing so, it implies a connection that enhances both social and natural capitals, rather than diminishing them. The apparent next question is: How can regenerative development be translated into architecture and construction?

According to our knowledge, regenerative approaches to the built environment represent an evolving multidisciplinary research field with a steadily growing knowledge base. Many scholars credit the landscape architect John T. Lyle and his book *Regenerative Design for Sustainable Development* with shaping regenerative development and design as distinct disciplines.[11] The regenerative process begins at the macro-scale (e.g., the bioregion, watershed or landscape) and continues down to the local scale.[12] While the availability of natural materials is a fundamental requirement for the concept of regeneration, it also necessitates considering historical, cultural, ecological and economic patterns of the ecosystems from which materials for construction are extracted.

Achieving regenerative building projects requires a deep understanding of the unique narrative of a place, enabling the creation of locally tailored solutions to foster regenerative outcomes for the future.[13] In this context, Pamela Mang and Bill Reed emphasise the importance of a connection to place by proposing a shift from being architects who aim to control their environments to becoming gardeners who care for a place with a whole-system understanding. Thus, regenerative design solutions, developed from the unique characteristics of a place rather than a set of universal best practices, regenerate rather than deplete underlying life support systems and resources and aim to integrate the flows and structures of the built and natural worlds.[14] In the context of a co-evolutionary partnership between socio-cultural and ecological systems, encouraging participatory processes that involve all relevant stakeholders and ensuring their co-investment in a project from the beginning is crucial for regenerative design.[15] In addition to community engagement, all aspects of life, including human, other species and ecological systems, should embrace a sustained commitment to stewardship in regenerative design.[16] In this context, Raymond J. Cole identifies two shifts in the temporal and spatial scope of the design process: from thinking of buildings as artefacts to thinking of them as adaptive processes over time; and from a focus on the individual building and its site to the neighbourhood within which the building exists. The aim is to identify opportunities for synergistic regenerative interactions over time.[17] Thus, regenerative design emphasises viewing the building as a process and adapting to local demands, particularly the needs of communities. While transforming the built environment is essential, it must be adaptable to surprises and uncertainties over time. Unlike nature, which adapts instinctively to survive, the built environment requires deliberate transformation to survive and evolve. As a result, adaptations within the built environment must be an integral part of the regenerative design concept due to the dynamic nature of social-ecological systems.[18]

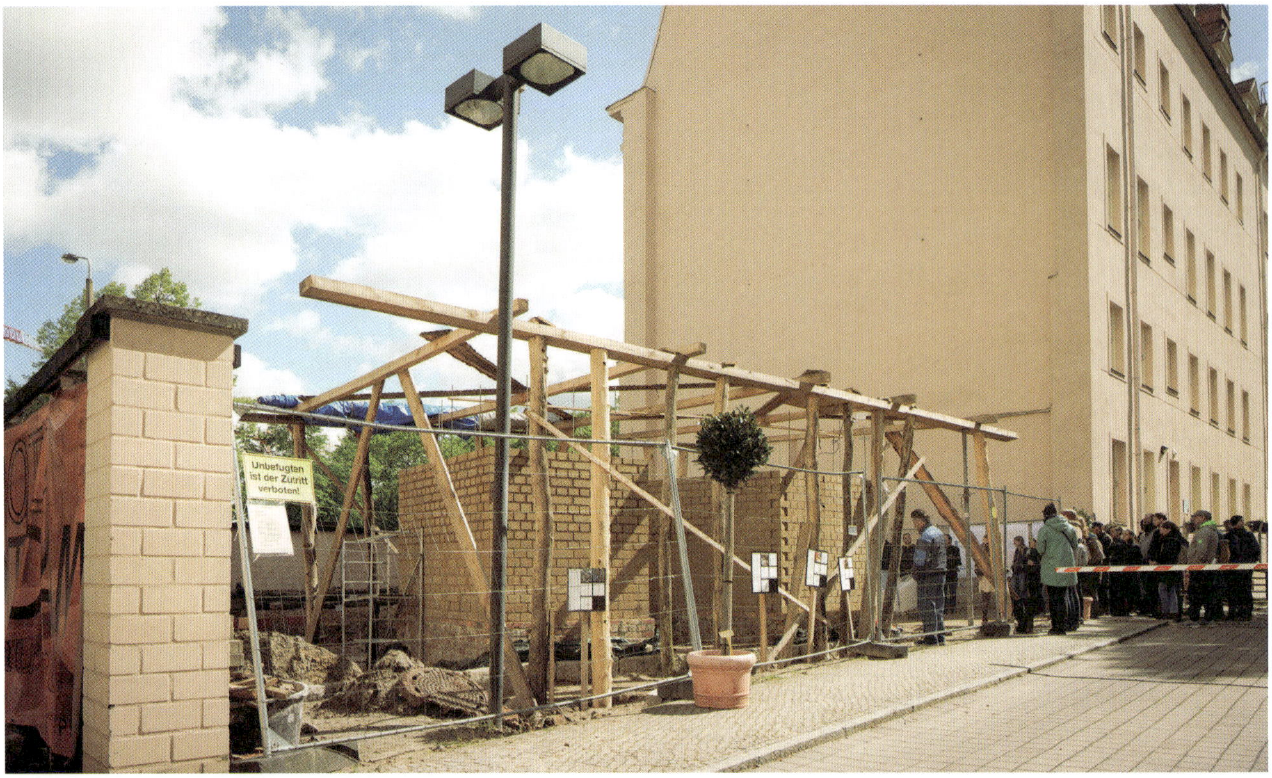
Unbefugten
ist der Zutritt
verboten!

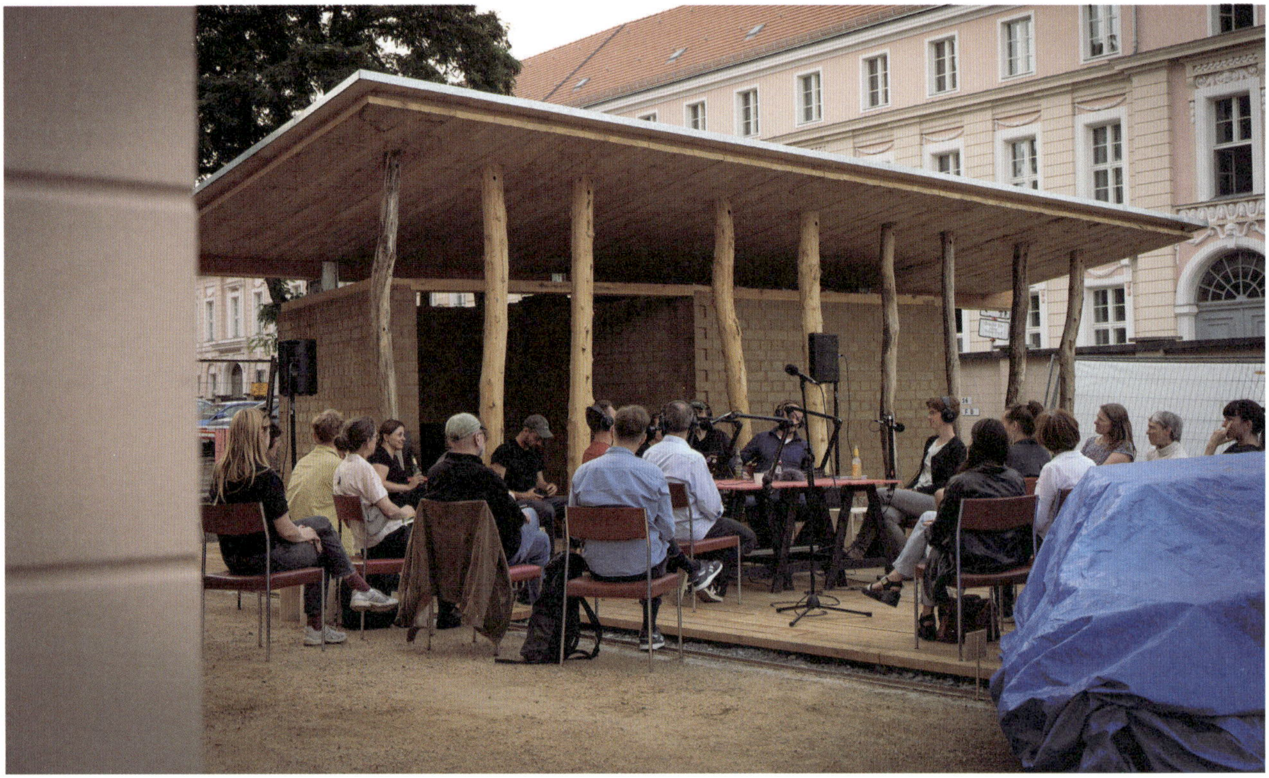

We conclude this part of the literature review with the following collection of principles that are key for a regenerative built environment:

1. Holistic Value Chain Approach
Regenerative design considers the entire lifecycle of buildings and infrastructure, from conception to demolition, ensuring that every stage contributes to the health and vitality of both human and natural systems. This includes systems thinking to recognise the interdependence between these systems.

2. Respect for Place
Regenerative built environments are designed to work in consonance with natural processes, therefore a careful consideration of both the place of construction and the place of resource extraction (usually in the wider bioregion) is required.

3. Positive Environmental Impact
Unlike the sustainability paradigm, which aims to reduce negative impacts, regenerative design seeks to create positive impacts by restoring and enhancing ecosystems and biodiversity. In construction, this can be achieved by balancing out the extractive resource use through sustainably sourced renewable materials or reuse/recycled components in the context of a circular economy.

4. Community and Stewardship
Regenerative built environments focus on human well-being, involving local communities, human and non-human actors as well as socio-spatial dynamics in the design process to ensure that developments meet the needs of people and nature alike.

5. Adaptability and Resilience
An important component of the regenerative paradigm is to design buildings and infrastructures that can adapt to changing environmental and social conditions and contribute to the resilience of ecosystems.

Critical positions regarding a regenerative built environment almost unified address its implementation gap across various dimensions. Both Peter Clegg and Joseph Tainter raise concerns about the appropriate scale of implementation. Focusing solely on the urban context can be misleading, as this could refer to the city, neighbourhood or building scale, while a 'scalar contradiction' is emphasised between the aspirations of regenerative designers and the realities faced by practitioners implementing projects.[19] In a comprehensive literature review, Kimberly Camrass raises similar concerns, mainly focusing on challenges to operationalising regenerative frameworks. For example, she notes the need to understand the impact of different decision-making structures within the built environment, the lack of sufficiently specific frameworks for engaging stakeholders across various sectors and the need to understand how regenerative aspirations and measures of success could be incorporated into existing planning and evaluation frameworks. According to Camrass, a range of authors emphasise the necessary changes in architectural practices when working with regenerative design and more case studies are needed to demonstrate practical implementation.[20]

Activating the Regional Bioeconomy for Construction
ProtoPotsdam is a small temporary pavilion that works as a laboratory for nature-based and circular construction. It is situated on a continually expanding demonstration site open to the public, featuring cutting-edge research while also hosting events and interdisciplinary debates about the future of construction. It was made possible by the collective vision of everyone involved to change prevailing ways of constructing. In its function as transformation laboratory, it is part of the ReBuilt project that aims to advance the novel concept of a regenerative built environment and demonstrate its practical implementation. In addition to the Berlin-Brandenburg region, this research project employs a comparative lab approach with other demonstrator buildings in the contexts of Bali-Denpasar in Indonesia, Thimphu-Paro in Bhutan and Western Cape Region in South Africa. The goal is to explore and disseminate the various dimensions of regenerative construction. The following case study addresses the problem of scales by covering aspects related to material, value chains and emissions.

We see ProtoPotsdam's focus on regional material value chains, including their processes, human and non-human actors and infrastructure, as the key component for achieving significant results regarding the benchmarks of a regenerative built environment. Additionally, the case study provides insights into the practical aspects of regenerative construction, addressing the aforementioned implementation gap. In the following, a primary example of regenerative design and construction is presented in detail, illustrating the central concept of the regenerative paradigm, the relationship between socio-cultural and ecological systems, in practical terms.

Fig. 1 (Above): Podcast live recording event at ProtoPotsdam pavilion. Image Courtesy of 414films.

Fig. 2 (Below): Podcast live recording event at ProtoPotsdam pavilion. Image Courtesy of 414films.

Local Materials and Value Chains

1. Historic Foundations

The plot was originally occupied by a half-timbered construction from 1724, which was replaced by a multi-storey brick building in 1778. At that time, the foundations made of limestone blocks were reinforced with brick masonry. This building was destroyed in World War II and the plot has remained empty ever since. As part of the analysis of the specific conditions of the building site, the ProtoPotsdam project team discovered that the historical foundations of the destroyed building are largely still preserved and usable. To minimise the use of materials in the foundation, the architectural design of the pavilion was aligned with the position and load-bearing capacity of the historic foundations. Hence, the robinia columns were anchored to the historic strip foundations.

2. Reuse Fired Bricks

Despite their popularity in Germany, where 30% of approved building projects use fired bricks as their principal construction material, bricks have the disadvantage of a substantial primary energy demand during their manufacturing process, which today commonly relies on fossil fuels. Within the paradigm shift towards a regenerative built environment, fired bricks will find utility only as a recycled building material. However, the recovery of bricks is currently labour-intensive and cost-inefficient, highlighting the omnipresent competition between economic and environmental sustainability. A new understanding of our building stock as a potential resource for building materials can drastically contribute to the decarbonisation of the building sector. The reused bricks sourced for ProtoPotsdam originate from a deconstructed farmhouse in Schwedt (Brandenburg), erected in the late 19th century. The pavilion showcases the practical application of reused building materials and, upon its deconstruction, will reintroduce the utilised resources back into the construction sector without downcycling. The use of lime mortar instead of cement mortar can significantly simplify the deconstruction process, thus promoting the recyclability of the material.

3. Compressed Earth Blocks

An examination of the conventional sourcing, processing and disposal of mineral materials by the construction industry reveals potential for innovation. Notably, within the Brandenburg region, an annual amount of approximately 500,000 cubic meters of uncontaminated excavation materials as waste is documented. In many cases, this waste material can be used to produce unfired, compressed earth blocks, providing a viable alternative to conventional, climate-damaging masonry materials. If produced without further additives, compressed earth blocks can be completely recycled, pointing the way to circular building practices. The research on local earth blocks culminated in the licensing of an earth block made from excavation material from a large construction site in Berlin. These blocks are now being used for the first time in load-bearing construction in the ProtoPotsdam pavilion.

4. Regenerative Timber Roof

As the most commonly used bio-based building material in the region, wood plays a pioneering role in the transition to a regenerative construction industry. By sequestering carbon during its growth phase, timber can be utilized in buildings to actively contribute to climate restoration by serving as a carbon sink. Currently, coniferous softwoods are primarily used in construction as they grow fast and straight. Additionally, their lower density compared to hardwoods make them easier to process industrially. However, the resulting monocultures, which extend over large parts of Brandenburg, are not resilient to climate change impacts and do not foster healthy ecosystems. This is evident in the annually increasing volume of damaged wood and the growing incidence of forest fires. To ensure that our forests become more resilient to the effects of the climate crisis, a transformation towards more mixed forests and regenerative forest management is needed. The spectrum of wood species used by the construction industry must therefore diversify, sorting methods need to become more differentiated and efficient utilisation is essential. Various applications are being explored in the ProtoPotsdam Pavilion, including using branch-rich sections, various hardwood species, smaller trunk diameters and young wood.

5. Round Timber Columns

The ProtoPotsdam Pavilion uses load-bearing round timber columns, a centuries-old building method. Almost any type of wood, even 'weak' wood, can be used as round timber columns if the load force is applied vertically. Due to its contact with the ground, the base of the column poses the greatest challenge because moisture and exposure to air accelerate the process of wood rot. Therefore, very weather-resistant and hard robinia wood was chosen for this pavilion. Despite its excellent properties for outdoor use, robinia wood has not yet received standardised approval in Germany. This is due to the low demand for robinia wood in the construction industry and the lack of infrastructure in sawmills to process it. Consequently, robinia wood must be classified in the lowest strength class for structural calculations. The use of robinia columns in the ProtoPotsdam Pavilion reflects the untapped potentials caused by the lack of standardised approval.

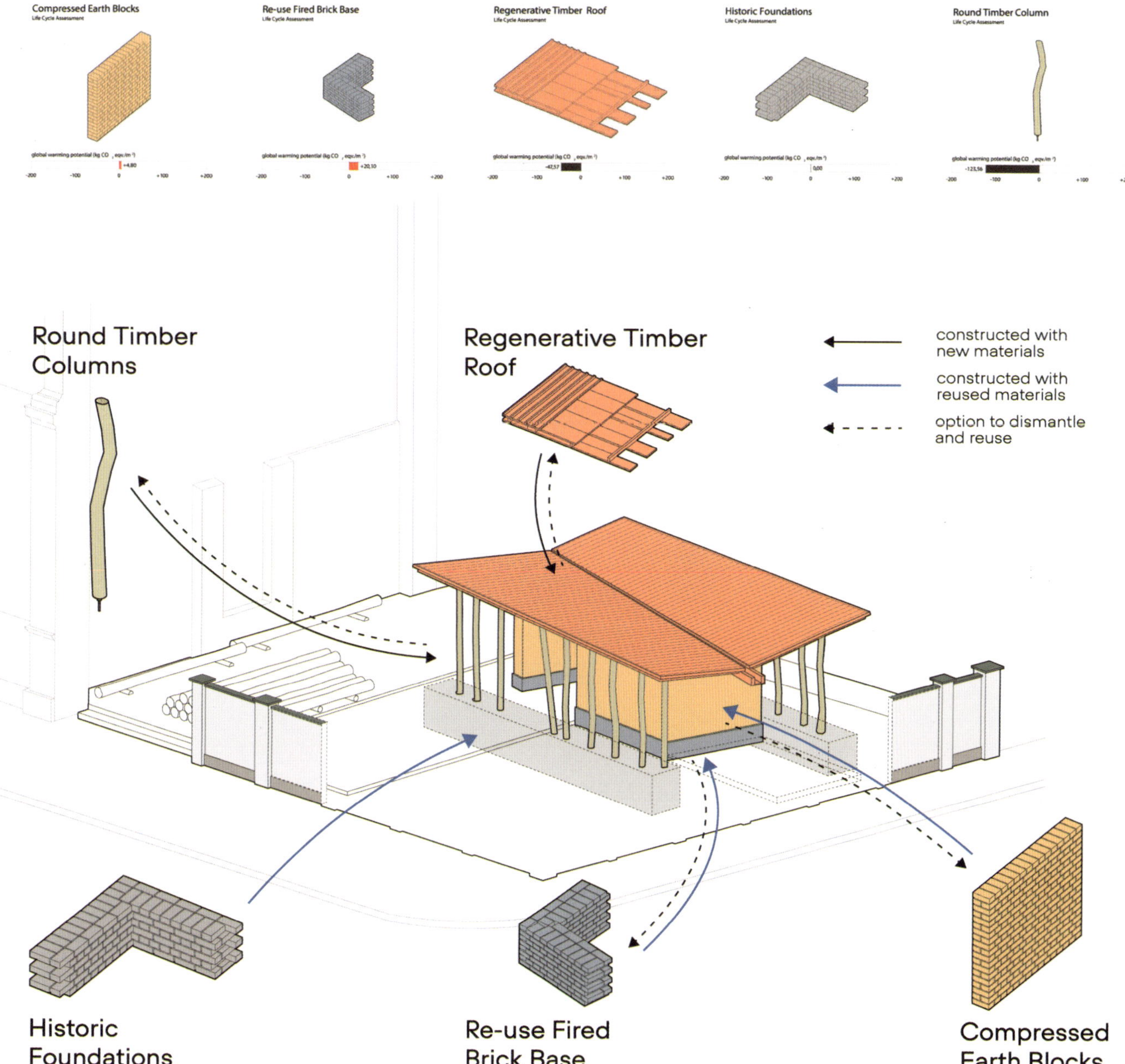

Fig. 3 (Above): Environmental impact of the single components, calculated per m2 or m3. Image Courtesy of Bauhaus Earth.

Fig. 4 (Below): Details of all the construction materials. Image Courtesy of Bauhaus Earth.

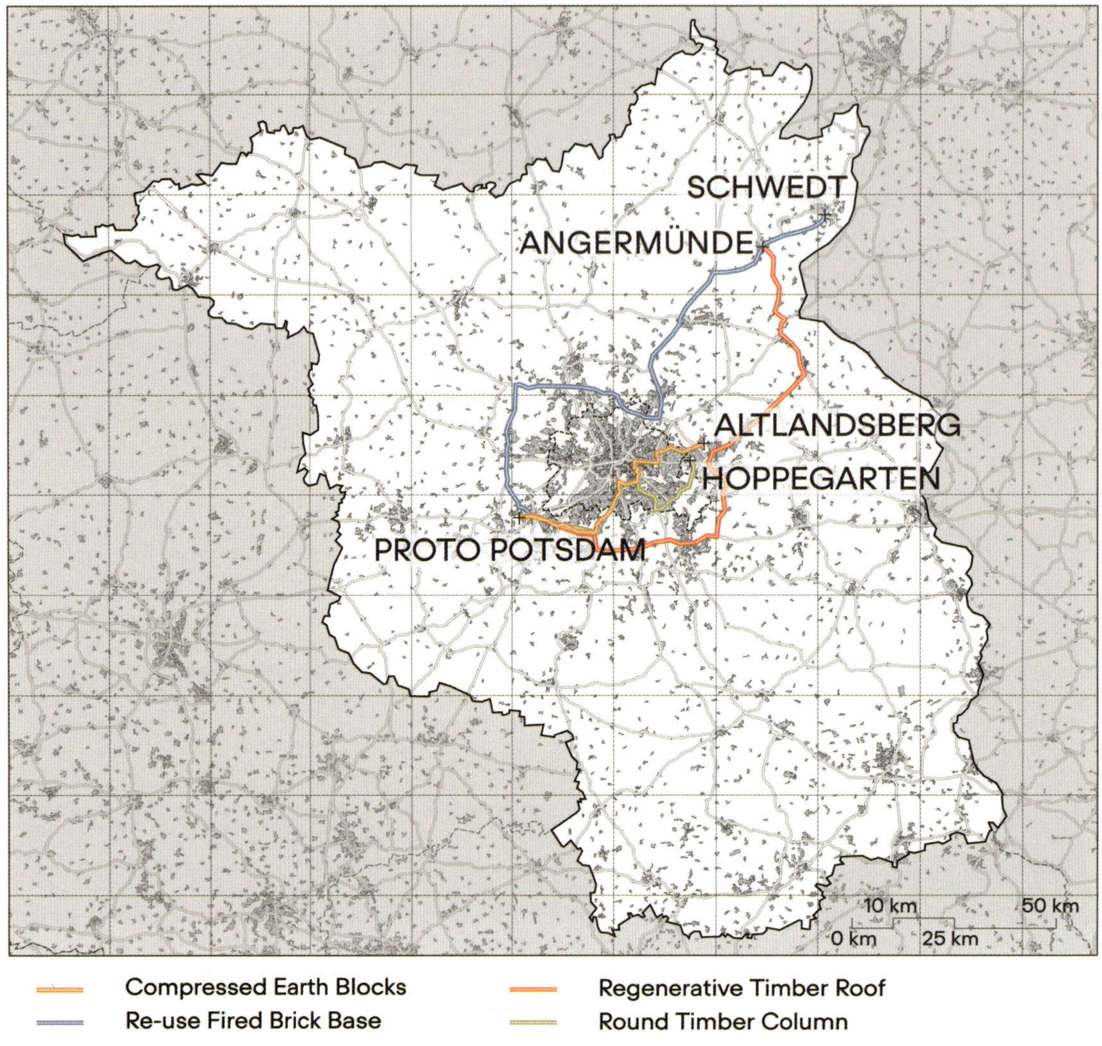

Regional Resource Availability and Sustainable Harvesting

The use of regional renewable raw materials offers the potential to reduce the environmental impact of construction by reducing resource consumption, greenhouse gas emissions in production and transportation and negative externalities such as non-recyclable waste while sequestering carbon over the long term. The Berlin-Brandenburg region provides a variety of locally grown resources that are already partially used as construction materials. A recent assessment identified wood, hemp, straw, flax/linen and thatch/reed, as regionally available renewable raw materials, which can be cultivated on available agricultural land or are already cultivated there.[21] In Brandenburg, approximately 37% of the land is covered by forests and sustainable value chains have been established, particularly for pine, which constitutes 70% of the region's most typical tree species.[22] By far the highest potential for a future renewable construction value chain lies with hemp due to its uncomplicated cultivation, high growth rates and biomass yield, lack of need for pesticides and multiple possibilities for processing its components (fibres, shives, grains). However, many renewable raw materials do not allow for scaling similar to that of conventional building materials. Additionally, many of these renewable raw materials are niche products and currently lack a broad distribution and information network.[23]

Fig.5 (Above): Regional value chain perspective. Image Courtesy of Bauhaus Earth.

Global Environmental Impact

In recent decades, the frequency and intensity of climate events have increased as a consequence of accelerated global warming. High levels of greenhouse gas emissions in the air are threatening fragile ecosystems and vulnerable communities. Despite global efforts and agreements to reduce greenhouse gas emissions, outcomes fall short of the critical 1.5 degree Celsius threshold outlined in the Paris Agreement.

Negotiated under the United Nations Framework Convention on Climate Change (UNFCCC), this international treaty was adopted by nearly every nation in 2015 to address climate change and its negative impacts. It aims to limit global warming to well below two degrees Celsius above pre-industrial levels.[24] Projections for 2100 indicate the need for a paradigm shift in development and climate change mitigation strategies, including moving beyond mere net-zero targets to actively work towards achieving negative carbon emission balances.[25] However, the current pathway of construction is far from a systemic transition towards being carbon negative.

In contrast to the global trend, the analysed case study shows that storing CO_2 in building stock while drastically reducing embodied emissions for construction is possible by employing regional nature-based and reused materials. The five main components of the ProtoPotsdam pavilion were analysed using a LCA. Accordingly, the historic foundations did not cause any emissions, both the reused fired bricks and the earth block masonry have minor emissions, while the round timber columns and the wooden roof have a significantly negative emission balance (see Fig. 3). When calculating the volumes of all the building components based on the LCA analysis, the entire building achieves an environmental impact of in total-7 266 kg CO_2 equivalent.

Compared to the same calculation using conventional materials (25 696 kg CO_2 eqv.), this makes a significant difference despite the small scale of the pavilion. This clearly underlines that when using regenerative and reused building materials, a positive environmental impact (the lower, the better) can be achieved.

Towards a Continuous Care for Materials

The regenerative built environment is a progressive approach in design and development that aims to create spaces and systems beneficial to both people and the planet. This concept is well-established in academic literature, emphasising a shift from merely sustainable to actively regenerative practices. In short, its goal is to reconnect human activity with the Earth's natural systems, characterised by the following key principles: (1) holistic value chain approach, (2) respect for place, (3) positive environmental impact, (4) community and stewardship, (5) adaptability and resilience. These notions are all reflected in the ProtoPotsdam case study, which is first and foremost a small-scale experimental pavilion and a symbol for the *Bauwende*, the material turn in construction. However, it impressively shows the potential of locally sourced nature-based value chains using either reused or renewable bio- or geo-based materials. By analysing a realised regenerative building, this article addressed open points in the current discussion about regenerative design and development, specifically the problem of scales and the implementation gap.

By detailing five principles of regenerative design, thoroughly analysing regenerative construction practices in the case study and examining various spatial scales, we addressed the central research question on how to transition from extractive to regenerative construction practices. It became clear that the configuration of ProtoPotsdam's material value chains are the defining factors that make the case study a regenerative project. These operate at different scales, they use local building materials, consider regional resource availability and achieve a positive environmental impact, which is connected to the global climate debate. This renders a discussion about what is the 'ideal' implementation scale for regenerative design obsolete. All addressed scales are important and are specific to the regenerative development logic. We see the focus on entire value chains (resource management and extraction, infrastructure, transportation, production, use and re-use) and thus a whole-system perspective on architecture as the most relevant addition to the existing literature. This is a tangible way to translate the conceptual regenerative development paradigm into practices of the built environment.

Regenerative construction practices require the attitude of gardeners who on a continuous basis care for, maintain and re-interpret architecture and its embedded material stock. In the interest of a healthier human-nature relationship, architecture must be more deeply entangled with its regional resource base, which may have implications for its processual approach, aesthetic, construction details and maintenance cycles. This means, as the literature also suggests, that the current role of architects must evolve towards curating entire value chains rather than merely controlling the parameters of the built environment. We can confirm that further research is needed into the scalability of regenerative practices in construction to bridge the gap between aspirations and reality.

Acknowledgements: We would like to thank Christian Gäth, Micha Kretschmann, Gediminas Lesutis, Angelika Drescher and Florian Förster from Bauhaus Earth for reviewing earlier versions of this paper, Kéan Koschany for preparing the diagrams and map as well as the *Inflection* team for productive comments.

01 UNEP, 2021 Global Status Report for Buildings and Construction (Nairobi, 2021), 1-104.
02 UNA-UK, Climate 2020: sustainability (London: Witan Media Ltd, 2020), 1-82.
03 UNEP & Yale Center for Ecosystems + Architecture, Building Materials and the Climate: Constructing a New Future (Nairobi, 2023), 1-138.
04 UNEP, 2022 Global Status Report for Buildings and Construction (Nairobi, 2022), 1-100.
05 Charlotte Malterre-Barthes, Who is it that the Earth belongs to? (London: Sternberg Press, 2021), 85-96.
06 Leah V. Gibbons et al., Regenerative development as an integrative paradigm and methodology for landscape sustainability (Switzerland: Sustainability), 1910-1929.
07 Josette M. Plaut et al., Regenerative design: The LENSES framework for buildings and communities (London: Building Research and Information, 2012), 112-122.
08 Chrisna Du Plessis, Towards a regenerative paradigm for the built environment (London: Building Research & Information, 2012), 7-22.
09 Srinivasula Venkata Mohan et al., Urban biocycles-Closing metabolic loops for resilient and regenerative ecosystem: A perspective (Amsterdam: Bioresource Technology, 2020), article number 123098.
10 Du Plessis, Towards a regenerative paradigm for the built environment, 7-22.
11 John T. Lyle, Regenerative design for sustainable development (Hoboken: John Wiley & Sons, 1996), 1-352.
12 Du Plessis, Towards a regenerative paradigm for the built environment, 7-22.
13 Kimberly Camrass, Urban regenerative thinking and practice: a systematic literature review (London: Building Research & Information, 2022), 339-350.
14 Pamela Mang and Bill Reed, Designing from place: A regenerative framework and methodology (London: Building Research and Information, 2012), 23-38.
15 Raymond J. Cole et al, Regenerative design, socio-ecological systems and co-evolution (London: Building Research and Information, 2013), 237-247.
16 Mang, & Reed, Designing from place: A regenerative framework and methodology, 23-38.
17 Cole et al, Regenerative design, socio-ecological systems and co-evolution, 237-247.
18 Ibid.
19 Peter Clegg, A practitioner's view of the 'regenerative paradigm' (London: Building Research and Information, 2012), 365-368.
20 Joseph A. Tainter, Regenerative design in science and society (London: Building Research and Information, 2012), 369-372.
21 Camrass, Urban regenerative thinking and practice: a systematic literature review, 339-350.
22 Florian Schröder, Analyse nachwachsender Baustoffe in der Region Berlin-Brandenburg (Eberswalde: HNEE, 1-9.
23 https://lbholzbb.de/wald-und-ressource-holz.
24 Schröder, Analyse nachwachsender Baustoffe in der Region Berlin-Brandenburg, 1-9.
25 UNFCC, The Paris Agreement (2015), 1-60.
26 Franck Lecocq et al., IPCC, 2022: Climate Change 2022: Mitigation of Climate Change. Contribution of Working Group III to the Sixth Assessment Report of the Intergovernmental Panel on Climate Change (Cambridge and New York: Cambridge University Press, 2022), 409-502.

CLIMATIC ARCHITECTURE

IN CONVERSATION WITH PHILIPPE RAHM

Interview by Abbey O'Regan, Alexandra Khomenko and Jarel Cheah

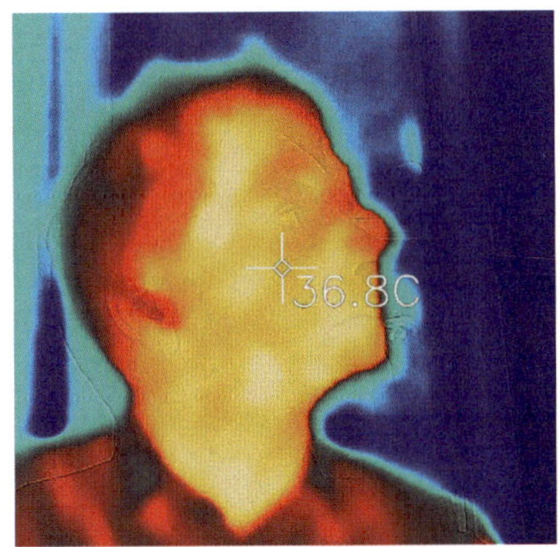

Philippe Rahm is a Swiss architect and principal architect in the office of Philippe Rahm architectes, *based in Paris. His work, which extends the field of architecture from the physiological to the meteorological, has received an international audience in the context of sustainability. He is the 2024 Treseder Fellow at the Faculty of Architecture, Building and Planning at the University of Melbourne, and in August he visited to give a lecture on the fundamentals of his research and design methodology to tackle today's climate crisis.*

Inflection *Vol. 11 editors had the pleasure of sitting down for a conversation with Philippe after his public lecture at the Melbourne School of Design. Throughout the interview, Philippe provided insight into the growing relevance of his practice at the turn of the millennia, shared some thoughts about bridging traditional climatic approaches with the extremities of the climate crisis, and outlined the need for resettling the discipline of architecture to focus on its intrinsic climatic qualities.*

To start at the beginning, your interest in physiological architecture dates back to the early 2000s, arguably around the time where the profession had neglected these needs as informing design process. What sparked your interest in the relationship between architecture and physiology?

Before 2000 there was the introduction of the mobile phone, the computer screen, and so on. The screen of the computer was like a new window. You have access to all this information through the screen. At that moment I was thinking, it's not only information we have access to through the screen, but also the radiation that comes from the screens to your eyes. It means you have some sort of physiological effect from the screen to the human eye, you know, it's not natural.

At the same time, the new technology that arrived in the 1990s was used by architects like Zaha Hadid, Greg Lynn or Frank Gehry to do these geometric forms; the 'blob.' But for us, we weren't so interested in the form generated by softwares, but more in the physiological effects of all this new technology. It meant looking at how the space was affected by some invisible part of the technology. Traditionally, as an architect, you are designing in black (the wall) and white (the space). It's very abstract and it means that space appears as nothing. Everything instead is about the solid and you don't design for the void, when in reality, the void is full of particles, chemicals, humidity, temperature, and so on. We were thinking at that moment, as architects, what happens when we start to question the void?

You have to remember; I was educated in a very narrative-driven period. A good example is how we learned about windows. If you are doing a vertical window, it's more like a Parisian window. If you are doing a horizontal window, it's more like a New York window. We were educated to choose the proportion of the window according to the cultural meaning. Nobody at that moment was talking about how the window relates to the physiological needs. What would be a better quality of light, for example. If it was better for the occupant's health to have a horizontal window or vertical window? So, at that moment, yes, it was not so popular, and I have to say that it's because the philosophical or intellectual dominance at that period was really a cultural one, and not a physiological one.

Above: Philippe Rahm, thermal portrait. All images courtesy of Philippe Rahm architectes.

You recently published a book titled *Climatic Architecture*. How did you bridge your early interests and experimentation in physiology into a work that started to seriously consider climatic conditions as design tools for architectural composition?

Even though we knew about global warming in the 1990s, I didn't really take it that seriously until 2005. But what we had already been doing by studying the quality of space, light, humidity, heat, and so on, was corresponding to the new regulations to economise energy and reduce CO_2 emissions. *Passivhaus* in Germany or *Minergie Label* in Switzerland, for example, asked us to deal with thermal insulation, heat regulation, air renewal and airtight barriers. All our research aligned well with these interests, and our projects had a new goal. Before, the goal was about improving health and to make clean air or good light. But this was quite niche. Now it was more to talk about global warming and architecture, not only from a technical point of view, but how it integrated into design. We are architects — we can design the climate.

One element that was crucial to understand was convection. Hot air moves up, and cold air moves down. With that you can make a section. Because you understand this; if you are doing a high ceiling, it will be warmer up there and colder down at the floor level. This is quite important because before this we had no form, it was just mechanical ventilation and heating blowing air around a room, or artificial lighting. But then we start to understand, OK, with the double flow air renewal system, if you introduce new air somewhere, then you can create a 'river' of air and the building can form a river of high-speed air renewal somewhere, and low-speed air renewal somewhere else, whatever is needed. By changing the form of the building, you can control these things. It gave new direction to how we thought about architecture. That was the moment when our projects moved to this kind of more climatic architecture.

Would you say then it's not so much then about controlling climactic factors, but more about analysing, adapting, framing the climate...how would you phrase it?

Yes, it is the idea that climate can be the driving force of the design. In reality, architecture is constructing a micro-climate. All buildings have a 'fake' climate. They are designed to be warmer when it's cold, cooler when it's too warm. If I have to introduce ventilation to create flows of air, how can I better design this flow of air, and place function according to that?

There's obviously a vernacular and historical quality to this design approach, in terms of relying on climatic conditions to inform spatial qualities, form, materiality and so on. But how does that approach continue to evolve as we deal with things like global warming and climate change, where our climate becomes less like it was historically and vernacularly?

You're right, and it's a question I'm quite interested in at the moment. My Italian colleagues of Fabulism and I have just applied for the Bahrain Pavilion for the 2025 Venice Biennale. The theme of the pavilion is 'heatwave.' Our idea was to challenge our current ways of living. It's super-hot in Bahrain, and with temperatures continuing to rise, maybe we need to switch to primarily living at night. Another solution could be to stop living on the surface of the planet and to go underground where it is cooler. If you go down five metres underground, you find a moderate temperature that is the average between winter and summer. The underground is something that has always been very popular in places like Iran and North Africa, for example, as a method of cooling down by building and inhabiting troglodyte houses or towns.

The title of the proposal was going to be *In Favour of Night and Underground*, or something like that. After we pitched the idea, the director of the jury said to us, "it is super-hot during the day, but now it is super-hot during the night too, and although it is a good idea, you cannot really cool down anymore during the night." The heatwave is also increasing the temperatures at night — maybe it is too late.

It's true that the solutions of the past no longer fit to the new, changing climate. We know that global warming is slowly moving our climatic conditions more north in the Northern Hemisphere, and more south in the Southern Hemisphere. If you want to find the vernacular solution in Paris, you must look to the vernacular from

Opposite: Taichung Central Park, also known as Jade Eco Park. Taiwan, 2012-2020 by Philippe Rahm architectes, Catherine Mosbach, and Ricky Liu & Associates.

the North of Africa, not the one in France, because that vernacular solution of France is maybe now suitable for the North of England. The model for the future is still the past model, but just from a different region located more in the respective south or north.

Could you share an example of a project where your emphasis on climatic factors fundamentally altered the design outcome?

The Taichung Central Park in Taiwan is quite interesting in terms of its different types of climatic responses. It is a response that is different from a typical climatic engineer point of view. This point of view would only want to do a 'good' climate; one that is good if the temperature is 22°C, there is 50% relative humidity, the light is 600 lux, things like that. But for us, the idea of diversity is important, and we accept variations in space. The project started by defining the three existing climatic conditions of heat, humidity, and pollution in terms of their variations.

When we started the project for example, we were quite interested in the areas of pollution. The city is polluted, like every city in the world. And we say, okay, we will try to clean some areas. But some will stay polluted. And we will accept this polluted area. As we like to say: form follows the climate, and the function for the form follows the climate. So, in this case, we will put the children's playground in the less polluted area. But in the most polluted area, we will place the BBQ and the smoking area. The client didn't want to hear about that, saying they will not create a polluted area, but in end, if you must place a BBQ somewhere, you know it will be better not to place it in areas with cleaner air. But politically, that was not acceptable, and took a lot of convincing.

We also proposed areas with a lot of trees around the naturally windier parts of the site, so it will be cool because of the shadow and the wind. But we are also proposing areas with no wind and a lot of sun without trees. It means that you are free to decide. Maybe you want to go out under the sun at noon, I don't know why, but it can be your decision. We don't want everybody to have to live in 22°C at 50% humidity. We are not all the same, so we want to keep this freedom of diversity by creating a diversity of microclimates and a gradient of climatic conditions.

So, that diversity is both a climatic diversity and an experiential diversity?

Yes. The master plan of the park created a diversity of micro-climates and a diversity of experiences in different areas of the park that we could freely occupy, depending on the hour of the days or the month in the year. It is why in a lot of my projects I try to work with gradation. There is a gradient of cold to warm, or dry to humid, or light to darkness — you know, to give some different qualities depending on what you prefer at that moment.

Is it difficult to create variations in gradient in a smaller and more contained environment, say like a house? At the urban scale, like a masterplan for a park, it's quite easy to understand, but how do you think it changes once you move indoors?

We made some projects for housing that introduced these ideas of gradation, where you had more cold areas and more warm areas. But we also saw the house as stretched out between a dry area, like the bedrooms, and a more humid area, like the bathrooms and kitchens, which produce a lot of water vapour. You have this kind of geography inside the house that is linked to these different qualities. The aesthetic can come from that too. There is this sort of poetic potential in thinking of the house in terms of managing climate gradients.

But to answer your question, I think the idea of gradation in a small house can be more complicated, because we have behaviours that are linked to the rise of fossil fuel energy. Everybody wants their own room, and they want it to be comfortable all of the time. But maybe if we think differently, we can imagine another way of living.

Right: Thermal bubble, layers of insulation. Plan drawn by Philippe Rahm architectes for the refurbishment of a mountain house in Switzerland, 2006.

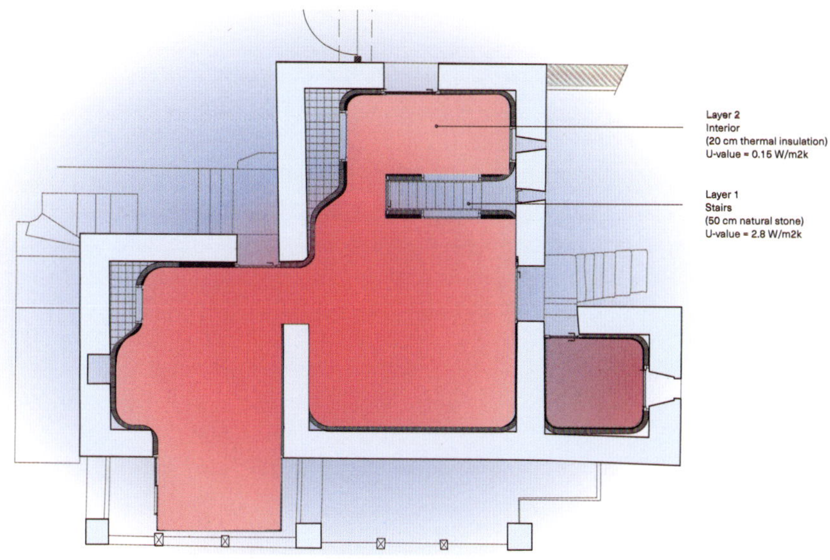

Where do you position yourself on the emerging 'after comfort' discourse, which talks about economising energy and moving away from mechanical heating and cooling?

It's an interesting position, and maybe in twenty years the energy will be so expensive we'll have to talk about it! I did a project with thermal insulation that was not following the wall but instead was creating an independent 'bubble.' Which meant that there were areas that were not inside the insulation because they did not need to be. For example, the stairs. You have undetermined spaces in between the external façade and the insulation that are without heat. Maybe it's a natural fridge, or some storage, or however you choose to use it. But it was an idea to use thermal insulation separately from the façade, and thinking about how it would change how we use when we don't rely on the machine to heat and cool.

Is it adaptable at all? Can you change how the insulation is placed to create new spatial arrangements?

No, it was more definitive. We looked at the space and said, okay, here is where we will place the insulation.

During the 1960s, there was a big interest in adaptive partitions, where we thought you can move the partitions and change things. But then in the 1980s nobody was changing the partition because it was too complicated. Sometimes it would break, and so on. So, when I was educated everyone was saying, okay, we have to forget this kind of moving partition because it wasn't working. It was very much this generation of "okay you must build a wall and just make it one way."

It's coming back strongly now, this idea of adaptable and flexible design, but sometimes it needs too much intervention. Or it's too sophisticated, and it becomes broken and doesn't work.

So, you prefer to design for a way that would work most of the time, as opposed to having to be changed to meet a number of different scenarios?

Yes. The adaptability and flexibility is based on the climatic conditions. You know, it's to say, here it will be warmer because there you have the sun. And here it will be colder because you have no sun. So sometimes you can create diversity which is just already happening. You're conditioning these spaces based on the environment. And it comes back to this idea of the gradient. You don't need to rely of adaptable and flexible design so much if you've got a gradient.

WILD FUTURES AND POLLINATOR ARCHITECTURE

Rafael Luna

...wilderness stands as the last remaining place where civilization, that all too human disease, has not fully infected the earth. It is an island in the polluted sea of urban-industrial modernity, the one place we can turn for escape from our own too-muchness. Seen in this way, wilderness presents itself as the best antidote to our human selves, a refuge we must somehow recover if we hope to save the planet.[1]

While this quote from William Cronon's *The Trouble with Wilderness*: *Or, Getting Back to the Wrong Nature* originates from an American context, it encapsulates the palpable change in the reality of the built environment that constitutes today's state of planetary urbanisation. Wild nature has become a background condition, a residual space in an ever-expanding network of infrastructures that have proliferated the growth of humans living in cities across the globe.[2] This ongoing process of expansive urbanisation engraves a paradoxical condition where infrastructure facilitates our collective assemblage for settlements around the world while at the same time, infrastructure displaces natural ecosystems that are essential for the survival of life at a global scale. This requires a recalibration of the built environment in a balancing act that mitigates between the natural wild and the constructed form through new architectural typologies and tectonics. In this sense, architecture must act as a green infrastructural hybrid capable of regenerating, producing, and managing resources such as energy, clean air, clean water, food, and biodiversity. While architecture must still satisfy occupancy, this architectural mutation of rewilding must also not rely exclusively on systems as add-on elements, but as integral productive elements that form part of the language and composition manifested through methodologies that translate green parameters into new architectural tectonics of bio-regeneration and pollination.

Pollinators are an essential component to maintain wild ecosystems as much as they are essential to sustaining our way of life in our constructed environments. Wild pollinator architecture must then reverse-engineer ecosystems and habitats that have been lost to urbanisation, which are quantifiable through satellite urban mapping programs. Projects such as the *Atlas of Urban Expansion* and the European Union's *Copernicus Land Monitoring Service* gather evidence of the continuous urban growth overtaking large expanses of land.[3] These programs have been collecting data on urban growth for several decades with the intent to help manage such expansion and better assess land usage. The Land Monitoring Service, for example, aims to understand water cycles, Earth surface energy variables and the contrast between vegetated versus unvegetated land. The programs demonstrate a growth —year after year —of urbanity, population, and a depletion of resources as large conurbations start forming megacities.

Above: Wild Futures - Hoverfly found pollinating in winter. Image courtesy of Yvonne Davila.

The UN Principles for Responsible Investment (UNPRI), another mapping program, has identified hotspots of natural resource depletion to be used as the basis for analysis of risk aversion. As stated in the UNPRI methodology brief: "As natural capital is depleted, it loses its capacity to support the ecosystem services upon which businesses, economic activities and broader society depend."[4] Rather than seeing the natural resource depletion areas as risk centres, they can also be targeted study areas for a new biodiverse urbanism with infra-architectural hybrid typologies that regenerate natural resources; incentivising new industries and investment markets. The UNPRI identified the global biodiversity hotspots to be the Great Plains in North America, the Southern cone of South America, Southern Africa, Central Asia and Australia. Policy-wise, the majority of regions would have to coordinate between several countries to protect the different ecosystems. Australia, on the other hand, presents an interesting opportunity as a case study for exploring a hybrid bio-urbanity and wild architecture as the biodiverse region lies under the jurisdiction of one country.

In the Australian context, the Atlas of Urban Expansion has been tracking urban growth only for the City of Sydney: "The urban extent of Sydney in 2014 was 162,527 hectares, increasing at an average annual rate of 1.5 percent since 2000. The urban extent in 2000 was 130,313 hectares, increasing at an average annual rate of 1.6 percent since 1991, when its urban extent was 113,035 hectares."[5] Yet, the city of Melbourne has overtaken Sydney in population, increasing the development pressure in the metro region. The preparations for the Olympics have also driven an increasing speed of urban development in Brisbane. Added to the population projections of Australia reaching between 29.2 and 30.8 million people by 2032, and between 34.3 and 45.9 million people by 2071, the east coast will face the pressure to urbanise to satisfy an already tight housing market, risking the disruption of its rich biodiversity.[6] The projected built environment must then be designed to balance cohabitation between humans and biodiversity through the direct integration of shared multi-species spaces.

To combat the degradation of resources and regenerate ecosystems back into urban settings, an array of cities launched urban greening strategy plans in the 2010s, such as the *Barcelona Pla Natura* (2021–2030), *Plan Biodiversite de Paris* (2018–2024), *Strategie Stadtlandschaft Berlin* (2012–2050), The London Plan (2021), Montréal durable (2016–2020), PlaNYC (2011–2030) and the Greening Sydney Strategy (2023).[7] These comprehensive plans target solutions for heat island effects, air pollution, green equity, water runoff management, biodiversity and the beautification of cities through the implementation of manicured green infrastructures. These plans aim to build resilient cities that can combat unforeseen risks in public health and safety. From the Greening Sydney Strategy: "We have identified community health, climate change and urban heat, and biodiversity and nature as the key risks to our city. Green infrastructure plays a vital role in mitigating these risks."[8] There is a human-centred focus on these green plans that require a shift in the specific parameters needed to increase strategic biodiversity. Pollinators need to be addressed within all these plans in a more targeted agenda for the success of greening, food production, and flourishing biodiversity. As the US Department of Agriculture notes:

> *Three-fourths of the world's flowering plants and about 35 percent of the world's food crops depend on animal pollinators to reproduce. That's one out of every three bites of food you eat. More than 3,500 species of native bees help increase crop yields. Some scientists estimate that one out of every three bites of food we eat exists because of animal pollinators like bees, butterflies and moths, birds and bats, and beetles and other insects.*[9]

This statistic is corroborated by the Food and Agriculture Organization of the United Nations (FAO).[10] Following the development of multilateral and international policies like UN Sustainable Development Goals and the Paris Agreement from 2015, the EU generated the EU Pollinators Initiative as a parallel initiative to the EU Biodiversity Strategy 2030 in recognition of the need for an independent focus of study, strategy and implementation.[11] With constant urban growth, intensive farming, and changes in land use (among other factors like parasites), the population of wild pollinators is threatened to a level of extinction. This could have devastating ramifications for food production and life on Earth as a whole. Organisations like the United States Department of Agriculture (USDA) have launched reports like the Annual Strategic Pollinator Priorities Report, to determine returns-on-investment from forage and habitat that benefits pollinators within agricultural lands, rangelands, federal forests and other working lands.[12] This signals a need for a new type of constructed refuge to be integrated into farming fields.

One key distinction that the EU Pollinators Initiative has made is the need to study how to strengthen and restore pollinator networks within agricultural, rural, and urban environments. While research focused on most pollinator initiatives is being conducted for best practices in agriculture and landscape management policies for agricultural and rural environments (as seen in the USDA initiative), little has been done to integrate pollinator ecosystems into the urban territory through architecture. Solutions for the preservation of bees have relied on constructing rural bee farms and promoting bee hives as artificial habitats. However, these solutions are more difficult to implement in an urban context because of site restrictions, and the natural conditions to sustain their networks at a larger scale. Their communities rely on the composition of native plant species, and interactions with a larger network, which is significantly disrupted in urban settings. To regenerate and protect these networks as integral parts of future cities, it is imperative to study vernacular pollinator tectonics to integrate them as parameters for contemporary architecture that not only promotes biodiversity and protects these fragile ecosystems within an urban context but also conditions the parameters for contemporary wild architecture of biomaterials, and biomimicry.

Methodologies for Green Architecture

At the turn of the 21st century, the regeneration or integration between nature and the built environment gave shape to new design methodologies based on reestablishing new roles for elements, systems and forms in architecture. Perhaps the most canonical methodology for understanding a holistic ecological green architecture that blends the wild with the built environment comes from Ken Yeang's thesis *Designing with Nature: The Ecological Basis for Architectural Design.* Yeang started working on ecological design in 1971 when green architecture and sustainability were seen as speculative futures, claiming, "Designing with Earth's ecological problems refers to the future and is therefore both prognostic and hypothetical."[13] His thesis, later published in 1995, delineated the strategies for integrating ecosystems within architecture to solve what has now become an imminent threat. Through this publication, Yeang makes the following distinctions between green architecture and sustainable architecture. Sustainable architecture adheres to meeting the construction demands while maintaining a responsible approach to using materials not to compromise the resources of future generations. Yeang sees this as a hypothetical approach as the state of resources can be projected, the future is not guaranteed. In green architecture, ecology influences the design process and spatial systems, and defines ecology as the study of the interactions of organisms, populations, and biological species. This brings the misconception of defining the site of intervention as being a physical, geographical boundary, rather than a larger ecosystem. An ecosystem is formed by both the physical and the biological with a defined trophic structure, biotic diversity and materials cycle. The impact of design is not restricted to the site's legal boundaries as the biosphere and ecosystems are not isolated systems but have spatial interlocking properties. Hence, it is necessary to assess the impact not only on the immediate environment but surrounding ecosystems with architecture working as a dynamic system that supports an environment beyond the physical site.

Yeang also states that the complexities of our environment must be understood holistically in the design process. This must include all the components of an ecosystem: inorganic substances, organic compounds, climate regime, autotrophic organisms, heterotrophic organisms, and decomposers. Architecture must be understood as part of a living and functioning ecosystem. He states: "In many instances, it has been found that it is the designer's simplistic understanding of the ecology of our environment that has resulted in many of the present environmentally insensitive urban land-use patterns and the present state of progressive degradation of the environment."[14]

Although Yeang differentiates between an ecological approach to architecture and a sustainable one, it does not mean that they cannot work together, as Yeang still mentions the need to understand the material flow, their life cycle and the use of finite resources. This poses the question of how architecture can use fewer materials but perform more efficiently while being a part of the larger ecosystem. This perhaps requires architecture to perform as a transformative responsive environment that interacts with both the biotic and abiotic.

Precedents in Green Architecture for Restoring Ecosystems

Yeang's own explorations of ecological architecture rely on the use of the vector as a design strategy. This is evident from his earliest works like the Mesiniaga Tower in Malaysia to more recently completed projects like the Solaris Tower in Singapore. The need for green to work as a continuous biotic system relies on the continuity of inorganic substances (H_2O, CO_2), organic compounds (soil), climate regime (sunpaths), autotrophic organisms (plants), heterotrophic organisms (animals), and decomposers (fungi). This translates into a singular ramping vector system that gives form to the topology of the buildings by wrapping around it. This would be similar to a single surface project, where the ground is used to form the massing of the building. The large Fukuoka Prefectural Hall (1990) from Emilio Ambasz emulates this condition of continuing the ground from the surrounding park to create an artificial hill that houses civic programs within it. The sectional drawings from this project reveal a continuous ecosystem that explores the 'green over grey' thesis for recovering the soil which the building occupies while connecting to the surrounding green square.

Limitations in space might not allow for a vectorial continuity of ground, yet the topology of the ground can be used to form an ecological building whether it continues from the ground level as a single surface or is separated from it by cutting the ground, pixelating the ground, or rotating the ground vertically. These strategies are evident in Renzo Piano's California Academy of Science, Stefano Boeri's Bosco Verticale, Jean Nouvel's One Central Park, and Vo Trong Nghia's House for Trees. All these projects are committed to the restoration of green ecosystems inside their respective urban environments. The different site conditions are then translated into different design strategies for treating the ground.

Renzo Piano's California Academy of Science from 2008 uses a section of the ground as the building itself and elevates it to form the building. The ground is conceptually a piece of the surrounding park that serves as an ecological plate covering 37,000 square metres and planted with 1,700,000 native species.[15]

Stefano Boeri's Bosco Verticale (2014) presents a pixelated repetition of ground through oversized balconies that can hold larger species of trees. The two towers house: "A total of 800 trees (480 first and second stage trees, 300 smaller ones, 15,000 perennials and/or ground covering plants and 5,000 shrubs), providing an amount of vegetation equivalent to 30,000 square metres of woodland and undergrowth, concentrated on 3,000 square metres of urban surface."[16]

Jean Nouvel's One Central Park (2014) rotates the ground to use it as a facade system where green becomes an element to dematerialize architecture. The facade is covered with 50 percent of vegetation with the aim to extend the surrounding park onto the building. Hydroponic walls and low profile horizontal planters and support cables integrated into the tower's facades support a variety of climbing and spreading plants.[17]

Vo Trong Nghia's House for Trees (2014) conceptualises a house as a series of oversized planter pots that can hold trees and serve for water management within a small urban lot. The pots themselves are both spaces for the plants above and spaces for the inhabitants inside.

Through these few precedents, it can be concluded that the scale in which the ground is used can compose a formal logic, as well as an architectural elements logic that can guide a spatial system for multi-species biotic and abiotic environments. Building further on these precedents towards an ecological architectural methodology for restoring pollinator networks in urban environments, the elements for pollinator architecture need to be reconsidered scientifically to accommodate specific pollinator communities and not just ecosystems in the generic sense. In addition, the architectural elements and system for holding the ground and its pollinator ecosystem is not to perform a singular role (spatial, ornamental, semiotic or performative) but rather a hybridised productive role. Meaning, a structural element can be spatial, ornamental and performative, for example.

Prototyping a Pollinator Architecture

To experiment with an ecological architectural system for strengthening, restoring, protecting and producing pollinator networks, *Wild Futures* was envisioned as an experimental prototypical design for a home following the parameters for pollinator communities. The project is contextual to Australia's complexity of having a rich biodiversity and the pressure of a growing population and urbanity. As previously established, Sydney is growing at an annual rate of 1.5 per cent. It is expected that between 119,400 and 138,550 new homes could be built over the next five years (2022–23 to 2026–27).[18] The housing market has been affected by disruptions in supply chains experienced globally from the Covid-19 pandemic and the blockage of the Suez Canal in March of 2021, along with global inflation, rising material costs and labour shortage. For these reasons, the typology of a house was selected for this study as housing will be a major contributor to urban growth and in parallel the detriment of biodiverse ecosystems due to the anticipated demand in an already existing housing shortage.

To contextualise this study for Sydney, an understanding of native pollinator ecosystems is needed to translate the specifics of pollinator habitats as architectural tectonics. This was done through a collaboration between the faculty of science and the school of architecture at the University of Technology Sydney with Dr Yvonne Davila, specialist in pollinator ecologies, and Dr Rafael Luna, director of the Infra-Architecture Lab.

To build an ecosystem for cohabitation between humans and pollinators, spatial parameters were extracted from the cavity-nesting solitary bees and their particular nesting habitats. Some of these parameters include the diameter of their nesting holes ranging between 3 to10 millimetres and should be between 100 to 150 millimetres in depth.[19] These cavities must be inclined at a slight angle to prevent water entering and pooling inside the nesting hole. The materials for nesting holes should be natural and untreated. If artificially built, the cavities must be spaced out, be stable so as to not move much in the wind, and be kept out of the rain with roofs or overhangs that protect their entrances.

Aside from the parameters for supporting cavity-nesting bees, there are also parameters for the flowering plants. A variety of native plant species were selected based on a database search of the species utilised by pollinators in Sydney. The list of plants was curated to include species that have diverse flowering periods to have a structure that could provide food resources for pollinators all year round. The plants can be mixed to produce a diversity of flower morphologies, sizes and colours that can attract not just solitary bees but also birds and butterflies. The plants must stay relatively short, within a 50cm height.

These 18 species were selected for the warmer months: Baeckea imbricata, Baeckea virgata, Brachyscome multifida, Brachyscome angustifolia, Clematis glycinoides, Darwinia citriodora, Dianella tasmanica, Goodenia albiflora, Goodenia ovata, Grevillea rosmarinifolia, Hibbertia procumbens, Hibbertia dentata, Pelargonium species, Pimelea sylvestris, Pultanea pedunculata, Scaevola calendulacea, Scaevola striata, Westringia fruticosa.

23 additional species and nursery varieties were selected for colder months: Brachyscome multifida, Goodenia hederaceae, Pimelea sylvestris, Scaevola aemula (pink flowering), Goodenia macmillanii, Platysace lanceolata, Viola hederacea, Westringia 'Low Horizon', Hibbertia vestita, Pimelea linifolia, Correa 'Little Cate', Grevillea 'New Blood', Grevillea 'Mt Tamboritha', Grevillea 'Gin Gin Gem', Scaevola stricta, Leucophyta brownii, Chrysocephalum apiculatum, Melaleuca thymifolia.

Through these preset parameters, a prototype of prefabricated elements was developed as a timber system that addresses the need for targeted greening and affordable housing. The whole system is composed of bee hotel I-beams and planter box-beams. The box-beams will hold the soil and plant species and will be connected horizontally to form continuous ground rings. Its dimensions in millimetres are 2400 by 500 by 500 based on the length of plywood and the width and depth needed for the soil to plant flowering species. The I-beams provide shelter for the solitary bees and stack vertically on top of the planter box-beams forming a structural system that can be assembled between a couple of people. The dimensions for a bee-hotel I-beam are 750 millimetres length

by 150 width by 500 height. Since this becomes a stacking system, the species of flowering plants need to stay under 500 millimetres in height. The dimensions and holes for the bee hotel cavities form a randomised pattern of holes between 3 to 10 millimetres in diameter as previously noted. This makes the I-beam not only structural but also performative and ornamental. Its design as an I-beam also protects the holes from the rain.

To address affordability, material life cycle, and material waste, both elements are fabricated using 19 millimetres construction-grade plywood as the primary material for structure, interior and exterior finish. The pieces are cut with a CNC with specific joint patterns to minimise the use of any other assembly material. Sikaflex 116 was used to glue all the pieces together. Each piece is painted with Crommelin Enhance Penetrating timber sealant for weather protection, and the planter box beams are treated with an extra layer of Crommelin Elastoseal as a rubber membrane to protect the plywood from the soil and water. The I-beam sits on top of the box beam connected with a wooden peg, Sikaflex-116 bond, and screws. This minimises the use of additional materials, reduces waste, and keeps the cost of construction down. As the system stacks, it also forms a self-watering trickle system where the planter above drips excess water to the planter below to conserve water usage. The I-beams are placed at random angles between 90 and 45 degrees to stabilise the lateral forces. The system has been tested through a pavilion demonstrating how targeted ecological parameters can restore damaged ecosystems, in this case, the pollinator community. Through the repetition of just these two elements, the system can achieve spatial variations, spatial effects, and optimised usage of resources while creating a productive piece of architecture.

Opposite: Wild Futures - Pavilion elevation. Image courtesy of Finn Marchant.

Top Left: Wild Futures - Pavilion interior. Image courtesy of Finn Marchant.

Top Right: Wild Futures - Pavilion plant detail. Image courtesy of Finn Marchant.

This project proposes a new concept for the role of elements in architecture. The vernacular breeding, feeding and nesting places of pollinators can serve as architectural parameters

for the tectonics of productive elements and systems that can produce a 'wild' architectural language. Walls, columns, windows, or slabs do not have to be static or independent elements. These can be optimised to serve multiple roles to minimise the use of materials. Using nature as an enclosure reconceptualises walls and windows as transformative and responsive elements with variant opacities that can change with time. This project demonstrates the need for a specific targeted "Green Architecture" that could pair up with urban policies for city greening, requiring a deep understanding of native urban pollinator networks that exist in an ecosystem along with their corresponding habitats of indigenous plant species to promote this much-needed symbiosis between humans and pollinators.

The ongoing planetary urbanisation has not only created social injustices of relocating populations for the sake of urban redevelopment, but it has also created ecological injustices by displacing species and depleting their natural environments. To promote the regeneration of ecosystems —in this case, pollinator ecologies —targeted ecological architectural models could serve as a framework for future methods to reintegrate biodiversity within the urban context. While the need for urbanisation and housing development will keep increasing, the aim is to show the need for new tectonics in architecture that demand productive elements, a certain functionality to ornamentation, and new composition methods for holistic ecological forms.

> *...because of humanity's pervasive influence, no area can be completely isolated from its direct or indirect effects. No part of the earth could be termed to be completely natural; some human modification of the environment has occurred, if no more than a minor change caused by chemical fallout from air pollution.*[20]

It is an inevitable condition that architecture must evolve as humans will need to coexist within natural wild environments in an act of planetary wild regeneration. We are all sharing a singular biosphere and every act of building links us at a planetary scale.

Above: Wild Futures - Exterior rendering of a Pollinator House. Image courtesy of HARP Collective.

Below: Wild Futures - Interior rendering of dining room in a Pollinator House. Image courtesy of HARP Collective.

01 William Cronon, *The Trouble with Wilderness : Or, Getting back to the Wrong Nature* (New York: Norton, 1995).

02 "Urban Development," The World Bank, published April 2023, https://www.worldbank.org/en/topic/urbandevelopment/overview#:~:text=Today%2C%20some%2056%25%20of%20the.

03 Marron Institute of Urban Management and the Stern School of Business of New York University, "Atlas of Urban Expansion," published 2016, http://atlasofurbanexpansion.org/.
European Environment Agency, "Urban Atlas Land Cover/Land Use 2018 (Vector), Europe, 6-Yearly," The Copernicus Land Monitoring Service, 2018, https://land.copernicus.eu/en/products/urban-atlas/urban-atlas-2018.

04 UNPRI, "Mapping Natural Capital Depletion," May 12, 2021, https://www.unpri.org/nature/mapping-natural-capital-depletion/7338.article.

05 Marron Institute of Urban Management and the Stern School of Business of New York University, "Atlas of Urban Expansion - Sydney," n.d., http://atlasofurbanexpansion.org/cities/view/Sydney.

06 "Population Projections, Australia," Australian Bureau of Statistics," 2023, https://www.abs.gov.au/statistics/people/population/population-projections-australia/2022-base-2071.

07 Amalia Calderón-Argelich, Isabelle Anguelovski, James J.T. Connolly, and Francesc Baró, "Greening Plans as (Re)Presentation of the City: Toward an Inclusive and Gender-Sensitive Approach to Urban Greenspaces," *Urban Forestry & Urban Greening 86* (August 2023): 127984. https://doi.org/10.1016/j.ufug.2023.127984.
Karen Sweeney, Phillip Julian, Matthew Sund, and Carl d'Entremont, *Greening Sydney Strategy* (NSW: City of Sydney, 2021).

08 Ibid. 13.

09 "The Importance of Pollinators," US Department of Agriculture, accessed April 30, 2024. https://www.usda.gov/peoples-garden/pollinators#:~:text=Pollinators%20visit%20flowers%20in%20their.

10 Food and Agriculture Organization of the United Nations, "Background," 2024, https://www.fao.org/pollination/background/en/.

11 European Commission, "Pollinators," Environment., Accessed April 30, n.d., https://environment.ec.europa.eu/topics/nature-and-biodiversity/pollinators_en.
European Commission. 2020. "Biodiversity Strategy for 2030." Environment.ec.europa.eu. European Commission. 2020. https://environment.ec.europa.eu/strategy/biodiversity-strategy-2030_en.

12 Office of the Chief Scientist U.S. Department of Agriculture, "USDA ANNUAL STRATEGIC POLLINATOR PRIORITIES REPORT 2022," U.S. Department of Agriculture, published 2022, https://www.usda.gov/sites/default/files/documents/annual-pollinator-report-2022.pdf.

13 Ken Yeang, *Designing with Nature: The Ecological Basis for Architectural Design*, New York Mcgraw-Hill: 1995), 1.

14 Ibid. 9.

15 Renzo Piano Building Workshop. "RPBW Architects - Renzo Piano Building Workshop," 2024, https://www.rpbw.com/project/california-academy-of-sciences.

16 "Vertical Forest Milan," Stefano Boeri Architetti, 2018, https://www.stefanoboeriarchitetti.net/en/project/vertical-forest/.

17 "One Central Park - Ateliers Jean Nouvel." Ateliers Jean Nouvel, 2014, http://www.jeannouvel.com/en/projects/one-central-park/.

18 "Sydney Housing Supply Forecast," NSW Government, n.d., https://www.planning.nsw.gov.au/Research-and-Demography/Sydney-Housing-Supply-Forecast.

19 "Aussie Bee Website Homepage," Aussie Bee, accessed 2024, https://www.aussiebee.com.au/.

20 Ken Yeang, *Designing with Nature: The Ecological Basis for Architectural Design* (New York Mcgraw-Hill, 1995), 11-12.

SOME UTILITIES, A COUPLE OF STAIRS, AND VERY FEW DOORS

João Paupério and Maria Rebelo
atelier local

The architecture of a city reveals an ecology of its own. From this perspective, typology is essentially the formal embodiment of its socioeconomic and cultural habitus. In Valongo, the city where we are based and conduct most of our work, the architecture of the house attests to this idea. It unveils a productive and ecological history that spans from the Portuguese inland to the neighbouring city of Porto (Portugal), as it produced most of the latter's bread between the 18th and 19th centuries. With the rise of industrialisation, the city of Porto began to produce bread in the city centre. Old houses in Valongo, where bakeries used to operate, were transformed in their character. It was in one of these houses that, regenerating its mixed-use purpose, we decided to establish ourselves in 2021.

Our practice is thus located in a peripheral town in a country itself that is relatively small and on the periphery of Europe. In the aftermath of the 2007-08 financial crisis, inadequately addressed through substantial investments in the tourism industry, major cities in Portugal now contend with a widespread housing crisis affecting more than just the most underprivileged classes.[1] Reflecting this context, our early commissions have been notable for their ordinariness. We have mostly been engaged in small house refurbishments for a lower middle-class population directly or indirectly displaced from the city centre of Porto.

In *Figures, Doors and Passages,* Robin Evans opens his essay with a striking line that has been a motto for our practice: 'the most ordinary things contain the deepest mysteries.'[2] The particular significance of this epigraph is methodological in nature. By examining the formal structure of various domestic settings from Renaissance palazzos and villas to Alexander Klein's *Functional House for Frictionless Living* (1928), Evans unveils how distinct ways of living have existed over time. Contrary to their understanding as "universal and timeless requisites for decent

Opposite: House in Valonga III. Image courtesy of Francisco Ascensão.

Top Left: House in Valongo II. Image by author.

Top Right: House in Valongo V. Image by author.

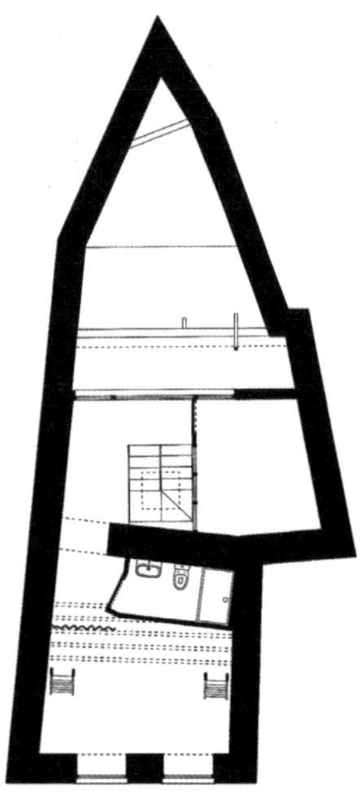

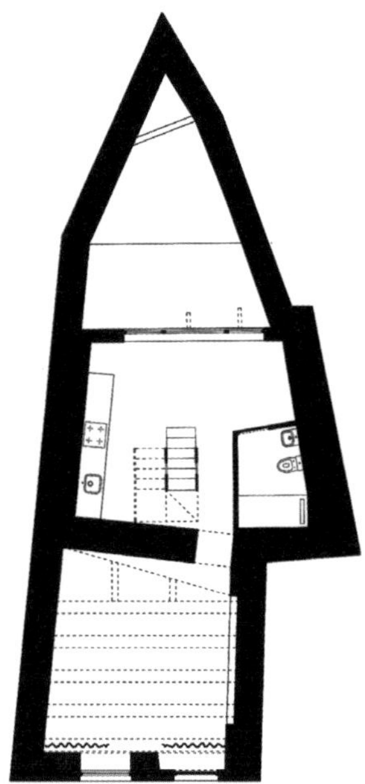

living," he argues that conventional layouts of contemporary housing represent specific forms of life situated in concrete places and particular moments in history.[3] Often working with modest aesthetic aspirations and limited budgets, Evans' ideas have provided us with the means to overcome banality and suburban boredom.[4]

Valongo, derived from the Latin *Vallis longus* [long valley], holds more significance than mere toponymic interest. The valley is defined by an extensive 'anticline,' a geological feature that has influenced its economy for centuries. A mineral-rich subsoil has yielded various raw materials, from gold mining during the Roman Empire to the present-day extraction and processing of slate. In fact, most of the property partition walls, and rear facades in the old town were constructed using stone-on-stone slate, with granite reserved for main facades, window stonework and nobler buildings. Besides, Valongo occupied a strategic position between Porto and inland agricultural regions where cereal was produced. Its valley was traversed by a river flowing through steep terrain, offering ideal conditions for harnessing hydraulic energy, while surrounding hills provided abundant firewood for ovens producing bread.[5] Between slate and bread, its economy and tectonics are interconnected and better understood in parallel.

This exploration of Valongo's socio-natural history leads us to a specific type of domestic architecture. The small-scale character of these bakeries was closely tied to their family-run operation. As households grew and new couples were established, they started new bakeries at home. These houses thus embodied a material heritage resulting from the convergence of labour (bread production) and an abundance of local materials (slate). And as soon as we began working on them, we realised that not only their facades but also their interior arrangements shared some common traits.

Slate partition walls, spaced five-to-six metres apart, typically supported a single-span wooden structure. Long before Le Corbusier, these houses had already embraced the *plan libre.* A thick slate wall of over 60 centimetres often replicated this structural logic, dividing houses longitudinally. In some cases, window remnants suggest that these may have originally served as rear facades before being extended. On the ground floor, rooms with a more public nature faced the street, welcoming the outside world. Adjacent to these rooms, a wide corridor allowed human and animal access, often linking the street to backyard subsistence gardens. Identifiable by unusually large doors on the main facade, this corridor provided ample space for donkeys transporting produce to go inside in an inverted *mise-en-scène* of Pieter de Hooch's painting 'A Boy Bringing Bread' (c. 1663). Additionally, a staircase under

a skylight granted access to the *piano nobile,* where daily life occurred besides work in a large polyvalent space looking onto the street, which sometimes featured smaller bed alcoves for an extra layer of privacy. Finally, at the rear end of the ground floor, traces of smoke on the robust wood structures register what was once a more or less open space for bread production.

As we mentioned in the introduction, industrialisation hindered this domestic economy, eventually leading it to disappear. More or less transformed, many of these houses are now decaying and, in most cases, underused or even vacant. Yet, as remote working once again questions the spatial relationships between home and work, their formal structure holds open potential for enriching those peripheral territories in the face of the contemporary economy, definitively overcoming the functional division of modern urban planning from the already existing building stock.

Upon encountering these houses, in particular the one we came to inhabit, we found them significantly transformed by the increasing functionalisation of life during the twentieth century to which Klein was referring. Corridors, interior rooms with no natural light, as well as closed kitchens became commonplace. Oral testimonies and material traces, however, revealed that the evolution of these spaces often retained a blend of work and domestic life, with ambiguous rooms offering varying degrees of privacy. Unravelling the mysteries of these ordinary houses provided potential clues for their architectural regeneration. To regenerate the domestic complexity of their past lives meant transcending a strict division and functionalisation of spaces, aiming to retrieve their original spatial qualities. This involved recognising their character within a specific time and place, allowing for the restoration of their original versatility, albeit re-imagined through newly fictionalised spatialities. The first step towards this goal was to restore the breadth implied by their original structure. Instead of compartmentalising spaces and defining them by function, our approach adopts an alternative spatial topology. Utilitarian cores are judiciously placed within use-less spaces, which can be either more inclined towards private or shared uses depending on characteristics that take advantage of the existing, such as their position in relation to the street or the rear garden.

Opposite: House in Valongo II. Plans by author.

Top Left: House in Valongo II. Image by author.

Top Right: Pieter de Hooch, *A Boy Bringing Bread*, c.1663, oil on canvas. Image courtesy of The Wallace Collection, London.

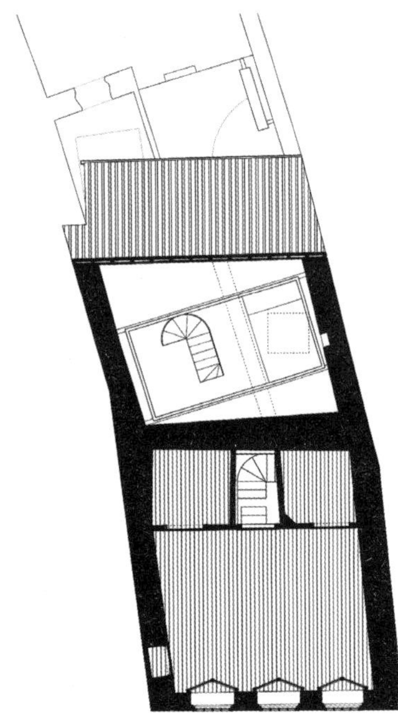

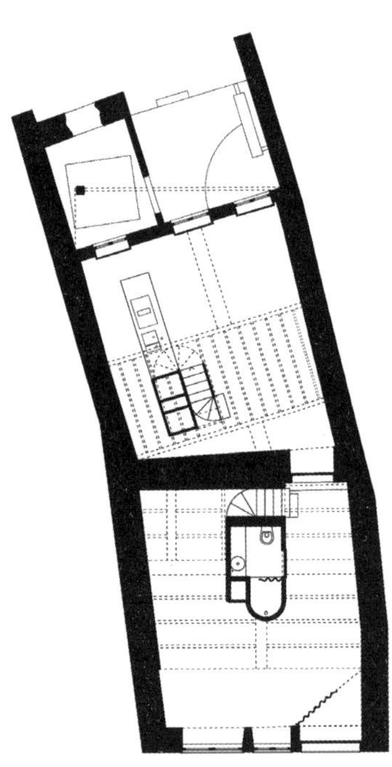

From a formal perspective, this approach creates an architectural space focused on preserving the original perimeter intact and organising, through minimal gestures, a number of utilities shaped after their practical purposes. Akin, for instance, to Saint Jerome's wooden study, depicted by Antonello da Messina (c.1475), where objects are stocked for convenience, and the rest of the space is liberated, or else to the cells that artist Absalon conceived before his death, for him to live in the middle of several metropolises while isolated from society and living with the bare minimum. Alongside these, of course, one positions an occasional door or a much-needed staircase to organise the resulting space. In the case of our studio-house, we have even added a second staircase to multiply our possibilities. The arrangement of spatial distances within the house may regulate several layers of privacy in a rather subtle and fluid manner. Depth is fundamental. In fact, in one of our built proposals, one can move from the street to the bed without needing to open or close a single door other than the front one. To do so, one enters directly into the main living space, then crosses a 70-centimetre-thick threshold into the kitchen area just to find a strangely positioned staircase to reach a winter garden. On the upper floor, one moves once again through a 70-centimetre-thick threshold to find a shared open room with a double-height pitched ceiling, where two single beds are placed above in a hanging mezzanine for children, liberating the room below for all sorts of uses.

The development of these projects has coincided with the emergence of new labour dynamics resulting from the COVID-19 pandemic. For many, working from home has become a reality once again, and our proposals' typological subversion to undo the over-compartmentalisation of space while keeping the possibility for different layers of privacy longs to address these new forms of housing. This strategy has allowed us to create more generous spaces with a reduced economic and ecological footprint, and promote more direct forms of life liberated from meaningless or obsolete domestic conventions such as a strict separation between day and night activities.

By presenting our proposals for the refurbishment of this type of houses, this essay argues that the regeneration of old productive centres such as Valongo lies in the polyvalence of its building types. In a way, it seeks to address the possibility of the 'city as a combinatory' of interconnected activities instead of zoning policies.[6] The truth is that we have found on the margins an opportunity to live together, which, due to the pressures driven by financial capitalism, has unfortunately become unattainable in the city of Porto. But also, of course, we found it in the possibility for their architectural re-invention by subverting its limitations with minimal gestures. A strategy that, in the face of the pressure being exerted by gentrification

in Portuguese cities, could constitute a relevant and ecological alternative to resist and restore proper urbanity to territories that have since been suburbanised.

Opposite: Studio House in Valongo. Plans by author.

Above: Living room of Studio House in Valongo. Image courtesy of Francisco Ascensão.

01 Ana Cordeiro Santos, *A nova questão da habitação em Portugal* (Coimbra: Actual Editora, 2019).

02 Robin Evans, "Figures, Doors and Passages" (1978), in *Translations for Drawing to Building and Other Essays* (London: Architectural Association Publications, 1997), 55-91.

03 Ibid. 56.

04 It is worth noting that Rossi's specific writings on the periphery has played a similar role. Aldo Rossi, "La Città e la Periferia" (1961), in *Scritti scelti sull'architettura e la città 1956-1972* (Milano: CLUP, 1975) 158-174.

05 These facts are part of Valongo's popular culture and have recently been incorporated into the redesign of public space, notably through commemorative plaques marking some of these old bakeries and biscuit shops. For a first and fairly structured historical review, see: Joaquim A. L. Reis, *A Villa de Vallongo* (Porto: Typographia Coelho, 1904).

06 Jean Renaudie (2014), *La ville est une combinatoire* (Ivry-sur-Seine: Movitcity édition, 2014).

DIALOGUE WITH THE PAST

IN CONVERSATION WITH NERI AND HU

Interview by Jarel Cheah

Above: Lao Ding Feng Beijing. Image courtesy of Zhu Runzi.

Below: Lyndon Neri & Rossana Hu. Image courtesy of Jiaxi Yang & Zhu Zhe.

In the context of intense urbanisation and development in China, Neri and Hu's architectural ouvre situates itself within the the aftermath of demolition, and erasure of traditional, urban and cultural fabric. Their ethos of working with the existing goes beyond government-designated historical buildings, advocating for the consideration of buildings deemed ordinary or mundane by legislation.

Based in Shanghai, the city's cultural, urban, and historic contexts function as a point of departure for design inquiries that span across a wide spectrum of scales. Alongside their design practice, Lyndon Neri and Rossana Hu have been deeply committed to architectural education and have lectured across the globe in various universities and professional forums, including University of California, Berkeley, Harvard Graduate School of Design, Yale School of Architecture and others.

At the time of the interview, Neri and Hu presented Liminality in the 2023 Venice Architecture Biennale, which consisted of adaptive reuse projects that represent the practice's research in different ways of working with the existing.

The questions posed to them were undertaken as a series of emails between two continents and different time zones attempts to investigate the intersection between their design practice and theoretical explorations of adaptive reuse. Neri and Hu's dialogue subsequently imparts to us their philosophical approaches to practice.

In the 2023 Venice Biennale, your exhibition was titled *Liminality*, What informs this interest?

In recent decades, living and traveling extensively throughout Asia, we observe the alarming trend of Asia's major metropolises becoming more and more alike. In China, this phenomenon is exacerbated by the sheer scale at which its process of urbanisation and modernization has occurred. Practicing in China, at this critical moment, we find ourselves caught between "the optimization of advanced technology and the ever-present tendency to regress into nostalgic historicism." Nostalgia can be a problematic notion for some; it tends to be taken dismissively, as Charles Maier remarks: "Nostalgia is to memory as kitsch is to art."[1] But we feel strongly that there is a potential to be constructive with nostalgia, rather than merely reductive." Due to the fast pace of change we encounter in our environments, we predictably look towards the past as a stable time, often imploring it to inject some meaningful content to the present. Our interest in liminality stemmed from our attitudes regarding constructs of temporality and history. The works showcased speak to our understanding that each project exists as part of a time continuum, occupying a liminal space, suspended in 'permanent evolution,' each yearning to write its own anticipated fate.

As part of this exhibition, your work was described as "allowing one to traverse both physical and allusive thresholds, thus creating a visceral perception of the intersections of past, present and future." Can you expand on this?

As we imagine for ourselves what the future holds, we collectively occupy the liminal space of experimentation both in theoretical constructs and in design practice. Derived from the Latin word *limen*, which means 'threshold', liminality is a term used by cultural theorists, anthropologists and psychologists to describe spaces located in-between locations of cultural action. In today's post-colonial world, Homi Bhabha speaks about boundaries in culture as a place of liminality or 'third space' where translations and negotiations occur. Liminal space and the notion of the threshold represents a space of ambiguity that engenders new possibilities and change. These spaces become the very stage for transitory events. Although such spaces may lack definition and are often associated as residual spaces, the power of liminality lies precisely in their open-ended transitory nature that provides the agency for disrupting and challenging the status quo. Through investigating the untapped potentials of liminal spaces, which are often unprogrammed transitional spaces lacking detail and purpose, we aim to position newfound purpose and potency in the unfamiliar and the uncanny. As mentioned before, liminality also has implications on our constructs of temporality and history. St. Augustine, in his Confessions challenges the divisions of past, present, and future, but reframes the construct of time into three categories: the time present of things past (memory); the time present of things present (direct experience); the time present of things future (expectation). All temporal constructs are equally 'present' and valid within their own right. As we hope for the future in anticipation of changes to take shape, liminal spaces provoke us to reflect on our nostalgic roots. We may long for the arrival to our final destination, but we remain in fixed co-existence with the past and present.

How do you approach the process of working on the existing?

We have to ask ourselves what is the meaning behind the things we do. Research in this case becomes very important because it tells us certain things that help us rethink the whole process of design. Our attitude to renovation is similar to Svetlana Boym's assertion in that the 'toleration of disharmony' allow us the freedom to stitch the building as we develop the project. In our confrontation with this set of issues, Boym suggests 'off-modern' relationships between preservation and development, advocating for designers to engage with traces of the past: past authors, builders, failed projects, and revealing the traces of non-realized compositions. Referencing the concept of *pentimenti*, defined in art history as "a presence of traces of previous work," the suggestion here is that through experimental means of preservation and adaptation, we can exploit a "different logic of the ruin, which is not romantic, not baroque, not melancholic, but a form of toleration of disharmony – a toleration of plural modernities with which we live."[2] Boym's notion of 'off' doesn't mean to go outside, but claims that the off-modern attitude can recover the unforeseen past and chart unexplored territory of modern history.

There were some amazing models from the three adaptive reuse projects in the exhibition, how did the model start to inform how you work?

For this exhibition, the most interesting model is that along with site models, each project is represented by large conceptual models displaying sectional fragments capturing isolated moments of tension. Building off of fragments and relics of post-industrial, rural and urban heritage, these models highlight the role of representation in the dialectics between past and present, old and new, smooth and textured, refined and raw. For a project such as Nantou, the inspiration was drawn from the site itself – the urban density, the existing notion of collage and patina, the intricate network of labyrinthine alleyways and urban assemblage. The material experimentation that went into creating the sectional models followed the research on local materials and construction craft.

Could you describe any of the existing buildings you've worked on as prosaic?

Each project has its unique background and challenges. The fundamental thing for us is we try to find meaning in everything we do. The basis for adaptive reuse more often than not, are actually non-romantic relics from the past. These remnants nevertheless pose important questions in terms of sustainability and construction waste management, as well as deeper philosophical questions regarding originality and authorship.

There is inherent tension between functionality and the poetic when working with existing structures, sometimes architects like to retain something that might not make functional sense. How do you balance these conflicting realities?

We believe in architecture and design as a powerful cultural force. The functional aspects are less interesting for us, although as professionals that's the prerequisite - your design must work on a very realistic level. We believe in the subtext over the obvious and the poetic over the utilitarian. There are issues that we always explore such as issues like layering, transparency, texture, framing and materiality. Questions of culture and aesthetic philosophy concern us deeply and we also want to relate what we do to the everyday and the public. These explorations allow us to respond to the problem of this era. In addressing the off-modern, we also borrow from the notion of the monument, put forth by Aldo Rossi, who conceived the city as a living entity, constantly transforming and accumulating its own consciousness and memory. Rossi argued that architecture's value resides within the forms of urban artifacts, which continue to structure the city even after they have shed their functions.

Rossi was talking about urban artifacts in European cities, many still stand today. Are there monuments in China?

The studio investigates, in parallel, how notions of 'ruinophilia' in eastern thinking can provide new design strategies for adaptive reuse. Unlike European ruins, ancient Chinese structures were often constructed out of wood, leaving behind only their foundations as traces of their original grandeur. Evident in its etymology, the word for 'ruin' which evolved from the word *qiu* (connoting a mound of rubble) to *xu* (a signifier of emptiness), indicates that over time the concept of the architectural ruin was increasingly freed from external visual signs relying on allusion, rather than direct, literal representations.

Any closing remarks on how you would like to end?

A quote by Saint- Exupéry expresses both our design and life philosophy well: "We don't ask to be eternal beings, but we ask that things do not lose all their meaning."

1. Charles Maier's 1995 essay titled "The End of Longing."
2. Svetlana Boym, *The Off-Modern*, (New York: Bloomsbury, 2017).

Top: The Waterhouse at South Bund. Photo by Pedro Pegenaute. Bottom right: Physical model of the Waterhouse at South Bund. Photo by Sanif Xu. Bottom left: Nantou City Guesthuse fragment model by Sanif Xu.

REVITALISING SONGYANG

XU TIANTIAN'S PRACTICE

Andrea Crudeli

Amid China's rapid urbanisation, rural villages have increasingly faced marginalisation as significant portions of their populations migrate towards urban centres, driven by the quest for better employment opportunities and enhanced quality of life. They face critical challenges such as scarcity of social resources, limited educational facilities, and poorer medical conditions compared to urban areas. These disparities contribute to a significant quality-of-life gap between rural and urban populations. This exodus leads to a depletion of social labour and resources in rural areas, leaving behind an ageing population that struggles with limited access to healthcare and economic opportunities. Consequently, many villages face economic decline, a hollowing out of communities, and a loss of cultural heritage and vitality. This demographic shift has engendered a pivotal discourse centred on preserving the periphery of what is often regarded as authentic China: a cultural fabric rich in history, rituals, and traditions that now confronts the risk of extinction. The region of Songyang can be considered a paradigmatic example of this phenomenon.

Top Left: Caichai Village, Songyang. Photo by Wang Ziling.

Middle: Tofu Factory. Photo by Wang Ziling.

Top Right: Tofu Factory. Photo by Wang Ziling.

Located in the lush expanse of southwest Zhejiang province, Songyang spans 1,406 square kilometres and is mainly populated by rural dwellers. This region comprises many villages, each representing the enduring charm of Jiang Nan's last hidden treasures. In this bucolic setting, traditional agricultural practices frame the ancient villages, surrounded by a vernacular building environment. However, despite the picturesque heritage, mass migrations of population to urban areas has been a challenge.

In light of this context, it has become necessary to implement a strategy of urban development, accompanied by crucial societal transformations. These processes of territorial regeneration have become one of the most prevalent phenomena of the past few decades, motivated by political factors to embrace globalisation. The tensions and opportunities that emerge when modernity intersects with a vernacular context and the ways in which architects have sought to mediate this phenomenon have been a subject of research by Kenneth Frampton from the 1980s to the present. The architecture historian has studied the issue of modernising peripheral regions with his theory of Critical Regionalism since the 1980s.[1] His initial discourse introduced a critical perspective regarding the encounter between modern architecture's language and the peripheral areas' vernacular attitude. His dissertation, encapsulated in a six-

point design-driven agenda, promoted adapting the universal language of construction to the specificities of regional contexts. In this sense, Frampton's approach was both a critique and a directive, urging architects to foster deeply contextual sensibilities that are attuned to each locality.

Over the years, Frampton's reflections on architecture have evolved, particularly concerning the role of regionalism in a globalised world and how to define the cultural boundary of a region. In a seminal discussion, he highlighted the necessity of revisiting Martin Heidegger's concept of *raum*—a philosophical interpretation of space where a civilization manifests its presence.[2] Frampton intended this concept as a phenomenologically bounded space. In this territorial area, a self-legitimised community governs independently, thanks to historically, institutionally, politically, and culturally ingrained factors, towards the definition of a recognizable cultural identity. From his early essays, Frampton described this *raum* as cities or small regions; then, he expanded this concept to encompass macro areas after the developments of globalisation, including large portions of territories, such as countries.[3] This renovated notion of *raum* encourages a broader view of what constitutes a region, suggesting a more fluid approach that transcends traditional boundaries to encompass broader macro-areas of the globe. This is where the Songyang region finds a particular role.

Central to this story is the initiative led by Xu Tiantian, a Beijing-based architect and founder of DnA (Design and Architecture), who has undertaken a pioneering project in this countryside that scholars have called the "Songyang Story."[4] In response to the pressing challenges facing Songyang, an invigorating collaboration between the local communities and DnA began in 2014. The general regenerative design strategy encompassed comprehensive social, economic, and architectural principles aimed at rural revitalization. Socially, it emphasised community engagement, cultural heritage preservation, and youth reconnection through various educational and cultural initiatives. Economically, it promoted sustainable local economies by diversifying income sources with small-scale factories, incorporating e-commerce, and establishing collective economic models to ensure equitable benefit distribution. Architecturally, the strategy involved minimal yet impactful interventions, adaptive reuse of existing structures, and context-sensitive design employing local materials and traditional construction techniques.

Xu Tiantian, educated with an international mindset, received her Bachelor of Architecture from Beijing's Tsinghua University and her Masters in Urban Design from the Harvard Graduate School of Design. She had the ability to convey the international language of contemporary architecture and adapt it locally to Songyang, considering its peculiarities and needs. Because her "context remains China, and so her architectural narratives inevitably address aspects of the country's sociopolitical condition,"[5] towards the integration of modern architecture with the traditional vernacular attitude described by Frampton. The architect has interpreted the "Rural Revitalising Plan" proposed by the local authorities as a venture of architectural acupuncture to rejuvenate the rural heritage, stimulate economic growth, and integrate tourism into the rural fabric. Each intervention, delicately tailored to its village's unique historical and cultural context, transforms buildings into communal hubs, intertwining nature with the social tapestry of community life.

Operating on a restrained budget, this strategy eschews the grandiose for impactful community-centric revitalization, fostering sustainable development across the region, as Li Zhang wrote, "what the female architect Tiantian Xu dares to do that few others have done is develop a program-driven approach that optimises the health and wellbeing of the building's users."[6] These interventions not only address the functional needs of the communities but also respect and enhance the local architectural vernacular, interpreting perfectly what Frampton proposed as a critical mediation language. The architectural interventions in Songyang serve primarily as venues for social activities, laying the groundwork for a "regenerative transformation" of the rural social structure. These buildings are designed to be multifunctional public spaces that host various community events and activities. They act as hubs for social interaction, cultural preservation, and economic development, thereby revitalising the community. This approach not only addresses the immediate social and economic needs of the villagers but also fosters a sustainable, long-term regeneration of the rural area's social fabric by enhancing community engagement and restoring local heritage.

Remarkable examples of an extraordinary capacity to graft modernity within historicized contexts include the Tofu Factory, the Brown Sugar Factory, and the Wangjing Memorial Hall. The use of local construction techniques reinterpreted with modern technology, the focus on preserving the local light, and a topological approach that incorporates the geographical dimension into the architectural scale are all factors converging towards an architecture that is attuned to the identity of place. Moreover, the economic revival of Songyang County is exemplified through the transformative initiatives at Pingtian Village Center. Since its completion in 2015, the centre has become a catalyst for the burgeoning local homestay business and a vibrant hub for a fabric dyeing studio, which serves as an incubator for entrepreneurial training in e-commerce. This innovative model rejuvenates the local economy and bolsters community spirit and pride, marking a significant departure from traditional economic activities. The revival efforts in Songyang involve a meticulous regeneration process, which is informed by a detailed analysis of the existing architectural framework. This includes identifying which structural elements, such as columns and beams, should be replaced using the traditional Chinese "Sun-Mao" or Tenon and Mortise system. This method ensures rapid reconstruction while maintaining cultural fidelity and structural integrity, which is crucial for sustaining the region's architectural heritage.

These ventures underscore a broader strategy to redefine the rural-urban interface, incorporating urban innovations into rural settings through initiatives like tea education programs that engage urban students. This strategic approach aims to maintain the region's rural identity while enhancing its appeal to urban dwellers, promoting an experiential continuity that integrates the allure of rural living with the conveniences of urban accessibility. Additionally, these efforts are crucial in restoring ecological balance. Revitalising local economies through sustainable building practices is also a key objective, ensuring that new developments are environmentally friendly and economically beneficial. Enhancing social equity and community well-being is prioritised by creating spaces that are accessible and beneficial to all community members, thereby fostering a sense of inclusivity and cohesion. The transformation of the Pingtian Village Center, which has quickly become a focal point for public gatherings and cultural events, exemplifies these principles. In a notable development, two young entrepreneurs from Hangzhou revitalised a local workshop into a thriving dyeing studio, which has become especially popular among the youth. This initiative highlights the potential of adaptive reuse, turning old buildings into vibrant community hubs while preserving their historical significance.

The same regenerative strategy has been adopted for the Shimen Bridge renovation. The project, along with the nearby Wangjing Memorial and Wang Village, is poised to turn an abandoned local connection into a cultural and touristic node along the Songyin River. Through a simple architectural intervention, consisting of a wooden framework and new flooring, the bridge is repurposed from a derelict transport relic into a vibrant community asset, intertwining the historical narratives of Shimen and Shimenyu villages into a cohesive and dynamic future. This initiative not only preserves but celebrates the shared heritage of the communities, positioning the bridge as a symbol of renewed communal life and a testament to the sustainable integration of tradition with modernity in the fabric of Songyang. These examples elucidated a design strategy that was not only responsive to the immediate context—socially, culturally, and environmentally—but also resonant with specific geographical and cultural traditions, involving Framptonian design-driven topics, such as topology, tactility, and tectonic, towards what can be defined as a specific Chinese critical regionalist approach.

Top: Pingtian Farming Museum. Photo by Wang Ziling.

Middle: Pingtian Village Center. Photo by Wang Ziling.

Bottom: Shimen Bridge over Songyin River. Photo by Wang Ziling.

01 Kenneth Frampton, "Towards a Critical Regionalism: Six Points for an Architecture of Resistance" in *The Anti-Aesthetic. Essays in Postmodern Culture*, ed. Hal Foster (New York: Bay Press, 1983).

02 Martin Heidegger, "Building Dwelling Thinking," in *Poetry, Language, Thought* (New York: Colophon Books, 1971).

03 Kenneth Frampton, "Critical Regionalism revisited," UW Department of Architecture Lecture Series, University of Washington, Seattle, Washington, May 16th 2013.

04 Hans-Jürgen Commerell and Kirsten Feireiss, *The Songyang Story: Architectural Acupuncture as Driver for Socio-Economic Progress in Rural China* (Zurich: Park Books, 2021).

05 Aric Chen, "DnA_Design and Architecture DnA founder Xu Tiantian puts downroots in her native China", *Architectural Record* 197 (2009): 34.

06 Li Zhang, "Alternative Modernity, Rural Rediscovery and What Next," in *Architectural Digest* 256 (2018): 134.

THE MILL

CONTESTED HERITAGE

Ariani Anwar

Industrial Relics

As major cities shift from centres of manufacturing to post-industrial zones, the abandoned shells of former industrial sites raise the question of heritage 'value' and 'use.' There is a pervasive stillness in these sites – their buildings standing as frozen remnants of the former bustle of employment and manufacturing. Their architecture represents an era characterised by optimistic visions of 'progress.' Often constructed using innovative technology, these buildings were designed to house the vast machinery required to operate the factory or other industrial activities. With expansive internal volumes and skeletal exposed steel structures, they are often vast and monolithic buildings. Yet, as industrial functions move elsewhere (or are no longer relevant in contemporary manufacturing) these sites are at great risk of demolition. As the commercial realities of land prices put pressure on yields it is perhaps not surprising that we are witnessing the loss of these buildings. Maybe they are no longer deemed 'useful' and have no heritage 'value.' But these relics of an industrial past offer insights into our cultural history and lie rich with potential for sustainable, adaptive reuse.

Adaptive Re-use – Latent Potential

There is a certain mesmerising quality of adaptive reuse projects that transform defunct industrial monoliths into significant public spaces. Take the highly acclaimed conversion of the Bankside Power Station into the Tate Modern gallery in London by architects Herzog & de Meuron. Not only did this create one of the most visited contemporary galleries in the world, but it also had a radical impact on the cultural and social character of the South Bank and Southwark areas. The adaptive re-use of the iconic power station included the conversion of the turbine hall, boiler house and central chimney. The turbine hall alone has since housed some of the world's most innovative site-specific art installations, such as Olafur Eliasson's *The Weather Project* or Doris Salcedo's *Shibboleth*. As contemporary artists delve into an era of site-responsive art installations, the vastness of these former industrial buildings offers a unique opportunity for intervention that is hard to come by in the traditional white/black-box museum.

In Australia, the conversion of the White Bay Power Station in Sydney's inner west represented a landmark opportunity to retain and celebrate the industrial heritage of the city. As one of the largest power stations servicing the city, it was listed on the NSW State Heritage, National Trust of Australia and National Estate registers.[1] After a significant amount of community advocacy in 2000 it was acquired by the NSW government and confirmed that it would be retained for cultural and creative purposes.[2] Strategic interventions and conservation works have been undertaken to allow public access and in 2024 it was opened to the public with installations as a part of the Biennale of Sydney. With a vision to become an important cultural site for the city, this project represents a catalyst to showcase the opportunities for the adaptive re-use of former industrial sites in Australia.

One of the key challenges for adaptive reuse projects is the development of financially sustainable strategies to fund the renovation and ongoing maintenance of the building. Yet, it is heartening to see successful examples emerging around the world. Of note are the many projects in the Netherlands that have implemented innovative strategies to enable the ongoing financial independence of the projects. For instance, the *Van Nelle Fabriek* in Rotterdam is a modernist factory built in the 1920s. In 2002 it was converted into an event space, office and museum and it has now been recognised on the UNESCO World Heritage list.[3] Or the Westergas industrial district in Amsterdam. Developed in 1885 this site comprised of 17 industrial buildings that once supported the production of gas used for lighting in the city.[4] Following the closure of the factory in 1967 the heavily contaminated site was mainly used for storage until 2003 when it was decontaminated and transformed into a lush, green cultural district.[5] Today, it is a thriving community site, housing creative entrepreneurs, food venues, a hotel, exhibitions, markets and a lively program of cultural events and festivals.

Opposite: 1954 Boiler House, Fairfield (now demolished). Photo by Ariani Anwar, 2016.

Melbourne's Lost Heritage – The 1954 Boiler House

The dilemma around the adaptation of former industrial sites is no less current in Melbourne. Historically, the city has been a major centre of Australian manufacturing. By 1881 two-thirds of Victoria's 2500 factories were in Melbourne and the manufacturing industry was dramatically shaping its architectural landscape.[6] Today, we are witnessing a rapid change in the character of the city's former industrial zones. Where brickworks, paper mills and textiles manufacturing once stood we now see the reclamation of these sites for residential, leisure and retail purposes. Some would say their demolition is part of the evolution of a city. But this represents an irrecoverable loss of layers of history – the silos, chimneys and other function-driven architectural forms – that create the unique character of the skyline.

A recent example is the demolition of the 1954 Boiler House designed by Mussen, Mackay and Potter at the Amcor Paper Mill. Located in Fairfield, Victoria, 8 km northeast of the Melbourne CBD, it was one of the largest sites of the Australian Paper Mills Ltd. that operated from 1921 to 2012. The site specialised in the production of paper and cardboard manufacturing, including a waste-paper recycling system. Crucially, the paper-making and pulping process was integrated with the production of energy through the construction of two power stations on the site. Water was pumped in from the Yarra River to cool the boilers and then was used by the paper manufacturing system.[7] The construction of the 1954 Boiler House signified a milestone in technological and mechanical development on the site, with a unit able to power a town of 30,000 inhabitants.[8] Originally classed as a 'Grade B' structure in the 1998 *City of Yarra Heritage Review* for its "technical and architectural significance" it was one of the few recognised heritage buildings.[9] According to the listing the "demolition of these buildings would adversely impact upon the cultural heritage of Yarra by its built environment and historic urban fabric."[10]

The 1954 Boiler House once stood as a recognisable silhouette on the skyline. The building was characterised by a vast internal volume for the main turbine and was filled with an abundance of diffuse natural light due to extensive glazing. The heritage significance of the building focused on this five-storey curtain wall, which was considered one of the "earliest known examples in Melbourne."[11] With glazed panes and framing members hung from the supporting steel frame, the curtain wall would have provided natural light for workers and machine maintenance. From outside, the industrial equipment hovered, suspended within this glass volume, and had an almost sculptural quality – a lantern glowing on the Fairfield horizon. Unfortunately, after the mill ceased operating in 2012 the glazing was significantly vandalised. In 2014 the site was sold, and an urban master plan was announced for a large-scale infill development including the construction of over 2,500 residences, retail and community spaces. As a part of the master planning process in 2016 a local consultation was held, and several community letters revealed a strong desire for the demolition of the Boiler House. There was opposition to the building's retention, with claims that its "heritage value [was] spurious" and that it had "questionable' aesthetic appeal."[12] There were also concerns about contamination from the building as asbestos had been used in the framing of the curtain wall.[13] Later that year, prompted by a hearing by Heritage Victoria to determine the future of the Boiler House, a ministerial decision was made to approve its demolition. The site is now one of the largest urban infill developments in Victoria and the 1954 Boiler House was demolished in 2023.

The Mill – An alternative to demolition

The Mill is a speculative architectural proposal that considered an alternative future for the 1954 Fairfield Boiler House. Within the context of the approved masterplan, it proposed an adaptive reuse strategy rather than the demolition of this significant landmark.[14] This project was undertaken in 2016 when the future of the site and the demolition of the heritage listed Boiler House came under review by Heritage Victoria. It included a historical 'fiche' to research and understand the history of the site which was used to support the case for its retention and submitted to Heritage Victoria as evidence in the hearing. In this alternative vision for the site the 1954 Boiler House is retained.

By proposing an adaptive re-use strategy for Boiler House and its surrounding landscape, *The Mill* critiqued the tabula rasa approach and celebrated the opportunity to showcase the history of the site. A range of landscape interventions are proposed around the Boiler House to assist with the bioremediation of the site. These included the integration of community programmes into found remnants across the landscape.

Within the Boiler House itself the architectural response is one of restraint. Targeted interventions in the historic fabric are designed as fragments with carefully chosen incisions, circulation routes and viewing platforms suspended within the existing vast vertical internal volume. Acknowledging the embodied energy in the structure, the framing is revealed, and remnants of the industrial fabric are retained and/or adapted.

Opposite: The Mill - Proposed Section. All Renders by Ariani Anwar.

Recognising one of the major challenges to the successful adaptive re-use of former industrial sites is the ability to fund the building's retention, a business plan was developed as a part of this project. This hypothesised a way to use the conversion of the existing boiler into a localised renewable energy source that could support the proposed creative and community spaces. Speculating on the opportunities for a local power source, the former coal-fired boiler infrastructure is converted into a renewable trigeneration plant. Utilising geothermal and solar sources the transformed power plant generates heat, electricity and cooling to power the building and its associated functions.

On the ground level the former condenser and firing floor is transformed into a collaborative research zone with fabrication workshop, exhibition display and presentation zones. Above, private ateliers are co-located with a community glass house and event space. The proposed community services such as an indoor garden, maker spaces and workshops are intended to create a vibrant hub for the surrounding new residential development.

Suspended on the upper level, a public bath house re-interprets the former use of the building and connects with the closed loop energy-water system. Utilising the surplus heat and steam from the energy production systems, the public bathhouse becomes a new place for gathering and recreation.

As a hybrid of community, private and commercial activities, the building is reimagined as an integrated system of production, leisure and gathering.

Concluding Thoughts

A city is a complex and layered entity. Industrial sites are embedded with narratives of the past and contribute to the history of a city. Yet, as we have seen from the successful examples around the world, it takes a strong vision, strategy and community support to ensure that they are retained.

The 1954 Boiler House is an important case study for the management of former industrial sites in Victoria. There is no doubt that the requirements for upgrading existing facades to meet the stringent contemporary building standards

Top: Workshop.
Middle: Steam Room.
Bottom: Wintergarden.
Opposite: Proposed Site Plan.

likely made the retention of the building technically and financially challenging. This was compounded by the lack of public appreciation for the building and highlights a broader challenge around the conservation of industrial 20th century buildings, that perhaps do not fit within the established understanding of heritage 'value.'

By reflecting on the recent demolition of this building we must ask ourselves: what is the cost of its loss? The loss of the significant embodied carbon, the loss of the cultural heritage of an era in our city and the loss of unique spatial volumes that are hard to come by in a highly competitive and yield-oriented development market. Given the commercial pressures that are pervasive in the Australian property market, in many ways it is not surprising that Victoria is also witnessing the loss of these industrial behemoths. But, as the demand for greater density increases, we should be mindful of the potential that is dormant in the adaptive re-use of these industrial sites before they are erased for good.

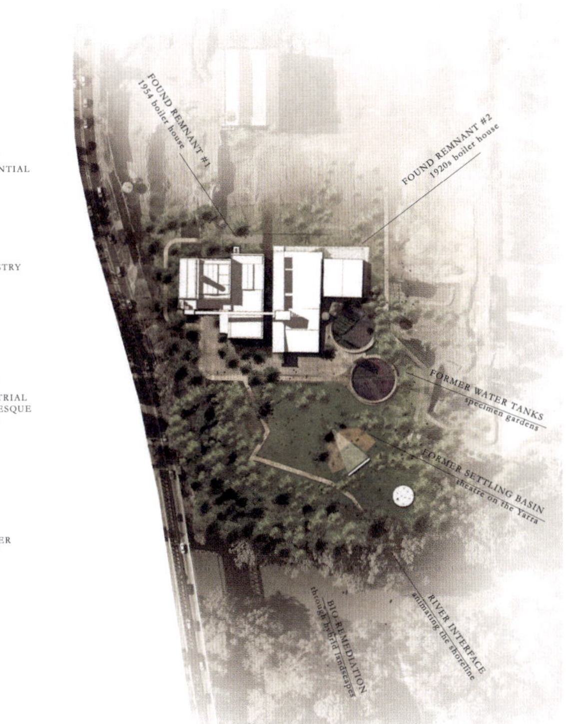

01 "The Story of White Bay Power Station" White Bay Power Station. Date accessed 06.08.2024. https://www.whitebaypowerstation.com/

02 Ibid.

03 "About Van Nelle" Van Nelle. Date accessed 07.08.2024. https://www.vannellefabriekrotterdam.com/en/events/about-van-nelle/

04 "About" Westergas. Date accessed 07.08.2024, https://westergas.nl/en/about/

05 Ibid.

06 Tony Dingle, "Manufacturing". E-Melbourne - The Encyclopaedia of Melbourne Online, The School of Historical & Philosophical Studies, The University of Melbourne, July 2008. Date accessed 07.07.2016. http://www.emelbourne.net.au/ biogs/EM00896b.htm.

07 Author unknown, "History - Fairfield Paper Mill", Australian Paper Manufacturers Limited, APM archives, the University of Melbourne.

08 Ibid.

09 Allom Lovell and Associates, "1954 Boiler House" in *The City of Yarra Heritage Review*, (Melbourne, 1998), p. 159.

10 Ibid.

11 Ibid.

12 West Alphington Residents, Inc. "3.0 Retention of 1954 Boiler House & Machine Room 6" in Submission to the City of Yarra, AMCOR Development, March 2015, (Melbourne: 2015), 6.

13 Sophie Pender, Glass & Glazing, (Farnham: Ashgate, 2011) 75.

14 The Mill was an independent research project completed at the University of Melbourne, under the supervision of Professor Alan Pert.

LOOKING BACK, MOVING FORWARD

RESTORING LOCAL CONSTRUCTION STRATEGIES IN EAST AFRICA

Francesco Stassi and Secil Taskoparan Stassi

Regenerative architecture encompasses a broad scope of approaches, ranging from reuse, recycling, and restoration strategies in the design and construction of the built environment to the regeneration of neighbourhoods, economies, and connections. We, the authors, are a group of architects with extensive experience designing and implementing various projects across East Africa, ranging from health and education to residential and hospitality. As foreign architects with Caucasian backgrounds, we are aware of the privileges and power dynamics inherent in our everyday lives and work. We recognize the importance of carefully navigating our roles when practising on someone else's land, rich with histories, traditions and stories. Our projects are guided by ongoing reflections and begin by asking how design decisions across the lifespan of a building can contribute to preserving cultural heritage, upholding community traditions and fostering positive socio-economic regeneration in a just and meaningful manner. Our decade of experience in East Africa, particularly in Rwanda, has proved that design and construction processes can empower communities and celebrate and promote the vernacular built environment.

Rwanda is categorised as a low-income country with a Human Development Index (HDI) below 0.55[1] and faces challenges ranging from the cost of life and low-purchasing power to healthcare, nutrition and employment. Despite the challenges, fast and steady economic development and a growing young population have driven significant demand for housing and infrastructure over the last two decades, and the increased need for architectural services has attracted the interest and establishment of foreign and local companies. Among them is Active Social Architecture (ASA Studio), a registered firm in Rwanda that both of the authors have been involved with, either currently or in the past. In this article which reflects on our practice and other regional design consultants' efforts, we will discuss architecture's regenerative potential in reviving forgotten materials and construction techniques, and how decisions and actions during design and construction stages can cultivate socioeconomic empowerment. In doing so, we will highlight the potential of our profession to influence positive change by embedding social, economic and cultural considerations at each stage of architectural practice.

Learning from traditions and heritage

Rwanda has a rich architectural history and heritage spanning from the pre-colonial and colonial eras to post-independence and modernity. Here, we interchange the terms 'vernacular' and 'traditional' to refer to the pre-colonial era Rwandan architecture, before the colonisation under German and Belgian rule. Traditional Rwandan architecture can be characterised by using locally available materials such as papyrus, bamboo and clay, employing methods like wattle and daub, and thatching/weaving in combination. A notable example of this architecture is the replica of the King of Rwanda's residence from the pre-colonial era. In addition to its domed shape that was typical during pre-colonial times, the King's Hut showcases natural, local materials and craftsmanship techniques. The hut features clay floors, compressed earth in-built components, and a combination of locally sourced timber and woven fibres that create its dome-shaped structure. Despite being far from today's comfort standards, the overall layout, tectonics and woven panels provide a permeable, breathable envelope and shaded interior space.

The replica of the King's Hut represents one of the last remaining examples of traditional Rwandan architecture. The disappearance of vernacular architecture partially stems from the impacts of colonialism on the built environment. The newly built environment that emerged under colonial influence spread Western notions of beauty and modernism throughout the country and reshaped local

expectations regarding how architecture should look and feel. Consequently, materials commonly used in the West, such as concrete, steel and glass, have dominated preferences and become symbols of wealth, power and durability. At the same time, bio-materials and their applications have been seen as symbols of poverty and instability. The reasons why communities prefer certain materials and look over others are complex and influenced by social, technical and economic factors, therefore, they cannot be reduced to a single reason. However, as mentioned in the UN Environment Program report, even though transitioning to low carbon earth- and bio-based building materials is technologically possible, it is socially difficult to implement as many communities view concrete and steel as 'modern' materials of choice.[2] This choice of materials has also been confirmed with some community participatory activities, as bio-materials and woven fibres are often ranked lower in preferences than their modern counterparts.

The need to reintegrate local materials and traditional passive design strategies, especially when facing the climate crisis, has prompted architects to take action. Over the last decade, several architecture firms operating in Rwanda, including ASA Studio, BE Design, MASS Design Group, GAPP Architects, Studio TAMassociati, to name a few, have been actively working on reintroducing traditional construction techniques by reusing and re-appropriating traditional crafts into several projects in Rwanda. For example, the Nyanza Education Center, designed by Dominikus Stark Architekten and completed in 2010, showcased external doors crafted through weaving techniques. In the following years, working collaboratively with local cooperatives, ASA Studio used

Above: The King's Hut. All images by the author.

woven panels, leftover eucalyptus branches from logging and bamboo, banana and papyrus leaves in various projects for the construction of doors, ceilings, external shadings and light fixtures. Aside from the regeneration of traditional crafts back into the architectural scale, using bio-materials significantly reduced the construction cost compared to using imported products and helped lower the overall carbon emissions. In addition, breathable components such as shutters, ventilated ceilings and double facades enhanced the interior comfort without using mechanical systems. Finally, the integration of weaving into the interior and exterior designs of high-end hospitality facilities across the country presented natural materials as fashionable and desirable. This adoption of traditional materials in high-end hospitality demonstrates that architects play an active role in influencing perceptions around traditional construction methods and their widespread use in the built environment.

Iterative prototyping became the essential step in reviving the architectural heritage. Throughout projects like the Rugerero Health Center (ASA Studio) and Singita Kwitonda Lodge (GAPP Architects & ASA Studio), the experimentation process helped to understand the potential and limitations of the weaving method as a building component. Research and testing included: examining existing weaving methods; designing woven panels and their spacing; selecting materials, framing, and fittings; and assessing their suitability for shading, doors or ceilings. Most importantly, through collaboration with local artisans and cooperatives and expanding this technique to building and furniture design, the initiatives helped to preserve cultural heritage, increased economic opportunities and empowerment within communities, and promoted ecological sustainability. However, implementing and maintaining natural materials presents technical challenges. Fibre-based materials decay fast when exposed to harsh weather conditions, requiring their replacement with new ones every few years. Therefore, the temporality and the need for continuous maintenance led communities to prefer more durable materials and long-lasting finishes. However, we believe that the need to replace materials is a condition designers must work with when using bio-based materials. Architects can reframe the challenge of ongoing maintenance as a positive process when looking from an environmental and socio-economic perspective. As the fibres turn into compost, it benefits the environment and soil through recycling of organic resources. In addition, replacing materials on a regular basis presents an opportunity to form an ongoing partnership with the local artisans and communities and contribute to the local economy.
Besides the architectural practices actively designing and implementing projects in the country, several technical consultants and organisations promote the benefits of local natural materials, such as *EarthEnable*, *Enabel* (the Belgian Development Agency) and *Skat* (the Swiss Resource Center and Consultancies for Development). These organisations conduct nationwide programs to engage local communities and promote discussions about the advantages of using local and natural materials. Through demonstrations, outreach and dissemination initiatives of ongoing research, the efforts advocate for adopting appropriate environmentally sustainable technologies suited to the local climate. For example, in 2022, *Enabel* partnered with the Rwandan Government to establish a centre of excellence for bamboo in Rwanda, which promoted knowledge of engineered bamboo for the construction sector. The initiative led to the first international conference on bamboo for construction in 2023 and the development of new bamboo plantations in the country. In a related field, the collective *Local Building Materials Think Tank* has conducted extensive research on Adobe Block, leading to the legalisation of the *rukarakara* / adobe in the Rwanda Building Code in 2019.[3] The group further contributed to developing Rwandan Standards and technical guidelines for adobe blocks construction in Rwanda in 2022. Establishing the guidelines has paved the way for the widespread use of adobe blocks as a more ecologically sustainable, locally produced alternative to concrete blocks and bricks.

Top Left: Singita Kwitonda Lodge Main Lodge entrance - project of GAPP Architects + ASA Studio.

Top Right: Busogo school classroom - woven ceiling.

Below: Rugerero Health Centre - woven doors.

Intertwined regenerative systems

Reflecting on these completed projects and processes, we argue that regenerative architecture offers a transformative vision for the built environment, intertwining ecological, social and cultural dimensions. Integrating natural materials and promoting their use in design and construction has multiple interconnected regenerative benefits, including increasing societal acceptance and appreciation of natural materials, enhancing socio-economic empowerment and reducing carbon emissions in the Anthropocene era. Buildings currently account for more than 30 percent of process-related CO_2 emissions in Africa, and these numbers are expected to rise as the continent undergoes an unprecedented rural-to-urban transformation. Therefore, increasing the acceptance of appropriate technologies is a determinant to facilitate the shift from high-carbon materials to bio-materials to decarbonise the construction industry and regenerate the land and the environment.

Gaining community acceptance is particularly crucial in this process. Past 'unlucky' experiences have demonstrated that buildings may remain vacant in case of a lack of endorsement from the local communities. Achieving acceptance is particularly challenging without demonstrating appealing examples, conducting research and experimentation, and implementing participatory programs and building codes. From an economic perspective, using appropriate technologies and local materials can ignite a transition from an import-based system to a locally-driven supply system. Throughout the construction process, starting with the preliminary design stage and the decisions on structural systems, materials and finishes, the investment often moves abroad to countries such as Kenya, Uganda, South Africa, the UAE and India. However, in a more locally produced and supplied system, income may flow towards local producers and cooperatives. The redistribution of money to communities may then help to increase job opportunities, resulting in less poverty, more sustainable development and a more equitable distribution of profits.

The path is not straightforward, but despite the challenges, architects working collaboratively with other stakeholders can catalyse a positive shift by reintroducing forgotten technologies and craftsmanship. Ongoing efforts to revive traditional materials and construction techniques have laid strong foundations in this direction. A critical factor in sustaining and amplifying positive changes in the industry is implementing considerate and meaningful design, research and engagement strategies. Within all projects, the success of effective strategy comes from an active collaboration with communities, government entities, donors, producers and other stakeholders. Even though the challenges in navigating cultural preferences and industry norms remain, by promoting collaboration across stakeholders architects can play a role in land regeneration and help develop sustainable built environments, fostering equitable and resilient communities for future generations. Regeneration in the Rwandan context is multifaceted; it's a long, meandering path marked by challenges at every turn, but taking it one step at a time seems like a good start.

01 UNDP (United Nations Development Programme), *Human Development Report 2023-24: Breaking the gridlock: Reimagining cooperation in a polarized world* (New York: UNDP, 2024), p 276.

02 United Nations Environment Programme, *Building Materials and the Climate: Constructing a New Future*, (Nairobi: United Nations Environment Programme, 2023.

03 Local Building Materials Think Tank, *Best Practice in Adobe Block / Rukarakara Construction in Rwanda*, (2019).

Top Left: Workers preparing eucalyptus branches.

Top Right: Nyungwe Forest National Park HQ, ISSB wall and clay plaster prototype.

Bottom: Community participation activity in Nkanga ECCD Centre.

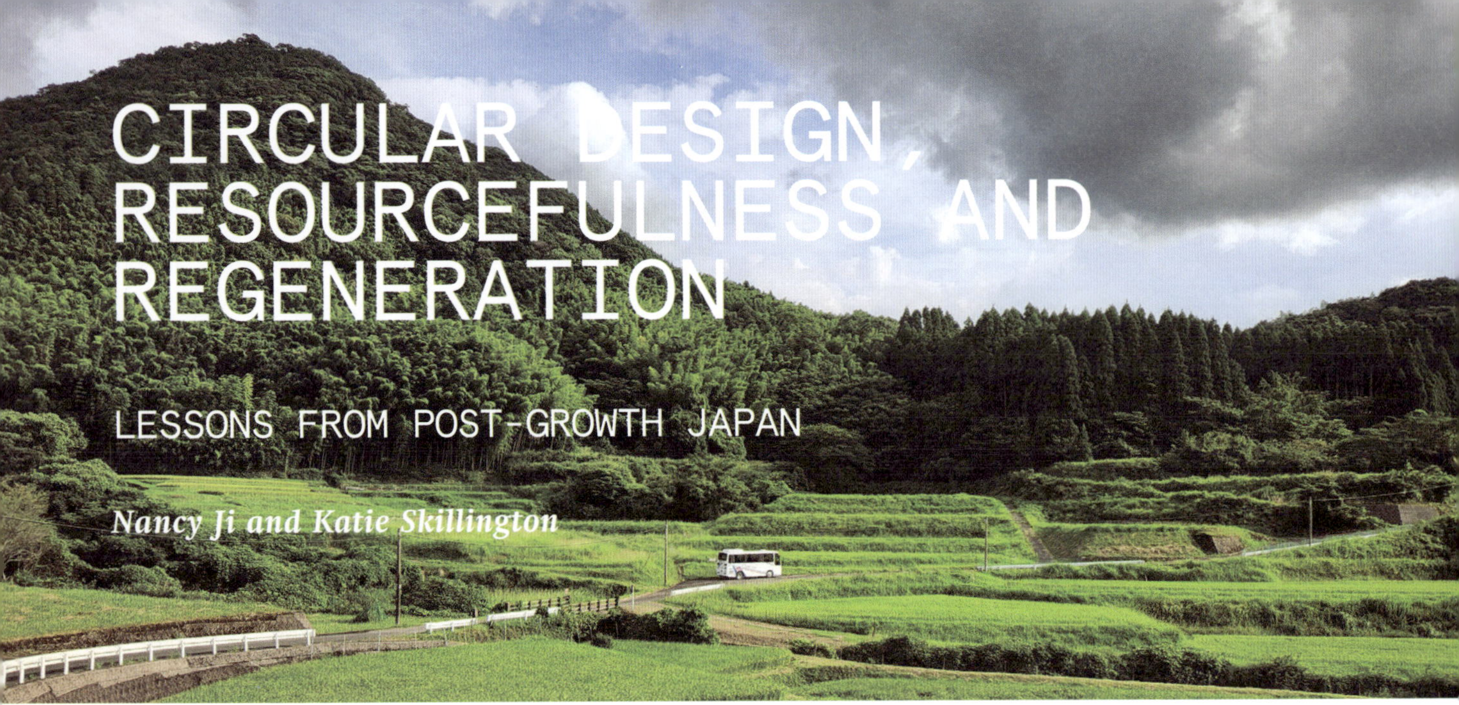

CIRCULAR DESIGN, RESOURCEFULNESS AND REGENERATION

LESSONS FROM POST-GROWTH JAPAN

Nancy Ji and Katie Skillington

Introduction

The deceleration of the Japanese economy has shifted its society from a previously burgeoning 'middle-class' – where economic growth, equality, and opportunity were the norm – to a post-growth era characterised by population decline, ageing, and the erosion of traditional models of life experience such as lifetime employment and property ownership.[1] The confluence of population shrinkage, socio-economic decline, and the depletion of natural resources have led to ongoing challenges including abandoned land, forests, and vacant buildings. There is a need to rethink alternative ways of living and working in a post-growth society.

Responding to such challenges, designers and other creatives in Japan are adopting strategies based on circular and regenerative design, resourcefulness and other place-based, socially engaged practices. Contemporary practices of circularity and regenerative design have deep roots in Japan's history where villages co-existed harmoniously with the natural landscape and eco-systems. The revival of circular principles and practices in post-growth Japan signify the emergence of a new kind of social design that prioritises people rather than growth.[2] This prompts us to question current growth-oriented practices and ask: What can we – as designers, citizens, economies, and nations – learn from Japan's post-growth revival of circularity, regeneration, and resourcefulness?

Fig.1 (Above): Bamboo Forests surrounding rice paddies in Fujimoto. All images by the author.

In light of this question, this paper showcases two case studies from Japan that are experimenting with models of practice that draw on social networks, resourceful use of materials, and alternative forms of exchange. We examine the case of Japan to offer insight into traditional and contemporary practices that engage with ideas of regeneration from a non-Western perspective. Given common challenges such as ageing populations and economic downturns experienced in other developed economies, Japan's post-growth era serves as a potential harbinger for what may come worldwide. To this end, we view the case studies not only as one-off examples unique to Japan but understand them as practices that can be adapted to suit a global context.

Post-growth Japan

Contemporary Japan is defined by its super-aged society and shrinking population.[3] This is in stark contrast to Japan's post-war boom and 'miraculous' growth since the late 1950s until the early 1970s.[4] Due to a housing shortage after the war, the government focussed on the urgent task of rebuilding. Mass construction became a key driver in Japan's high growth period (1955 – 1972) leading to rapid urbanisation and development. By 1973, the number of houses exceeded the number of households, yet construction continued to fuel economic growth.[5] The 1973 oil shock signified the end of the high growth period and the burst of the bubble economy in the early 1990s further slowed economic growth. Aside from the economy, Japan's population started to decline in 2010. Consequently, Japan has entered a 'post-growth era,' characterised by economic and employment precarity, an ageing demographic, and depopulation.

Yet, at first glance, Japan seems to be doing fine in this era. Infrastructure is well developed, quality of life is still perceived to be high, and construction has not stopped in urban centres where large redevelopment projects continue to bolster the economy. However, upon deeper examination – beyond the shine and splendour of urban metropolises – traces of post-growth emerge. Today, schools are closing due to low enrolments, abandoned shops and farmland scatter the countryside, and there are over 9 million vacant houses sprinkled throughout Japan, accounting for approximately 14% of all residences in the country.[6] An increasing number of people are questioning the growth-oriented model of development that seems to make less sense in the current post-growth era.

So, how does post-growth manifest in Japan? Some of the reflection on post-growth Japan follows the discourse around degrowth, which is defined as the "equitable downscaling of production and consumption that increases human well-being and enhances ecological conditions at the local and global level, in the short and long term."[7] Indeed, the two terms – post-growth and degrowth – are often used synonymously, as they both explore alternatives to the capitalist economy.[8] Kohei Saito, a Japanese philosopher from the University of Tokyo, discusses the concept of degrowth communism and analogises Marx's thinking to the degrowth movement in his 2024 book *Slow Down: The Degrowth Manifesto*. Saito's main argument is for a post-capitalist economy where people can still maintain a high quality of life and social well-being while living within planetary boundaries by slowing down production and sharing wealth. In practical terms, this means working less, consuming less, and ending mass production to eliminate wasteful practices. In an earlier study, Saito noted how Marx critiqued new developments such as chemical fertilisers which were invented to maximise profits to ensure growth. By using technological advancements such as fertilisers to increase efficiency, ecological sustainability was neglected. Harmful effects include pollution, ultimately resulting in land that became exhausted revealing the "irrationality and contradictions of the development of productive forces under the capitalist mode of production."[9]

What is needed, Saito argues, is a post-capitalist economy where any over-extraction of resources is eliminated. In Japan, traditional villages co-existed with the natural landscape and ecosystems known as *satoyama*. The term has various meanings but is widely understood as a concept to describe the harmonious co-existence between humans and nature. The satoyama concept describes a type of 'encultured' nature where humans play a key role in the care and management of natural resources. When examining circularity, resourcefulness and regeneration in Japan, we use this human-nature dynamic as a basis for understanding circular principles from the Japanese context.

Circularity, Resourcefulness, Regeneration

In the post-growth era, there is a need to shift towards more circular methods and approaches to economic development in terms of production, innovation, and creation. Generally, there has been much interest in concepts of circularity and regenerative approaches to design and architecture in recent years in response to the ongoing climate crisis, underscoring the importance of this concept to nations beyond Japan. We have observed that circularity, which is used synonymously with circular economy and circular design in this paper, is undergoing a kind of resurgence within post-growth Japan, albeit in niches of societal practice. The concept of circularity is inherently tied to related concepts of regeneration and resourcefulness. We first outline the key definition of circularity before introducing two case studies that adopt circular design principles in contemporary Japan.

Circularity definition

Circularity is defined as a system of practice or design that separates economic growth from resource consumption by reusing and minimizing the use of new resources, especially those sourced from the natural environment (adapted from EMF).[10] It opposes the 'take-make-dispose' system of economic growth that nations have been accustomed to since the Industrial Revolution. The connection between circularity, regeneration, and resourcefulness is inseparable. A circular system inherently fosters regeneration, continually aiming to replenish resources in each cycle without diminishing their quality or detrimentally affecting adjacent ecosystems. Similarly, resourcefulness is a key strategy to achieving circularity, as the reduction of resource flows into and out of a system would undeniably result in some kind of net benefit to the environment and the financial outcomes of the creator. Although there are questions surrounding the ability of circularity to absolutely decouple resource use from economic growth, its recent dominance in global dialogue around sustainable development sees circular approaches evolving and gaining prominence across various fields including the construction and building industry.[11]

Circularity and post-growth/degrowth have mutual goals and shared principles. Both aim "for human society to operate within the ecological limits of the planet."[12] Schröder et al believe that "degrowth can and should contribute to circular

economy principles, as circular economic principles can contribute to an anchoring of degrowth commitments in an inescapably resource-dependent world."[13] This means reducing extractive practices and replacing them with regenerative ones to restore the Earth's ecosystems. Some scholars have described circularity as a new sustainability paradigm acknowledging conflicting ideological differences as well as beneficial similarities.[14] We urge readers to be careful when engaging with the term as the worst would be for circularity to become the new buzzword after sustainability, which everyone uses yet has little real impact. To do so, it is useful to deepen our understanding of the term by studying real life cases across different cultures.

Circularity in Japan

The case of Japan offers valuable ideas on rethinking circularity. Japan has a long history of circular practices, particularly those embedded in everyday life. The kimono for example is an example of a 'loose-fit' architecture for the body; made from a single piece of cloth to minimise waste. The way the kimono is designed allows for optimum flexibility and adaptability permitting the wearer to freely adjust the length by how it wraps around the body. In addition, repair and mending were commonly adopted to prolong the life of textiles and objects rather than throwing them away. Methods of textile repair include sewing a series of layered patchwork known as *boro* (ぼろ) and *sashiko* (刺し子), which first emerged from practical origins to reinforce poor-quality cloth. Similarly, the art of *kintsugi* (金継ぎ) refers to the art of repairing broken pottery by using lacquer and powdered gold. This act of repair extends to the building scale where traditional wooden construction based on standardised dimensions made it easy to repair and replace individual elements. These include tatami mats for flooring, wooden frames for sliding doors and washi paper screens which could be removed easily, repaired, and then placed back again.

From a landscape perspective, the concept of *satoyama* (里山) has gained prominence in recent years. The term is comprised of the word *sato* (village), and *yama* (mountain). The term encompasses both the cultural and natural landscape and its resources comprising a mosaic of diverse yet interlinked elements such as village settlements, farmland, forests, streams, and rice paddies that collectively form a *satoyama landscape*. Similarly, a related term is *satoumi* where *umi* means ocean or sea. Both terms emphasise how natural resources from *satoyama* and *satoumi* are responsibly managed to cultivate a harmonious relationship between humans and nature (including plants, animals and non-human elements) through low-carbon, low-waste approaches that utilise available resources to achieve a balanced model of environmental stewardship.[15]

Due to industrialisation and urbanisation, *satoyama* landscapes have been deteriorating. Both biological and social processes are needed to achieve the ecological restoration of *satoyama* landscapes, one that is rooted in cooperation and local knowledge. Since the 1960s, the close relationship between humans and nature has weakened due to modernisation and mass migration of people moving from rural to urban areas. The adoption of fossil fuels and chemical fertilisers meant that firewood, bamboo and charcoal were no longer widely used to reduce the need to rely on forestry for everyday life. The underuse of forests has led to various challenges including the decline of biodiversity and the rise of invasive wildlife causing damage to crops and farmland.[16] The lack of forest management has resulted in the proliferation of bamboo which has contributed to poorer biodiversity outcomes, a decline in soil quality, and the loss of important cultural capital, such as *satoyama landscapes*.[17] To illustrate such challenges, we introduce the case of Satsumasendai in Southwest Japan as a case study.

The case of Bambooful

In the city of Satsumasendai, Kagoshima Prefecture, Japan, we (the authors) attended a week-long workshop called 'Bambooful.' Satsumasendai is a city of around 95,000 people as of August 2023 and has been experiencing a steady decline in population since the first census of 1950, which recorded over 150,000 people. Employment in this regional city is largely industrial; a nuclear power plant, a semiconductor manufacturing facility, and a paper mill with a single private tertiary education provider. Kagoshima prefecture has the largest area of bamboo groves of Japan's 47 prefectures.[18] This is evident in the landscapes surrounding the built-up areas of Satsumasendai where significant swathes of bamboo groves, largely abandoned and in a state of wild growth, envelope urban settlements and villages.

Bamboo, by virtue of its characteristics, growing behaviours and qualities is a bio-based material that has been identified as having significant potential in the circular economy.[19] As a rapidly growing, self-regenerating material that can be harvested without requiring replanting, bamboo has the potential to be a viable alternative to many non-renewable or synthetic products. The versatility of bamboo's application from construction to biomass for energy production to food means that all parts of the material can be found to have a purpose in the material economy. Leveraging the potential of bamboo and the challenging context of Kagoshima's prolific bamboo groves, Tokyo-based design consultancy Re:public Inc in collaboration with the Satsumasendai Tourism & Products Corporation organised 'Bambooful,' a workshop conceived as part of a sustainable tourism program supported by the Japan Tourism Agency.

Our workshop focused on bamboo that comes from the local mountains in an area called Fujimoto (Fig. 1). About 170 villagers still live in this small community experiencing ageing and population decline. Local stakeholders – including a local farm, Senmyo Noen, and the Fujimoto Community Association – joined the workshop to provide a local perspective. Joined by ten students from Hong Kong, the workshop started by taking us through the qualities of bamboo as a regenerative material, traditional ways of working with bamboo, and how bamboo forests are managed, harvested, and then processed for use in a variety of ways. The workshop was described by Re:public Inc Managing Director Ryota Kamio as one that "focuses on the intersection of circular design, indigenous knowledge, and communities." The bamboo forests of Fujimoto present a local and readily available resource but are currently abandoned due to a lack of villagers able to manage and care for the forest. Our goal was seeking to learn from this situation by exploring the potential of using bamboo as a construction material in order to contribute to ongoing forest management and care.

Upon visiting the Fujimoto area, the proliferation of bamboo became more readily apparent. Guided by Mr Senmyo (Fig. 2), a young farmer from the area, we noticed the density of the bamboo culms and the coolth of the bamboo understory. Mr Senmyo has been taking care of the bamboo forests of Fujimoto in recent years and is one of the few remaining villagers performing this voluntary task. Regular maintenance through harvesting and thinning is crucial in sustainable forest management.[20] We learned that although such practices enabled healthy growth of the forest, simply burning the bamboo was not sustainable in the long run and there was a need to find additional ways to use the resource in a meaningful way. Mr Senmyo burns some of the bamboo, and uses some of it in his agricultural work. Along with the other villagers, he sells most of the bamboo harvested to a production facility which processes it to generate biomass (Fig. 3).

A visit to a local bamboo processing factory called Hinomaru (Fig. 4), one of the last ones remaining in the region, opened our eyes to how fresh bamboo is treated and the various uses for bamboo. For example, in the making of bamboo strips: first, the large bamboo needs to be cut, then boiled, dried, and further sanded and cut before it is ready to use as a cladding material. Other uses include producing bamboo charcoal, including a version of which is edible and used by chefs in restaurants. Bamboo charcoal is also an effective natural fertilizer which helps to improve the quality of the soil. A community garden was established recently in the town to make use of this natural fertiliser and promote it to residents.[21]

Fig. 2 (Left): Local farmer and resident,Mr Senmyo, cutting down mature bamboo to allow the younger roots to grow.

Fig. 3 (Middle): Burning of Mature bamboo to allow younger roots to grow.

Fig. 4 (Right): Bamboo about to be boiled at Hinomaru factory.

Our experiences in Satsumasendai, Fujimoto and Hinomaru gave us insight into how *satoyama* principles worked on the ground and the potential of bamboo as a circular material resource. We learned the importance of managing the land as the first step, explored the possibilities of bamboo in craft and furniture making, and witnessed the eventual return of bamboo back into the land in the form of charcoal and fertiliser. Yet, there remains barriers to leveraging this resource which includes difficulties in finding people to manage the bamboo forests due to the depopulation, a trend that will undoubtedly continue if generous incentives are not offered to encourage younger generations to remain and live with the land. There also remains the question of long-term pathways for bamboo use. Once referred to as the 'poor man's timber,' bamboo has at least three International Standards for use in construction, yet its wide adoption in Japanese mainstream construction is not prevalent.[22] Acknowledging that bamboo has a range of uses in the restoration of traditional Japanese architecture, such as fencing or the restoration of traditional decorative elements, it remains a niche material that is largely used for interior finishes such as flooring. Circularity of bamboo *en masse* in the Japanese domestic context will only be possible if these barriers are considered and addressed.

In a similar vein, the proliferation of vacant houses, known as *akiya* (空き家), is another resource that has emerged in post-growth Japan. While many akiyas are in the countryside, there are cases of them found in urban centres. The preference for new housing coupled with the oversupply of housing overall has rendered many old akiyas little to no market value. Yet it is precisely the fact that people have been able to rent or purchase one for a low price, sometimes at no cost at all. The next case study introduces how circular design practices are being adopted in the regeneration of akiya.

Vacant House Regeneration

The transformation of Japanese rural and urban landscapes over the past few decades has been affected by the increase of akiyas in these locations. Villages and towns of once thriving populations and industries are increasingly becoming sleepy hamlets with akiyas that pose health and safety threats in this natural disaster-prone nation. In 2015, the Vacant Houses Special Measures Act was passed by the Japanese National Diet to help mitigate the increase of akiyas. However, some scholars have noted this measure as a 'whack-a-mole' situation whereby financial, moral and labour issues present as barriers to speeding up akiya identification and handling.[23] In most instances, the endgame from the perspective of the government is demolition, with little emphasis placed on reuse, renovation or adaptation. Yet, even in these circumstances, demolition is not always forthcoming, as neither the city, prefecture, nor current owners can raise the funds for demolition to take place.

Against this background, a new wave of akiya regeneration in the form of renovation and repair has emerged where various creatives are starting to experiment with a Do-It-Yourself (DIY) method.[24] They see the city and akiyas themselves as a source of locally available material and resource. With limited budgets, these akiya enthusiasts are finding alternative ways to renovate and give new life to existing buildings recalling the architect-bricoleur who embraces low-tech and DIY methods. Akiya regeneration is an example of adaptive reuse which challenge the need for demolition, calling for a closer examination of circularity, repair and maintenance.
In January 2024, a group of Master of Architecture students from The University of Melbourne travelled to Japan for two weeks and visited several sites involving vacant house regeneration. One of these sites was in Kobe, called Bison Village (Fig. 5) by Nishimura Gumi – an architectural

collective renovating a series of vacant properties in the area. The group is headed up by Mr Nishimura, a qualified architect who also worked in real estate before forming Nishimura Gumi. After graduating from University, Mr Nishimura said he had little savings and was renting an old warehouse to live in with friends for 15,000 yen a month. They renovated the warehouse with scrap material to make it habitable and soon began renovating other properties in the area, moving out and renting previous projects they renovated. In 2020, at the time of the COVID-19 pandemic, Mr Nishimura gathered friends and acquaintances who had time to spare to work on a larger project – a collection of several vacant buildings along a narrow street, which was later named Bison Village.

After a 10-minute hike up narrow streets we arrived at Bison Village and were greeted by Miyako, a core member of the Nishimura Gumi team. Miyako oversees the renovation process much like a project manager and is responsible for the day-to-day operations including managing the growing team of members and their work schedules. Miyako explained how Nishimura Gumi tackles the vacant house problem by targeting properties that have been neglected due to their poor location. Bison Village for example is located up on the hills on a narrow street with no car access. The inconvenient location allowed Nishimura Gumi to purchase seven vacant buildings along the street for a low price. The vision was to create a village like atmosphere made up of a mix of programs including residences (private residence as well as a shared houses), an artist-in-residence called Bison AIR, a co-working space, workshop and event spaces that can all be rented out, and a public gallery called Bison Gallery (Fig. 6). At the time of our visit, visiting artists from Vietnam had recently completed a two-week residency. Their work was shown not only in the main Bison Gallery but also across other sites turning the whole street into an art museum.

The style of renovation Nishimura Gumi adopts draws heavily on the architect as bricoleur approach. At the start, Mr Nishimura himself would go around the streets of Kobe to visit vacant buildings and salvage materials to use in his renovation. Now as more and more people know of his activities, he often receives calls from people all over the city who bring him various materials they no longer need. These range from building materials such as timber and glass to second-hand furniture and other items that may simply be viewed as waste. In Japan, it costs money to arrange for the disposal of large items to be collected by the local town. Nishimura Gumi often take offers from people who have excess or waste materials and repurposes them where possible. Examples that stood out include a wall remade out of reclaimed window frames pieced together like a puzzle (Fig. 7) and a kitchen island in the shared house made from sheets of crumpled copper strips. Nishimura Gumi's way of renovation emerges out of an assemblage of different elements making each project unique yet embody a cohesive aesthetic that draws on old and discarded materials.

Our time at Bison Village gave us insight into how circular practices are being carried out at the architectural and building level. Again, the process starts with the managing and coordination of the material itself. Nishimura Gumi mines the city for discarded materials and explores the possibility of how waste materials can be repurposed rather than having a preconceived notion of what the result would be. In the former tea house turned event space, the floor has been made from hundreds of timber offcut pieces each cut down and sanded before pieced together (Fig. 8). In the capitalist mindset, such a laborious process would be too costly to hire a professional builder to do. For Nishimura Gumi, the process of working together with various members is a social experience where everyone has a good time, often cooking and sharing meals in between working sessions. Many students and volunteers also often join to gain experience and have a go at D-I-Y style construction. In the post-growth mindset when time does not equal money, the shared experience of working and making together has opened new possibilities of building that can overcome the perceived high cost of alternative building methods that involve the preparation and reuse of existing materials.

Conclusion

The above two case studies demonstrate how circular design practices can emerge from a post-capitalist framework in Japan. Key learnings include the recognition of alternative economies that value non-monetary forms of exchange and the socio-cultural values to shape material, resource and labour. In the case of the bamboo forests in Satsumasendai, community members need to work together to manage the forest and consider end of life possibilities for bamboo. At Bison Village, we see an alternative building model as an ongoing process where diverse members work on a common goal to renovate vacant houses left behind by capitalism. Bison Village emerged from an organic building process involving diverse members from all walks of life, not only those with building or design skills. These include students,

Fig. 5 (Top Left): Entrance of Bison Village, a collection of vacant houses along a narrow laneway on a hill.

Fig. 6 (Top Right): Bison Gallery showing work from visiting artists from Vietnam who recently completed a residency at Bison AIR.

travelling artists, cooks, managers, and anyone else interested in participating in the renovation and associated activities either temporarily or long term. In both cases, there is a strong sense of environmental and material stewardship that acknowledges the need for shared responsibility to ensure not only the efficient use of materials but also how they can be continuously renewed or reused in the long run.

Finally, we note the need to recognize the real-life challenges of striving for circular principles on the ground. As students and professionals in the design field, we must not overlook the importance of tangible experience in the field, which includes direct hands-on 'doing' to fully understand the potential of natural and material life cycles. The social aspects of design processes, which are often overlooked, hold significant promise in moving towards a more circular and regenerative future. For example, there is a need to rethink how shared forms of labour can be an opportunity for social cohesion in the context of depopulation where social networks are increasingly fragmented, yet circular action is still required. Indeed, while this paper has focused on two cases from Japan, the lessons learned could extend to other countries that are experiencing depopulation and/ or fragmentation, such as Australia. Although Australia has been experiencing continued national population growth for decades, our sparsely distributed population, the expense of delivering infrastructure to the regions, and the economic appeal of major cities has consistently driven a rural depopulation pattern for decades. Yet, in these remote and rural areas, there remains natural, knowledge, and cultural capital that could benefit from similar hands-on 'doing' as witnessed in these Japan-based case studies. With progressively receding services and a legacy of governments instructing regions to be responsible for themselves, we cannot help but think that these lessons from Japan could help support Australian rural areas to work towards a circular and regenerative future.[25] As such, we encourage all to take lessons from post-growth Japan, which hint at promising ways forward by experimenting with circular design processes from the ground up drawing on principles of satoyama for the present day.

Fig. 7 (Above): A hole was punched into the façade to let in light, refashioned from reclaimed window frames.

Fig. 8 (Below): The new floor is pieced together from different sized timber offcuts.

01 David Chiavacci and Carola Hommerich, *Social inequality in post-growth Japan: Transformation during economic and demographic stagnation*, eds. (London: Routledge, 2017).
Yosuke Hirayama and Misa Izuhara, Housing in post-growth society: Japan on the edge of social transition (Routledge, 2018).

02 Christian Dimmer, "Place-Making before and after 3.11: The Emergence of Social Design in Post-Disaster, Post-Growth Japan," *Review of Japanese Culture and Society 28* (2016): 198-226.

03 Naoko Muramatsu and Hiroko Akiyama, "Super-Aging Society Preparing for the Future," *The Gerontologist*, Volume 51, Issue 4 (2011): 425 --432. https://doi.org/10.1093/geront/gnr067.

04 Koichi Hamada, Keijiro Otsuka, Gustav Ranis, and Ken Togo, eds. *Miraculous Growth and Stagnation in Post-War Japan* (New York: Routledge, 2011).

05 Toshihiko Hara, Population Prospects in Japanese Society. In *A Shrinking Society: Post-Demographic Transition in Japan* (Japan: Springer, 2015).

06 Ministry of Internal Affairs and Communications Report April 2024 https://www.soumu.go.jp/menu_news/s-news/01toukei03_01000119.html.

07 François Schneider, Giorgos Kallis, and Joan Martinez-Alier, "Crisis or opportunity? Economic degrowth for social equity and ecological sustainability. Introduction to this special issue," *Journal of Cleaner Production* 18,6 (2010): 512. https://doi.org/10.1016/j.jclepro.2010.01.014.

08 Olga Vincent and Amanda Brandellero, "Transforming work: A critical literature review on degrowth, post-growth, postcapitalism and craft labor," *Journal of Cleaner Production* 430, 139640 (2019): https://doi.org/10.1016/j.jclepro.2023.139640.

09 Kohei Saito, "The Emergence of Marx's Critique of Modern Agriculture: Ecological Insights from His Excerpt Notebooks," Monthly Review, Oct 01 2014, https://monthlyreview.org/2014/10/01/the-emergence-of-marxs-critique-of-modern-agriculture/.

10 Blanca Corona, LiB., Shen, Denise L., Reike, D., Jesús Rosales Carreón, Ernst WorrellRosales Carreón, J., & Worrell, E. (2019). , "Towards sustainable development through the circular economy-A review and critical assessment on current circularity metrics,". *Resources, Conservation and Recycling*, 151, 104498 (2019). https://doi.org/10.1016/j.resconrec.2019.104498.

11 T. Bauwens, "Are the circular economy and economic growth compatible? A case for post-growth circularity," *Resources, Conservation and Recycling*, 175 (2021): 105852, https://doi.org/10.1016/j.resconrec.2021.105852.

12 Patrick Schröder et al., "Degrowth within-Aligning circular economy and strong sustainability narratives," *Resources, Conservation and Recycling* 146 (2019): 190-191.

13 Ibid. 191.

14 Ibid.

15 Maya Ishizawa, "Cultural Landscapes Link to Nature: Learning from Satoyama and Satoumi," *Built Heritage* 2, 4 (2018): 7-19. https://doi.org/10.1186/BF03545680.

16 Miyanaga, Kentaro , and Daisaku Shimada, "The tragedy of the commons' by underuse: toward a conceptual framework based on ecosystem services and satoyama perspective." *International Journal of the Commons* 12, .1 (2018): 332-351.

17 Suzuki, Shigeo, and Nobukazu Nakagoshi, "Sustainable management of Satoyama bamboo landscapes in Japan." *Landscape ecology in Asian cultures* (2011): 211-220.

18 Valentina Maria Vasile and Ryota Kamio, "Bambooscape: Designing a Practice of Rural Futures: Bamboo architecture and spatial design." Proceedings of the Fab 23 Research Papers Stream (2023): 3-21. https://doi.org/10.5281/zenodo.8171638.

19 van der Lugt, P., & King, C. (2019). Bamboo in the Circular Economy: *The potential of bamboo in a zero-waste, low-carbon future*. (Policy Synthesis Report; Vol. 6). International Bamboo and Rattan Organisation (INBAR).

20 Valentina Maria Vasile and Ryota Kamio (2023). Bambooscape: Designing a Practice of Rural Futures: Bamboo architecture and spatial design. Proceedings of the Fab 23 Research Papers Stream, 3-21. https://doi.org/10.5281/zenodo.8171638

21 Ibid.

22 Ruiz Pérez, Zhong Maogong, Brian Belcher, Xie Chen, Fu Maoyi, Xie Jinzhong, "The role of bamboo plantations in rural development: The case of Anji County, Zhejiang, China," *World Development* 27, 1 (1999): 101-114. https://doi.org/10.1016/s0305-750x(98)00119-3.
Ana Gatóo, Bhavna Sharma, Maximilian Bock, Helen Mulligan, Michael H. Ramage, "Sustainable structures: bamboo standards and building codes," *Proceedings of the Institution of Civil Engineers - Engineering Sustainability* 167, 5 (2014): 189-196. https://doi.org/10.1680/ensu.14.00009.

23 Chie Nozawa, "Land and Homes and the Japanese: The issue of vacant houses and land with unknown owners today = What progress with preparations for closing houses," Japan Foreign Policy Forum, Jan 26 2022, https://www.japanpolicyforum.jp/society/pt2022012616580811841.html

24 Nancy Yao Ji, "Renovation Machizukuri in Contemporary Japan: The Cases of Suwa, Kokura and Onomichi," In *Proceedings of the Society of Architectural Historians, Australia and New Zealand:* 39, Nga Putahitanga / Crossings, ed. Julia Gatley and Elizabeth Aitken Rose, 214-30. Auckland: SAHANZ, 2023. DOI: https://doi.org/10.55939/a5026ptoed.

25 Juuditj Brett, "Fair Share: Country and City in Australia," Quarterly Essay Vol. 42, n.d., https://www.quarterlyessay.com.au/essay/2011/06/fair-share/extract.

OBJECT PERMANENCE & REGENERATIVE PROCESSES IN HERITAGE CONSERVATION

Claire Miller, Janice Yeung and Isabella Chow
Trethowan Architecture

Heritage is a practice in flux, encompassing a range of contested meanings and processes that are continually renegotiated. The questions of what to preserve, how, why and for whom, remain contentious and unfixed.[1] This regenerative quality emerges as existing values are re-defined, expanded upon and new audiences emerge. As a values-based endeavour, built heritage seeks to connect people to places and buildings that reflect a shared history, cultural identity or achievement. These values change over time as new shared histories develop and communities reaffirm what should be retained as representation. But what those values are varies considerably across the world, across local areas and within subgroups of a community.

In Victoria, contemporary heritage practice manages and preserves cultural artefacts through statutory protection, practical conservation and advocacy. A separate piece of heritage legislation recognises pre-contact Aboriginal heritage, however this discussion focuses on the state's post-colonial built heritage.[2] There is a tension within built heritage practice between the objectivity of heritage management and statutory controls, and the inherent subjectivity of the act of preserving. Changing community values mean that the lists of places that are protected are frequently renewed as the understanding of what constitutes heritage evolves. However, once places and objects are listed, the statutory controls provide a degree of permanence. The intention is that buildings, as representative of heritage values, may be retained for future generations to use and enjoy. However, retaining buildings requires maintenance and repair so they remain usable. A current challenge in the Victorian heritage industry is a diminishing skills base of traditional trades with the knowledge and material experience to undertake essential repairs and conservation work to heritage assets. In contrast, approaches to built heritage in Japan have preserved and safeguarded traditional skills, supporting their active use. A comparison of the Victorian and Japanese statutory approaches enables deeper consideration of preservation skills and their role in the retention of built heritage. This may reveal opportunities to regenerate practice in response to the skills gap and inform broader and more representative approaches to heritage protection that connect to process and intangible values, and encourage sustainable use.

Architecture can be understood both as object (a building) and as process (designing, making). In Victoria, the values-based system of identifying, classifying and managing heritage has historically favoured architecture as an object, rather than a series of processes. This is reflected in statutory frameworks that prioritise the retention, preservation and conservation of built fabric in a cautious manner of "changing as much as necessary but as little as possible."[3] Heritage values are considered inherent in the fabric of the place, such that the artefact signifies the processes of its creators and the legacy of its past and ongoing users.[4] Evidence of processes of designing and making architecture is therefore retained in the resultant object. The architectural object is a tangible form of heritage — it can be touched and measured, and has a physical presence. The architectural process is an intangible form of heritage — it is intellectual and relates to the practices, uses and meanings connected to people and culture. In prioritising the architectural object, we risk not maintaining the traditional knowledge and skills required for its preservation. Can heritage practice support architectural processes through object preservation? Could a greater understanding of architectural processes and their connection to intangible heritage practices allow for more holistic forms of preservation?

Ongoing discussions in academia and practice regarding how to define and manage built heritage provides context for

a comparison between parts of the Victorian and Japanese approaches and their outcomes. The Victorian heritage industry recognises that dwindling skills and knowledge of traditional trades threaten the future preservation of historic buildings. There is a shortage of traditional tradespeople with the required skills and material knowledge to appropriately undertake conservation or repair of significant heritage assets.[5] The reasons for this knowledge gap are varied. A 2010 audit of education and training opportunities in heritage trades pointed to several factors: a lack of formalised education about traditional skills in present-day training programs leading to a lack of knowledge in younger tradespeople; a concentration of specialist knowledge in the hands of a small aging professional group; and low demand for courses related to specialist knowledge in heritage trades where they were available.[6] Worryingly, if not addressed, this skills gap risks the future of our built heritage, as traditional trades are either lost, increasingly inaccessible or economically unviable (as low supply increases prices). Many in the industry, including professional bodies, organisations and businesses, understand the stakes and are actively contributing to addressing the skills gap through research, practice-based programs and education. Lessons may be learned from Japanese examples that include the architectural process — the act of making — as an essential element of built heritage.

Evolution of the Western Heritage Discourse

The Western definition of heritage has expanded over time to be more representative. The tools to identify, assess and manage heritage places, and the types of places that warrant protection, have been updated to reflect changing community values and conceptions of shared heritage.[7] Early built heritage practice prioritised superlative examples — the best, the oldest and the most monumental or remarkable buildings surviving from the past.[8] This approach emerged as an extension of the development of collections, through private antiquarians and museums, in the Enlightenment era.[9] However, as relationships and connections to the past change, the formal systems of heritage practice necessarily must evolve. Jean Hillier explores a conception of heritage that is a "continually renegotiated actualisation of assemblages of political and economic power, of exclusions and inclusions."[10] This regenerative quality reveals an

Top Left: Historically, the best, the oldest and most monumental buildings were often protected under early heritage legislation. The Royal Exhibition Building was first listed on the Historic Buildings Register (precursor to VHR) in 1982 and inscribed to the UNESCO World Heritage List in 2004. Image courtesy of The State Library of Victoria.

Top Right: Chapel in construction: Convent of Notre Dame de Sion, Sale. Constructed in 1893, with chapel and north wing added in 1901, the skills and trades originally used to construct the building have changed immensely in the past 100 years. The monolithic nature of brick and stone structures means they often require less frequent repairs and many of the skills and techniques originally used to construct these buildings have disappeared or have been replaced by modern techniques, leading to the scarcity or gap in the conservation skills required to appropriately maintain and repair many of Victoria's heritage buildings. Image courtesy of Bates, Smart McCutcheon Pty. Ltd. Collection, The University of Melbourne Archives.

Above: Ian Goddard of Wooden Inspirations leads several Como Approach Workshops, organised by the National Trust of Australia (Victoria). The workshops, which cover traditional joinery and cabinet making, from sash windows to door joinery, are intended to demonstrate best conservation practice. Trades, heritage professionals and members of the general public are encouraged to participate. Neisha Breen Photography, courtesy of the National Trust of Australia (Victoria).

inherent conflict within a system rooted in the classification of historical artefacts, that must respond to changing values in the present. Heritage is a "dynamic and contested social phenomenon" that is mediated through often-conflicting relations between past, present and future.[11] Efforts have been made to develop some consensus on how to identify and assess built heritage value, and how to manage places that have been identified. Founding documents such as the *Athens Charter* (1931) and the *Venice Charter* (1964) sought to provide guidance on the restoration and care of historic monuments and their settings as important historical evidence, more than just artworks from the past.[12] These efforts claim that historical monuments have universal value for humanity, an idea that was furthered in 1972 at the UNESCO World Heritage Convention which resulted in the World Heritage List and a set of universal heritage values.[13] Through the turn of the twenty-first century, criticism of UNESCO's universalising principles identified biases that prioritised examples that were European, Christian, urban and elitist.[14] Living cultures were notably excluded, as were conceptions of heritage that differed from the Western hegemony, in spite of UNESCO's claims of universality.[15] Since then, built heritage has broadened its scope beyond Eurocentric principles to include more intangible concepts such as social and cultural practice, and the spaces that enable ritual and everyday life for living cultures. Broader global discussions introduced the concept of cultural relativism and propelled understandings of heritage as relative to cultural context, but there remains a prioritisation of object over process in the Western approach. Challenges to universal values have enabled shifts in how heritage is defined and managed across the world, and its systemic biases.[16]

Heritage in Victoria

The Victorian approach to preserving and managing built heritage is informed by British and European precedents and is not without contention.[17] Historically significant places protected by legislation demonstrate the cultural values, assumptions and biases of those who developed the identification and assessment tools. However, ongoing discussions within the industry continue to recognise legislative biases and seek ways to redress imbalances.[18] The current framework is a values-based system that provides objective approaches to assess built heritage, mitigating the inherent subjectivity of the practice. This system is informed by the *Australia ICOMOS Burra Charter, 2013* and evaluates places against a range of criteria assessing values related to the building itself, the people who made it and the people who use it.[19] These are known as the HERCON criteria, introduced in the early twenty-first century, and they encompass historical significance; rarity; research potential; representativeness; and aesthetic, technical, social, and associative significance.[20] If a place or object is assessed to meet the significance threshold for one or more of these criteria it may be formally listed and afforded protection. The threshold is higher for state-listed places than those at a local council level, but the logic of applying the criteria remains.

The HERCON criteria provide an objective measure of values inherent in the fabric of the place and its ongoing use. Preserving those values is a matter of retaining the original fabric, or object.[21] The tangible architectural object, therefore, acts as a text through which to read the intangible values related to its makers and associated processes. This approach does not explicitly affirm that the architectural process itself should be preserved. Traditional acts of designing, crafting and building, which create built heritage objects, are not statutorily protected as culturally valuable in and of themselves. Evidence of intangible values related to designing and making architecture is retained in objects. However, without formal protection there is a risk that architectural processes related to traditional skills and knowledge will be lost, threatening the ongoing conservation and maintenance of architectural objects.

The risk of losing traditional skills has been recognised within the industry, but this risk has not been translated into legislation. In 2019 the National Trust of Australia (Victoria) developed the Como Approach to promote and disseminate traditional conservation skills and knowledge, providing opportunities for skills sharing and education through practical workshops and events.[22] However, as the National Trust is an advocacy and custodial body there is no statutory weight behind the Como Approach. The National Trust describes the challenge of diminishing skills as follows:

> *The National Trust recognises there is limited knowledge in the community about conservation processes and their necessity for providing good conservation outcomes. There is also a critical need to address the ongoing issue of a diminishing pool of skilled conservation practitioners, as well as limited avenues and opportunities for practitioners to share their knowledge and develop skills in the traditional trades and conservation practices. If these two issues are not addressed there will not be the conservation skills required to sustain cultural heritage values in Australia into the future.*[23]

This initiative is one component of a broader movement to promote traditional trades within the heritage industry. In 2024, the Heritage Council of Victoria, the independent statutory body providing legal protection for places and objects of state significance, partnered with the Lost Trades Fair, an annual event that has been running for the last 11 years showcasing traditional crafts and artisans across a range of skills and industries.[24] Propelled by shared concerns, the International Council of Monuments and Sites (ICOMOS) Australia and the Association of Preservation Technology Australasian Chapter (APT) have advocated for an Australian Heritage Quality Framework to be adopted by heritage stakeholders in an effort to create quality benchmarks for conservation work and improve training and access to practitioners skilled in traditional trades.[25] APT's Longford Academy and the University of Canberra's Heritage Conservation Summer School, for example, disseminates knowledge on practical conservation techniques and traditional trades.

Despite industry recognition of the skills gap, and while critical heritage theory and practical approaches increasingly include intangible values and architectural processes, the formal statutory system has not kept up. There is currently no formal statutory recognition for, or protection of, traditional trades within the Victorian system. There are few opportunities for training in traditional trades within the current TAFE and apprenticeship programs for the construction industry (for example, Certificate III in Heritage Trade Skills is offered concurrently with existing apprenticeships.)[26] Lessons can, however, be drawn from Japan, where a different conception of heritage has led to a formal system of statutory protection for architectural process, and where traditional skills and knowledge holders, essential for maintaining heritage places, are actively protected.

Japanese Perspectives

In order to compare the legislative framework of heritage protection in Victoria with that of Japan, it is important to first understand Japan's architectural traditions and approach to heritage conservation which encompass a much longer time period and range of traditions than Victoria's post-colonial built heritage. The clear distinction between object and process evident in Victoria is not found in Japan. In some ways, Japan's heritage buildings and construction processes form an indivisible whole.

Although traditional Japanese architecture has a rich tapestry of styles, techniques and materials spanning from pre-historic to recent years, the most common and traditional structures are associated with timber construction due to the nation's Sylvan landscape. The oldest standing wooden structure in the world, the Horyuji temple built in the seventh century, is in Nara, Japan.[27] Timber, while an abundant and versatile raw material, decays rapidly in Japan's humid climate. As a result, conscious efforts to document, repair and preserve significant wooden structures began as early as the Nara period (A.D. 710

to 784.)[28] Over the coming centuries, repair works for temples and shrines, in comparison to that of common structures such as residences, were viewed particularly seriously due to their spiritual connection to Japanese people, and their outstanding architectural and aesthetic values. Master carpenters (*miyadaiku*), who are experts trained for at least twenty years in using traditional construction techniques, materials and tools, are qualified to repair religious structures. In contrast, regular carpenters are only allowed to repair secular structures.

The late nineteenth century saw radical modernisation in Japan, as it transitioned from a feudalistic Shogunate regime to a centralised, constitutional monarchy. From 1868, the period known as the Meiji Restoration opened Japan to Western industrialisation but also led to the overzealous elimination of the country's traditional Buddhist establishment. Copious Buddhist relics and practices were irreparably abolished. Realising that the anti-Buddhist maelstrom threatened traditional cultural heritage, the government began calling for the protection of movable objects, including those associated with Buddhism, under their first piece of heritage legislation, the *Protection of Antiquities Order*, in 1871.

Evolution of the Japanese Heritage Legislative Framework

While movable cultural heritage was safeguarded from 1871, it was not until 1897 that built heritage was granted statutory protection under the Law for the *Preservation of Ancient Shrines and Temples*, and funds were provided to repair designated buildings.[29] This legislation was a prototype of Japan's modern heritage protection system which remains in use today, granting the government the power to designate and financially support built heritage. Generally, the legislation focuses on safeguarding the cultural significance of buildings, their authenticity and integrity through the use of original materials, structural systems and building techniques.[30]

In 1949, fire struck Nara's *Horyuji* temple, and led to the enactment of the 1950 *Law for the Protection of Cultural Properties* (the Law). It was at this time that the phrase 'protection' (*hogo*) was first used instead of 'preservation' (*hozon*).[31] Here, the act of utilising and maintaining cultural properties for long-term future use was emphasised over the preservation of cultural assets as objects from the past. As Japan's national standard for heritage protection, the Law has repeatedly been revised to categorise the designation of cultural properties in greater detail, not only covering built and natural environments but also arts, crafts, folk practices and individuals who are deemed holders of these practices, collectively known as Intangible Cultural Properties (*mukei-bunkazai*).

What has truly set Japan's legislative framework apart from its Western counterparts, including Australia, is the protection of a selection of traditional building conservation techniques following the 1975 amendment of the Law. It has since registered a selection of techniques under the sub-category 'Protection of Conservation Techniques for Cultural Properties.'[32] Recognising that they are considered indispensable for conserving cultural properties, the registration extends to individuals or groups who are deemed possessors of these techniques. One of the individuals who earned this status was the late Tsunekazu Nishioka, master carpenter who led the *Horyuji* temple reconstruction after the 1949 fire and revived a lost traditional tool, the spear-headed plane (*yari-ganna*). Currently, there are 84 registered techniques and 98 registered individual and group holders of these practices.[33] Notable techniques include traditional carpentry work, roof thatching and lacquer painting for structures. This legislative breakthrough offers formal protection for the processes involved in heritage conservation.

Japan's heritage protection system is regulated by the Agency for Cultural Affairs (ACA). Specifically, the Architectural Division of the Cultural Properties Protection Department in the ACA enacts the Law by designating, selecting, registering and safeguarding the most important cultural properties in the country. Each year, the national budget allocates funds to the ACA to undertake preventative and reactive measures that protect cultural properties across Japan, as well as to obtain public ownership of heritage places. Broadly, some key preventative measures include researching and documenting conservation practices, procuring materials and tools, educating and promoting the public, training and employing conservation professionals, and undertaking disaster prevention works. It is through this mutually dependent network of support between the preservation of built heritage and the availability of knowledge, materials, tools and personnel, that the long-term sustainability and protection of these assets is guaranteed. This holistic approach values and protects architectural processes and objects equally.

Japan and the International Heritage Discourse

Japan's heritage conservation approach emphasises the complete return of traditional timber structures back to their original appearance. This attitude shares similarities with the 'stylistic restoration' theory popular in the nineteenth century, which advocates for the total reconstruction of a building to a complete state, even one that may have never existed in its entirety.[34] This contrasts with the cautious approach taken in Victoria, and other Western jurisdictions, that advocates "changing as much as necessary but as little as possible."[35] Complete reconstruction is only to be undertaken

where original fabric cannot be salvaged for repair, and must be based on evidence, not conjecture.[36] Whereas, the Japanese approach, referred to as 'freezing preservation,' focuses on the importance of adopting original building techniques, materials and tools, and as such contributes to the safeguarding of architectural processes.[37] It is informed by the country's deep respect for carpentry techniques and the material character of timber specific to its climate, and plays a vital part in ensuring conservation knowledge and skills remain relevant in the future.

By the 1990s, tensions surrounding differences in conservation approaches adopted by particular nations sparked a wider discourse about cultural relativism and plurality, culminating in a conference held in Nara, Japan in 1993.[38] The conference challenged the Eurocentric idea of authenticity and instead addressed it as a nuanced, evolvable concept that can be articulated in different cultural contexts, advocating for the view that tangible heritage was inseparable from intangible elements.[39] This approach was then formalised by UNESCO's adoption of the *Nara Document on Authenticity* the following year, fundamentally changing the methodology for the recognition of World Heritage Sites, allowing culturally-diverse places to be inscribed.

Top Left: 'History of Kamakura: Building the Tsurugaoka Hachiman Shrine,' polychrome woodblock print (*surimono*) by Kubo Shunman (MET, JP2032). The woodblock print depicts carpenters constructing the Tsurugaoka Hachimna Shrine using a variety of traditional tools. H. O. Havemeyer Collection, Bequest of Mrs. H. O. Havemeyer, 1929, Metropolitan Museum of Art.

Top Right: The Horyuji Temple in Nara, Japan is understood to be the oldest timber structure in the world, dated to the seventh century. In 1949, a fire devastated the temple and lead to the enactment of the 1950 Law for Protection of Cultural Properties. Reconstruction of the temple was later led by master carpenter Tsunekazu Nishioka. Photograph by Yokoyama Matsusaburo, c.1872 © ColBase: Integrated Collections Database of the National Institutes for Cultural Heritage, Japan. Held by Tokyo National Museum.

Following the adoption of the *Nara Document,* the need to establish a global standard for protecting Intangible Cultural Heritage (ICH) was recognised internationally. Throughout the 1990s Japan played an active role in formulating the new framework for heritage conservation.[40] Twenty eight years after Japan enacted its national legislation to protect conservation techniques used for cultural properties and holders of these techniques, UNESCO adopted the *Convention for the Safeguarding of the Intangible Cultural Heritage* (2003), which includes various measures for ICHs from protection to revitalisation. While there had already been robust protection for traditional conservation techniques since 1975, Japan ratified 17 "traditional skills, techniques and knowledge for the conservation and transmission of wooden architecture in Japan" into the Convention in 2020. Japan believed that the ratification would, on an international level, "promote a more integrated approach that reveals the close connection between the tangible and intangible cultural heritage" so that people would "understand that some types of tangible cultural heritage cannot be transmitted without traditional skills and techniques."[41]

Discussion

There is a tension in heritage practice between its theoretical development, its continual evolution of values, its aim to provide permanence and its statutory frameworks. The values-based approach of the Victorian heritage system encourages the regeneration of practice through the continual re-evaluation of heritage values and the use of statutory tools such as registers and overlays to consider what heritage is. However, the architectural processes that underpin physical conservation are often left behind. Discussions and initiatives in Victorian practice acknowledge the value of intangible heritage and the fundamental need to preserve traditional knowledge and skills. However, the complex and lengthy process of formal recognition and legislative change are yet to follow. Intangible cultural heritage values related to traditional trades are preserved through their continued use such as by repairing and reconstructing heritage buildings. Active use of knowledge and skills is essential to maintain this aspect of shared history and cultural heritage in the built environment. The absence of formal legislation relating to physical conservation leads to a system that prioritises architectural objects over architectural processes. Traditional skills, knowledge and crafts can be lost when not actively used or formally safeguarded. Ultimately, the future of heritage places is at risk as appropriate means of physical conservation are lost or increasingly difficult to access.

Japanese examples demonstrate that the formal recognition of architectural processes and objects are seen as equally valuable. The statutory system values the methods of repair and preservation equally to the significant buildings themselves, contributing to the ongoing safeguarding of traditional skills and techniques. The symbiotic relationship between built structures in need of preservation and the availability of knowledge allows the sustainable continuation of built heritage as a process and an object. There are notable differences in the material and cultural contexts that separate the Japanese and Victorian systems. Nevertheless, Victoria can learn from the Japanese approach of including the preservation of architectural processes in the statutory framework. This could provide more systematic protection for traditional skills, techniques and knowledge, and contribute to the physical preservation of built heritage, ensuring the regenerative capabilities of heritage are capitalised in practice. This may allow for more sustainable forms of preservation, as the transmission of dwindling knowledge is encouraged, traditional practices are uncovered or re-learnt and fabric is regenerated through traditional avenues of production which often favour repair over replacement. Statutory interventions, informed by Japanese examples, may benefit the Victorian heritage system. Existing initiatives to preserve traditional skills demonstrate the urgency of resolving the skills gap, and the willingness of the industry to find solutions. Statutory protection of traditional skills would provide a formal framework to train and employ traditional tradespeople. The architectural process would be supported and balanced against the architectural object, as two parts of an indivisible whole.

Left: Traditional spear-headed plane (yari-ganna) being used to smooth a piece of timber at the Takenaka Carpentry Tools Museum in Kobe, Hyogo prefecture, Japan. The yari-ganna tool was revived by the late master carpenter, Tsunekazu Nishioka who led the Horyuji temple reconstruction. Image © 663highland.

01 GJ Ashworth, "Conservation as Preservation or as Heritage: Two Paradigms and Two Answers," *Built Environment* 23, no.2 (1997): 92.

02 *Aboriginal Heritage Act 2006* (Vic) https://www5.austlii.edu.au/au/legis/vic/consol_act/aha2006164/.

03 *The Burra Charter; The Australia ICOMOS Charter for Places of Cultural Significance,* 2013.

04 Sian Jones, "Experiencing Authenticity at Heritage Sites: Some Implications for Heritage Management and Conservation," *Conservation and Management of Archaeological Sites* 11, no. 2 (2009): 133-147.

05 Performance Growth Pty. Ltd. for Construction and Property Services Industry Skills Council (CPSISC) and Heritage Victoria, *Heritage Trade Skills Report,* August 2012, 21-22.

06 GML Heritage, La Trobe University and Donald Horne Institute, *HCOANZ Heritage Trades and Professional Training Project - Final Report,* September 2010, 125-127.

07 Michele Lamprakos, "The Idea of the Historic City," *Change Over Time, an International Journal of Conservation and the Built Environment,* 4, no. 1 (Spring 2014): 8-40. Refer also: ICOMOS *International Charter for the Conservation and Restoration of Monuments and Sites* (Venice, 1964).

08 Rodney Harrison, *Heritage: Critical Approaches* (New York: Routledge, 2012), 18.

09 Ibid. 23.

10 Jean Hiller, "More than meat: rediscovering the cow beneath the face in urban heritage practice," *Environment and Planning D: Society and Space,* 31 (2013):864, DOI: 10.1068/d6812.

11 James Lesh, "Melbourne's Federation Square and its Heritage Discontents, 1994-2002," *Fabrications* 31, no.1 (2021): 113, DOI: 10.1080/10331867.2020.1827545.

12 ICOMOS, 'Article 3," *International Charter for the Conservation and Restoration of Monuments and Sites* (Venice, 1964).

13 Harrison, *Heritage: Critical Approaches.* Refer also: Marc Askew, "The magic list of global status: UNESCO, World Heritage and the agendas of states" in *Heritage and Globalisation,* Sophia Labadi and Colin Long (eds) (Abingdon: Taylor and Francis, 2010).

14 Harrison, *Heritage: Critical Approaches,* 128.

15 Laurajane Smith, *Uses of Heritage,* (New York: Routledge, 2006): 11.

16 Harrison, *Heritage: Critical Approaches,* 115.

17 James Lesh, *Values in Cities: Urban Heritage in Twentieth-Century Australia* (New York: Routledge, 2023).

18 In 2023 the Heritage Council of Victoria sought public input into the types of cultural values most important to Victorians, or that are under-represented within heritage listings. Refer "Future Directions of the Victorian Heritage Register - Have Your Say!", published 24 October 2023, https://heritagecouncil.vic.gov.au/2023/10/victorian-heritage-database-technical-issues/.

19 *The Burra Charter,* 2013.

20 Planning Practice Note 01: Applying the Heritage Overlay, https://www.planning.vic.gov.au/guides-and-resources/guides/planning-practice-notes/applying-the-heritage-overlay.

21 Jones, "Experiencing Authenticity at Heritage Sites: Some Implications for Heritage Management and Conservation," 133-147.

22 "The Como Approach," accessed February 2024, https://www.nationaltrust.org.au/the-como-approach/.

23 Ibid.

24 Heritage Council of Victoria, "The Lost Trades Fair 2024," 27 February 2024, https://heritagecouncil.vic.gov.au/2024/02/lost-trades-fair/.

25 Australia ICOMOS, "Traditional Trades & Conservation", 15 May 2024, https://australia.icomos.org/resources/traditional-trades-conservation/.

26 Training.gov.au, *Accredited course details 10858NAT - Certificate III in Heritage Trade Skills,* https://training.gov.au/Training/Details/10858NAT Accessed 4 June 2024.

27 The Japanese Association for Conservation of Architectural Monuments, "Conservation Approach," The Japanese Association for Conservation of Architectural Monuments, n.d.

28 Knut Einar Larsen, *Architectural Preservation in Japan* (Trondheim: ICOMOS International Committee, 1994), 10.

29 Christoph Brumann, "Outside the glass case: The social life of urban heritage in Kyoto," *American Ethnologist* 36, no. 2 (2009): 278, doi: 10.1111/j.1547-1425.2009.01135.x.

30 The Japanese Association for Conservation of Architectural Monuments, "Conservation Approach."

31 Natsuko Akagawa, *Heritage Conservation in Japan's Cultural Diplomacy: Heritage, national identity and national interest* (Oxon: Routledge, 2015), 50.

32 Ibid, 52.

33 Agency for Cultural Affairs, "Bunka-zai wo sasaeru: Dentou no meisho" [Supporting Cultural Properties: Masters of Traditions], n.d.

34 Pamela Buxton, "Ruskin or Viollet-le-Duc?" published 12 May 2016, https://www.ribaj.com/culture/building-on-the-built

35 *The Burra Charter,* 2013.

36 Ibid.

37 Brumann, "Outside the glass case," 284.

38 Christina Cameron and Nobuko Inaba, "The Making of the Nara Document on Authenticity," *APT Bulletin: The Journal of Preservation Technology,* 26, no. 4 (2015): 31-34.

39 Akagawa, *Heritage Conservation in Japan's Cultural Diplomacy,* 115.

40 Ibid. 119.

41 "Nomination file No. 01618 for inscription in 2020 on the Representative List of the Intangible Cultural Heritage of Humanity," Intergovernmental Committee for the Safeguarding of the Intangible Cultural Heritage, December 2020, https://ich.unesco.org/doc/src/47956-EN.doc.

RESIDENCE AD&H

Britta Klingspohn and Heribert Alucha
Open Studio Architecture

As an architectural practice working on small-scale projects, we often wonder if we can make a meaningful contribution towards addressing climate change. Then again, the climate emergency we are facing extends well beyond the physical environment to encompass a complex entanglement of social, economic and ideological challenges. By reviewing a recent project through a regenerative practices lens, what we believe we can do is question current housing stereotypes based on real estate speculation and the economic model of unlimited growth. But let's start at the beginning…

Above: New link connecting the two existing houses. All photography by Open Studio Architecture.

Opposite: Link detail.

This unconventional project began as a conversation with a former client. Her daughter's family had become cramped in their small house in Melbourne's inner suburbs. The former client asked us whether we could possibly find a way of extending the building to better accommodate a couple, three children, a dog, a cat, a large collection of musical instruments and a versatile working space.

We began with a search for references for the atmosphere that we wanted to achieve. The house described in the film *The Last Days of Chez Nous* came to mind.[1] This house exemplified the dynamic fluidity characterising the collective lives of the people living in it. It was evocative of a time before the current housing speculation, where dwellings were not so much viewed as transactional commodities, but as 'homes' that supported informal ways of living. It quickly

became clear to us that the omnipresent 'back extension for a growing family' model was not going to be a good fit. We needed an alternative to this stereotype, which is based on an idealised notion of domesticity, hierarchical organisation and over-specialised spaces. Our initial studies exploring conventional additions were put to one side, and we changed our approach.

Our client, living in the house next door, was more or less in the opposite situation to her daughter's family. She had two spare rooms and a great deal of relatively unused space. This led us to ask ourselves whether, rather than thinking of the two separate dwellings as isolated entities, we could use the fact that the three generations were living in adjacent houses. As it was, the backyards were already communal. This new direction opened up new possibilities and we began to explore the idea of connecting the two buildings without transforming them into a single shared house. We took the two existing Edwardian era houses, including their extensions from the 1970s and 1990s, at face value; as 'found objects' devoid of any symbolic connotations. By distancing ourselves from a nostalgic approach tied to heritage conservation or restoration, we could focus on the elemental qualities of the existing rooms and their innate logic. We re-used and edited what was already there, adding another layer to the many changes that have accumulated, and continue to accumulate, over time.

Working from the inside, we created new openings and re-appropriated some of the rooms for new uses. One of the spare rooms was reconfigured as a bedroom for the teenage granddaughter. An old over-sized laundry was transformed

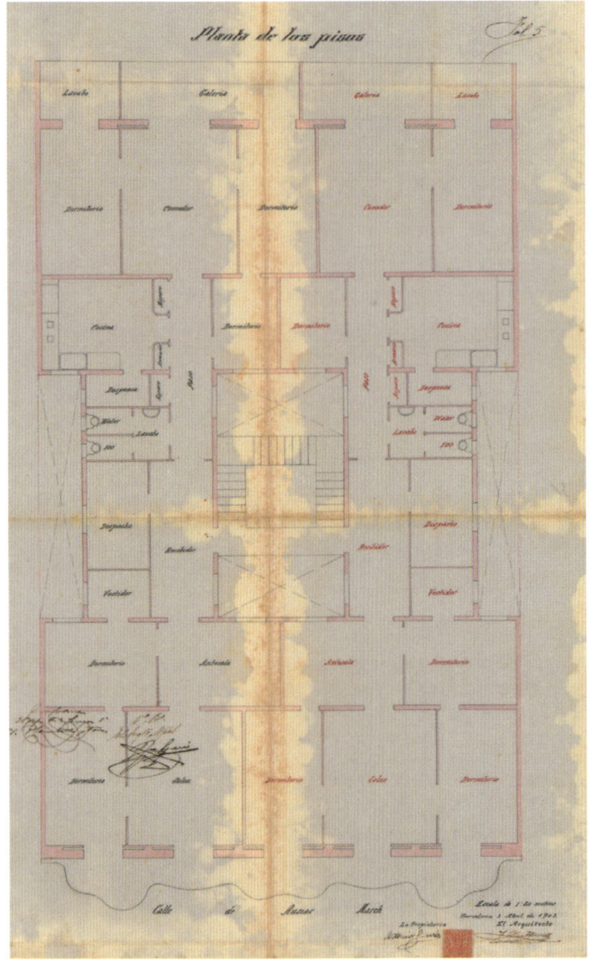

into a barrier-free bathroom. A series of communal spaces — a music room and a study — were used to connect the houses whilst providing a buffer zone between the two private and fully independent dwellings. These changes incorporated the under-utilised spaces without compromising the individual quality of the freestanding houses. All members of this extended family can now live, work and study without tripping over each other. The resulting combined floor plan has a quality that is reminiscent of the late nineteenth century Eixample apartments in Barcelona. With six to eight rooms totalling around $200m^2$, this type became a domestic tradition resisting spatial hierarchy through the almost-equal sized rooms with no predetermined program.

It is this fluidity and ambiguity that intrigues us most. By connecting the two residences using a series of generic spaces with minimal functional determination, we attempted to dissolve, to a certain degree, the original hierarchical layout of the houses. Their axial quality, the day/night zoning and the distinction between served/serving spaces thus begins to break down. The houses become a unified domestic space that is based neither on the traditional arrangement of corridor and rooms, nor on the modern open plan.[2] The reconfigured overall floor plan is more elemental, more a system of communicating rooms with a certain degree of homogeneity, distinguished by adjacencies rather than by spatial qualities. This insertion of a range of non-specific spaces with a degree of continuity and indetermination affords a more flexible type of habitation. It enables the family to benefit from the advantages of inter-generational living, such as mutual support and companionship, without losing their sense of independence and individuality. It is that fluidity and ambiguity that is so appropriate, fostering the closeness of family-oriented interaction, as well as the ability to retreat into private space.

Above: A late 19th cenutry Eixample apartment floorplan of the Antònia Burés building, completed in 1903. Drawing courtesy of the City of Barcelona Archives.

Below: A room that could be a study.

Opposite: Residence AD&H floor plans, showing the previous conditions on top and the alteration on bottom. Drawing courtesy of Open Studio Architecture.

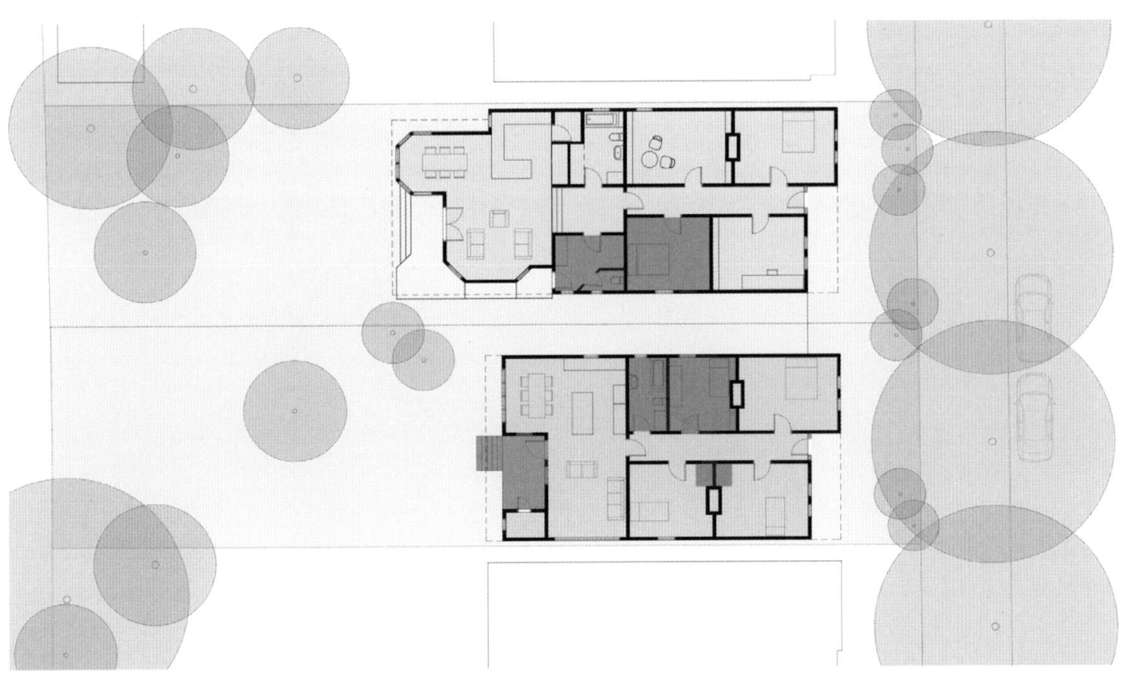

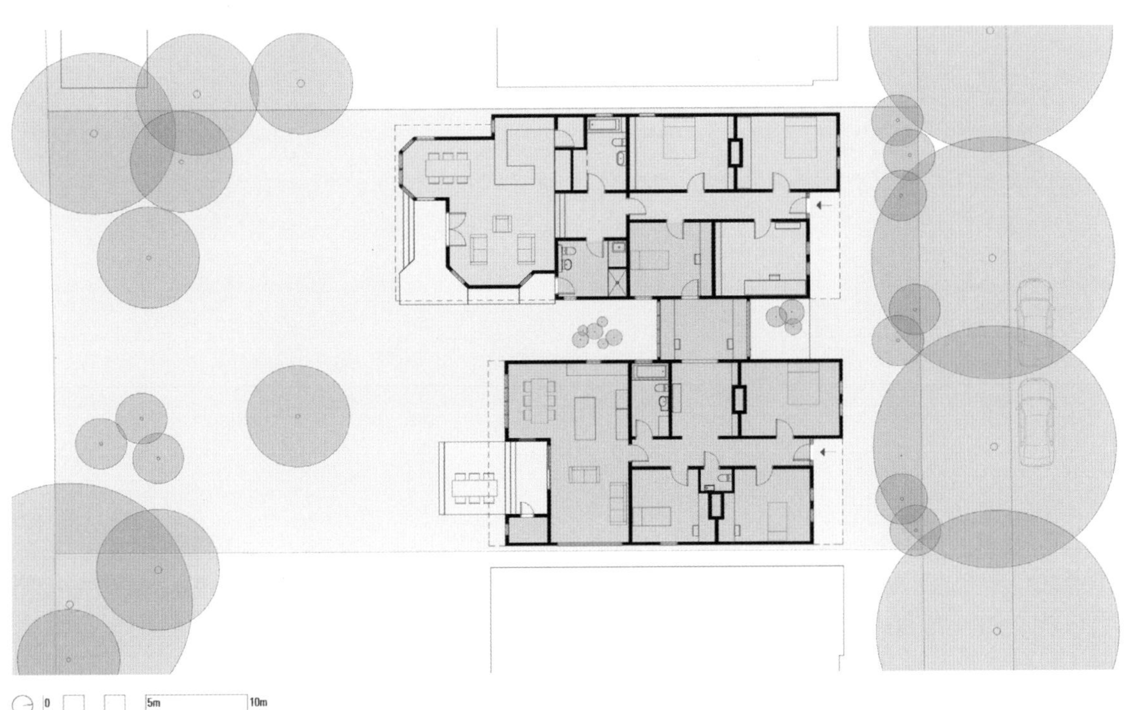
0
5m
10m

This particular spatial quality is also relevant in a broader social context. In an increasingly heterogeneous and individualised world, the 'typical inhabitant,' if one ever existed, is no longer a useful reference. Perhaps a 'neutralisation' of the floor plan (less hierarchical, less specific, less customised) can help redefine what domesticity today can be, and become a better fit for non-traditional forms of living such as shared living, living/working arrangements and alternative family structures.

Surprisingly, what made this new floor plan possible was nothing more than a series of small interventions. It brings to mind Oriol Bohigas' 'Benign Metastasis' strategy in which, akin to urban acupuncture, limited and concrete changes can radically regenerate their surroundings.[3] In our case, the addition of a mere 14m² and careful internal micro-interventions has fundamentally transformed the configuration of the two existing houses. The notion of reducing the scope of works is not only important for sustainability and housing affordability, but also has design implications for the approach taken with suburban residential extensions and alterations. It is always tempting, almost a default position, to demolish the existing and build something new, perhaps due to our training, market pressures, client expectations or just because it is easier.

What amount of work is necessary for each project? What is the correct dose of change? Mark Wigley, in his article *Towards a History of Quantity*, describes architecture as a theory of quantities that are calibrated to a historical time and a physical context.[4] These quantities are not only physical, such as size, density, materials and ornament, but also include ideas, images, effort and energy. It is an intriguing way of analysing how we work. It encourages us to rethink the relationship between effort and outcomes.

During the early stages of every project our studio undertakes, we tend to instinctively fear doing 'too much,' or being excessive. This could be a personal reaction to the 'maximalist' designs of the 1990s and 2000s, or resistance to the perpetual novelty and complete makeovers promoted by the real estate market. Most importantly, we question forms of excess because we find them at odds with the very idea of sustainability.

However, this idea of quantity in architecture has a flip side; one of 'too little.' There can sometimes be a propensity to not do enough, to reduce interventions to the strictly necessary. This kind of self-effacing action could open the door to a new dogmatic or functionalist approach that overlooks the intangible qualities of architecture.

What then is the right quantity? It is an elusive question. But we find that small-scale projects, because of the direct relationship with clients, shorter timeframes and generally modest budgets, can be an ideal place to look for an answer. This project in particular has shown us the potential for developing a greater sensitivity towards small and incremental changes as a tactic for finding the right balance between the 'too much' and the 'not enough.'

Above: North elevation. Drawing courtesy of Open Studio Architecture.

Opposite: A room that could be a music room.

01 *The Last Days of Chez Nous*, directed by Gillian Armstrong (1992, Fine Line Features).

02 Silvia Colmenares Vilata, "Ni lo Uno, ni lo Otro: Posibilidad de lo Neutro en Arquitectura" (tesis doctoral, Universidad Politécnica de Madrid, ETSAM, 2015).

03 Oriol Bohigas, "Metàstasi i Estratègia" in *Barcelona Espais i Escultures 1982-1986*, (Barcelona: Ajuntament de Barcelona, 1987), 11-12.

04 Mark Wigley, "Towards a History of Quantity," *Archis* Volume 2 (July 2005), 28-32.

BELIEVING IN GHOSTS

Jarrod Haberfield and Paul Walker

For those familiar with its forebear, a visit to the *new* Ravenscar House is attended by a haunting quality. The first Ravenscar House was designed in 1999 by architects Warren & Mahoney and built atop Scarborough Hill, overlooking the city of Christchurch. It was home for a wealthy couple and their eclectic collection of New Zealand art, and subsequently wrecked in the Canterbury earthquakes of 2011. A replacement building was conceived as a 'successor to and reminder of' its predecessor by architects Patterson Associates, and in an act of philanthropic largesse, the sequel Ravenscar House opened in 2022 on the flat lands of the city's cultural precinct (Fig. 1). The new location reflects a new purpose: the building displays to a visiting public the collection previously housed on the hill.[1] A new building that emerges from the ashes of another suggests a particular kind of regeneration, but the evocation of memory is always complicated.

The new building's status as a house is vague: the building is indeed a house apropos its name and zoning designation, however throughout the literature relating to its design and museological ambitions, the building is described as a 'house museum' – that is, part house and part museum. In a seeming attempt at legitimisation, the official biography of the Ravenscar House project by journalist and scholar Sally Blundell cites a series of 'usual suspect' house museum precedents: Sir John Soane's house (London), Fenway Court (Boston), Peggy Guggenheim's palazzo (Venice), Kettle's Yard (Cambridge) (Fig. 2), and the Lyon Housemuseum (Melbourne).[2] We learn from Blundell's commentary and interview transcripts with the architect that notions of living with art, and the balancing of private life with public viewership were central to the project's conception. Indeed, in the words of Andrew Patterson, the building's architect: "Far and away the best idea for the building was a house museum – all the stars aligned to a house museum."[3] While 'house museum' is an umbrella term that refers to many things – the house of a famous person, a famous building that happens to be a house, a house that displays a collection – Ravenscar does not fit in these categories. The thorny fact is that no one has ever lived there, meaning it is not a house at all: Ravenscar House is a museum.

The paradox that exists between Ravenscar's naming and its truth is more than semantic: the lack of clarity in its typological designation is mirrored by the visitor experience. In typological terms, an *actual* house museum is a hybrid (part house and part museum, as noted), and vacillation between the qualities of each parent type elicits a kind of experiential ambiguity; we experience concurrently or sequentially domestic versus museological space. At Ravenscar, where domesticity is barely manifest, the unsettledness pervades almost to the point of eeriness. Within a series of normative gallery spaces, interior scenes from the previous house are re-presented like stage sets. Complicating one's reception of the objects on display, the architecture is very 'now,' and the exhibition is very 'then,' which makes impossible any sense of transport to another time or place and creates for the viewer a particular temporal dilemma. An apt illustration is the assemblage of David Linley's bedroom furniture fashioned to evoke its previous Scarborough setting: we encounter damask wallpaper and plaid Roman blinds juxtaposed against a polished concrete floor, display plinths, and museum-standard track lighting (Fig. 3).

Fig. 1 (Opposite): Aerial view, Ravenscar House with Canterbury Museum opposite. Image Courtesy of Sam Hartnett.

Fig. 2 (Above): Interior view, Kettle's Yard. Image by author.

Ravenscar is rife with typological slippages that emerge as one discerns the links between the original and replacement buildings. Materials, finishes, and room functions are employed in Patterson's architecture to evoke 'glimmers' of the Scarborough building; alongside the art collection and the *mise-en-scene* of recreated furniture arrangements, we are encouraged to suspend our disbelief and engage with the benefactors' lives and former home (Fig. 4). As for the building itself, Patterson speaks of 'ghost rooms' that recreate in their plan dimensions the four key spaces of the original house: Library, Dining Room, Living Room and Main Bedroom.[4] The adjacencies between these rooms and the circuit that links them are completely reimagined, and it remains unclear whether this facsimile adoption of room plans is sufficient to experience in a convincing way the new building's ambition to memorialise the house on the hill. More successful might be the actual capturing of memory on the building's façade, where rubble from the original building which the earthquake shook into ruins provides aggregate for the new building's precast concrete panels (Fig. 5). Beyond the poetry of this upcycling, however, nothing in the formal or material expression of the new building recalls the original.

Fig. 3 (Top Left): Interior view, Main Bedroom. Image by author.

Fig. 4 (Top Right): Interior view, Dining Room. Image by author.

Fig. 5 (Opposite): Courtyard corner detail, precast panels with upcycled aggregate. Image Courtesy of Sam Hartnett.

The architect speaks of "integrating the building elements together three-dimensionally to create one cohesive 'home' form, as in a gabled house," but the gable reference is far from self-evident within the abstract language of the architecture, which instead evokes the image of a chamfered rock (Fig. 6).[5] And despite the 'reminder of the forebear' rhetoric, the very fine building is notable for the complete eschewal of normative building elements; roof plumbing, for example, is entirely absent from view. Absent, too, are any windows in the façade, removing every opportunity for the outside world to penetrate the interior, or for Ravenscar's program or objects to inflect their wider setting. Museums are often conceived as vaults, and here the idiom holds. Despite its 'house' moniker, the hermetic presentation of the architecture to the street is not 'housey' at all: a conventional house achieves its engagement with the world through windows, porches, verandas and front gardens that address the street and passers-by. Further, the unadorned prismatic form of the building neutralises any casting of shadows or discernible movement of light across its skin, affecting a sense of immunity from time – a sense only strengthened by the material palette of inert finishes that subvert ageing.

The spatial and lived experience of the typical museum is defined by temporality – at the hands of temporary exhibitions that change in series, or items from the permanent collection that rotate in turn from the darkness of the storerooms into the light of public view. Shifting our focus from architecture to curatorial agenda, we see that by contrast, the Ravenscar model suspends the building and collection in permanent repose. Numerous scholars – Theodor Adorno amongst them – discuss the risks of a collection that is frozen in time against its museum setting; for many, museums are where objects go to die, and the semantic link between 'museum' and 'mausoleum' is frequently made.[6] Maintaining dynamism, or a sense of contemporaneity, is a common challenge for collection museums and invites innovative curatorial approaches to ensure the institution remains vital.

At Melbourne's *Buxton Contemporary*, for example, the permanent collection of 354 donated artworks provides the starting point for exhibitions that are in turn appended by loaned and commissioned works. The DNA of the collection is manifest in every show, but freshness is assured, and solipsism eschewed.[7] At *Kettle's Yard* in Cambridge, meanwhile, the house and its collection are often deployed as a springboard for invited artists to make new work, like the 38 artists who in 2018 made original work for a major show titled *Actions. The Image of the World can be Different.*[8] Certain works from that exhibition (including Cornelia Parker's painted window) live on; in a curatorial sleight of hand, the serial and the momentary achieve permanence (Fig. 7).

In the context of its house/museum ambiguity, vault-like presentation, and changeless exhibition program, Ravenscar faces a grave risk. Aside from a library of fine books, the collection comprises art of some importance and furniture of uneven quality (fig. 8). The decision to partner with the local museum, rather than the Christchurch Art Gallery, is notable because the curatorial project of the former is defined by a kind of mothballed protectionism. Christchurch's Canterbury Museum – now undergoing a major renovation and extension – is best known for its wildlife dioramas and replica heritage streetscapes; both exist as vestiges or stage sets, and it is fair to observe that a vestigial quality defines the Ravenscar experience too. It seems that for Ravenscar House to catalyse an ongoing process of regeneration that keeps alive the memory of its benefactors and their beloved home, a curatorial program that rotates the collection and incorporates works from outside worlds might affect a welcome dynamism while making peace with the resident ghosts.

01 Sally Blundell, *Ravenscar House: A Biography* (Christchurch: Canterbury University Press, 2022), 7.
02 Ibid. 155-57.
03 Ibid. 159.
04 Ibid. 199.
05 Ibid. 201.
06 Theodor Adorno, "Valery Proust Museum," in *Prisms, trans. Samuel and Shierry Weber* (London: Neville Spearman, 1967).
07 Melissa Keys et al., eds., *Buxton Contemporary* (Melbourne: Buxton Contemporary, The University of Melbourne, 2018).
08 Sarah Lowndes and Andrew Nairne, eds., *Actions: The Image of the World Can Be Different* (Cambridge: Kettle's Yard, 2018).

Fig. 6 (Above): Exterior view, street elevation with roof forms (copyright Pattersons).

Fig. 7 (Bottom Left): Interior detail, Cornelia Parker artwork at Kettle_s Yard. Image by author.

Fig. 8 (Bottom Right): Interior view, Living Room. Image by author.

OPENING THE POSSIBILITY SPACE TO AN ARCHITECTURE OF CARE

Dylan Newell

Sitting in the sunroom with the Le family, adjacent to the 'working kitchen' and looking out toward an expansive, productive garden littered with colourful autumn leaves, it is challenging to imagine the hardships endured by this family of six over the preceding 18 months.[1] The atmosphere is serene, a freshly brewed coffee in hand, light conversation, the smell of fresh paint lingering in the air of the immaculately renovated house, with only the natural sounds of the garden interrupting us. Yet, as Tom tells me his story, it is hard not to be overwhelmed with stress just imagining the circumstances, let alone living through them. The Le's are a testament to resilience — the type of resilience often discussed in the literature, but rarely something one ever wants to call upon.[2]

Tom Le, a middle-aged father to four, walks me into the main kitchen in the heart of the house and proudly shows me all he has accomplished since the recent floods. He tells me how he stripped back the plasterboard up to 1.5 metres (the height the floodwaters reached) throughout the entire house (Fig. 1) and how, because the insurance company was unresponsive, he naturally ventilated the house for three months to allow it to dry. While dehumidifiers and heaters are best practice, without support, Tom could not afford to take these measures. Instead, he opened windows, stripped the walls and floor and brought in fans when he could. Once the house was dry, Tom proceeded to demould the house himself in preparation for the repair work.

After the flood, while their insurance company used drawn out stalling tactics to avoid a payout, the Le's were forced to find temporary accommodation which left them, paying rent on top of a mortgage and moving from place to place based on availability. Of course, nobody from the insurance company actually visited — what human could meet this family, see the situation and not want to help? Time, as the insurance company was well aware, was against the family; they needed to be home as fast as possible. Taking matters into their own hands and drawing on family and community, they began the process of repairing the home, with or without an insurance payout. It is clear how proud Tom is of what he's accomplished and under different circumstances he may have even enjoyed the process.

However, below the surface of the satisfaction one gets from the tactile experience of using your own ingenuity to make, repair, build and problem-solve, there is an underlying and unresolved scar left from the still ongoing ordeal.

Tom takes me on a house tour and tells me of how he: dug out the mud from under the house; installed moisture barriers; assisted tradie friends — as if he was an apprentice with electrical and plumbing works; re-plastered walls; tiled and waterproofed the bathroom; laid new flooring; and built cabinetry. YouTube, friends, his handyman brother and an unimaginably strong work ethic carried him through the ordeal. Throughout the process, the Le's had to continue to hold down jobs, go to school and undertake normal domestic work like cooking, washing, cleaning and educating. Their remaining spare time was spent repairing the home; weekends, holidays and evenings. Tom's proudest work and for good reason, is the kitchen built from factory seconds. The kitchen is a monument to what is undoubtedly a central part of the Le's domestic life; cooking, eating and family time. Tom sourced door panels, bench tops and appliances from factory seconds, then built cabinets to match what was available. He explains how the ends of the cabinets have fixed panels to accommodate the misalignment between the bench, room dimensions and cabinet door sizes, an ingenious and imperceptible method of using second hand joinery in lieu of custom made.

For anyone even notionally interested in repair, sitting with Tom uncovers innumerable design interventions likely impossible to conceive of without the hands-on experience he has endured. It is clear that without a strong network, none of this would have happened. Moreover, it is well-known by anyone who has attempted to renovate or repair that resources are notoriously difficult to source at the right time. Tom, however, seems to have managed this with enviable efficiency. Every time I visit, he shows me new resources for the garden and the house, which he has managed to gather from his community. The house sits on a sizable piece of land with a large portal shed erected for the sole purpose of storing collected materials.

Maribyrnong Floods

On the 14 October 2022, the banks of the Maribyrnong River broke, flooding suburbs in the lower reaches of the 160 kilometre catchment, which included Deep Creek and Jacksons Creek. This flood event was the third-highest on record for the catchment, reaching 4.2 metres and inundating over 500 homes, with the worst affected areas being the suburb of Maribyrnong and the Rivervue Retirement Village in Avondale Heights (Fig. 2).[3] The 2022 Maribyrnong River flood was considered a one in 50-year event, but in an age of emerging climate events, where flood drivers are increasing, this seems a disingenuous claim for authorities to make.[4] This statistic is seemingly more about obfuscating the gross incompetence of the authorities involved in their failure to adequately plan for potential disasters and the subsequent recovery and warn residents of the impending flood.[5] By labelling the flood a rare event, authorities are attempting, at least partially, to exonerate themselves.

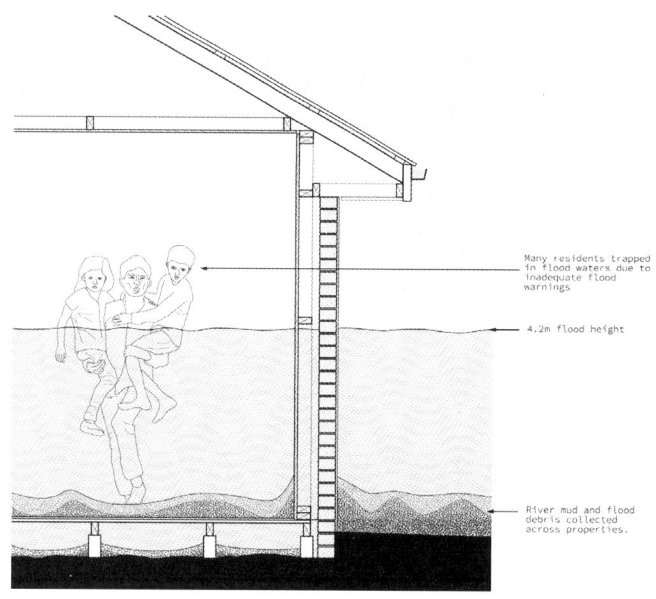

Fig. 1: A section through a house in Maribyrnong.Image by author.

The Climate Council of Australia has labelled the 2022 Eastern Australian floods, which includes the Maribyrnong River flood, the 'Great Deluge' and called them an 'unnatural' climate change disaster.[6] The residents of Maribyrnong are victims of climate change and as I will show later through the insurance response, are tangled up in what is becoming known as the polycrisis. I will argue that, through a framework of degrowth, architects can help map out a careful path through the polycrisis by opening up the possibility space to regeneration and repair. However, as the floods show, particularly through the insurance response, if the logics of capital continue to guide us, there will be no room for equitable regeneration. Particularly when, as Stéphane Hallegatte et. al. have shown in a recent literature review, poor people have a disproportionately greater chance of being affected by natural disasters and have reduced ability to recover from them.[7]

Furthermore, a 2020 report from the UN Office for Disaster Risk Reduction (UNDRR) has shown that, due to climate change, the frequency and severity of natural disasters has increased over the last 20 years, with a 175 per cent rise in events between 2000 and 2019 from the 1980–1999 period.[8] Therefore, we should expect that our built environment will continue to be adversely affected by increased floods, fires, heatwaves and storms and that it is not fit for purpose.[9] Moreover, recovering from natural disasters and adapting the built environment to the effects of climate change will become more difficult in an unplanned post-growth economy as capital becomes less accessible and more polarised. The Maribyrnong River floods, as I will show, already illustrates this trend, as insurance companies prioritise profit over human wellbeing in an economy fighting to maintain growth.

My involvement with the floods began when I met some affected residents at the Moonee Valley Repair Café, where I am investigating an improvisational architectural method that uses a framework of degrowth to regenerate buildings, landscapes and community through care, repair and maintenance. Shortly after meeting these residents, I was contacted by GenWest and engaged as a permaculture consultant. GenWest is an organisation that supports victim-survivors of family violence and runs social and education programs for people who experience inequity. They work in seven western local government areas, including Moonee Valley and Maribyrnong. The work I am undertaking with GenWest has been about consulting affected residents on their gardens and creating sketch plans and a general report for all residents. GenWest then uses this output to run community workshops and working-bees to help residents bring their gardens back into a manageable state.

For many residents, their garden is an important outlet for stress. However, little time has been left for gardening after the impact of the floods on the landscape, the time constraints of repairing their homes and often being physically dislocated from the home for over twelve months. Through this permaculture work, I have met many more people who have been impacted by the floods who have often generously and bravely shared their stories with me. Before I studied architecture I was a permaculture designer, which has influenced my research direction. While I am not a horticultural expert by any stretch, I draw architectural thinking to study living patterns and use that understanding to inform

Fig. 2: A map of the Maribyrnong River showing the extent of the 2022 floods and potential flood impacts under 2100 climate change condition.

a design outcome that works for the users; who, for the most part, know the space and their requirements better than anyone and just need it articulated as a design concept. The link between permaculture and architectural design thinking has huge overlap, being that permaculture was heavily influenced by Christopher Alexander's *A Pattern Language*.[11]

Degrowth

While it is easy to understand the links between the floods and regeneration, repair and community, the concept of degrowth can be more abstract. Furthermore, the link between architecture and degrowth is rarely understood and as Alejandro de Castro, a postdoctoral researcher in architecture has suggested, "architecture is almost antithetical to degrowth because architecture is about building."[12] Admittedly, given that most of the people I speak to are just trying to fix their house and "get back to normal," I frequently find the academic jargon I use in my writing (which seems appropriate from behind a computer screen) a little embarrassing. However, I will now try to draw out some of these links and illustrate why I believe the ethico-political concepts embedded in degrowth are important in finding a path through the seemingly perpetual polycrisis of the Anthropocene.[13]

Degrowth asks "how much is enough?" and in doing so, aims to challenge the growth imperative through a rigorous analysis of the biophysical metabolism. In answering this question, degrowth aims to bring the anthropogenic footprint back within planetary boundaries, while centering social justice and equality in its response.[14] Where the green growth approach argues for decoupling and dematerialisation, degrowth asserts that decoupling rarely occurs, never equitably, nor at a rate that will meet the net-zero time frame required for 1·5°C or 1·7°C of warming.[15] Therefore, degrowth aims to orientate productive forces on human wellbeing and the transition away from fossil fuels, instead of towards profits.[16] Within this context, it is important to recognise that degrowth concepts fit within the precautionary principle, which prioritises the minimisation of environmental degradation where scientific uncertainty exists.[17]

Underpinning the origins of the degrowth concept is *The Limits to Growth* report, which simulated exponential growth, reporting on critical indicators like pollution, resources use and industrial output. From the 12 simulations, the 'business as usual' (BAU) model, while not an exact prediction, was deemed the most likely scenario and indicated that industrial civilisation would begin declining early in the twenty-first century if the growth paradigm had not changed.[18] In 2004, the authors updated the data and World3 simulation, confirming that the world had stayed on track for the BAU model.[19] In 2011, professor of physical chemistry at the University of Florence Ugo Bardi revisited the data, reaching similar conclusions. In 2014, the applied physicist Graham Turner re-examined modelling based on up-to-date statistics and confirmed that collapse remains probable.[20]

In 2023, a team recalibrated the World3 model and once again the results indicated that the BAU overshoot and collapse scenario is likely to occur in the coming years.[21] Since its inception, degrowth, through a multitude of contributors, has worked toward an ethico-political theory that tackles the limits to growth in a way that is equitable and socially just.[22]

The BAU overshoot and collapse scenario can be understood as the 'polycrisis,' which includes climate change driven weather-related natural disasters. In the context of the polycrisis, the 2022 Eastern Australian floods represent a single crisis point, which, following from the Ancient Greek *krisis*, means a turning point where critical decisions must be made. The polycrisis, however, refers to the prolonged entanglement between multiple crises, including the crisis of capitalism, biodiversity loss, energy and the earth system. The turbulent interactions between each of these equates to an inextricably larger catastrophe that will thoroughly change the planetary system.[23]

As we navigate the polycrisis, political theorist Michael Albert asserts that we need to create qualitative maps that draw on quantitative modelling such as the *Limits to Growth* and speculate on possible paths through the turbulent feedbacks of each crisis.[24] Albert draws on the idea of the problematic to create these speculative maps, which he says emerge:

> *From the encounter between the core goals of a system —for example, to survive and flourish — and the intersecting challenges, tensions and obstacles that force the system to creatively adapt or transform in order to pursue these goals … A problematic thus determines the 'possibility space' for a given system and each possible trajectory for that system can be understood as a 'solution' to its problematic — a solution not in the sense of a 'fix,' but as a way of responding to these problems that creates a particular trajectory for the system.*[25]

It is within this possibility space that we find the potential for regeneration by drawing on the skills of designers to think through systems and imagine new pathways forward.

An Architecture of Degrowth

Degrowth has vast implications for architecture, most of which are beyond the scope of this article. In summary, my research indicates that reducing material use (especially steel and concrete), incorporating circularity and integrating more renewable material sources into construction is vital. Above all else, significantly reducing new construction, particularly in the global north, is essential for an architecture of degrowth. That is why my research is centred on repair and reuse, which appears to not only be the best path forward for architecture, but a vital step in preparing for climate change. Urbanisation, is one of the most intensively detrimental human activities on the planet, leading to deforestation, agricultural land conversion, habitat fragmentation, biodiversity loss and weather modification, while buildings contributed 21 per cent of global greenhouse gas (GHG) emissions in 2019.[26]

However, urbanisation is essential to growth. In 2020, construction alone, without including the extraction and manufacturing of materials, accounted for 13 per cent of global GDP.[27] As geographer David Harvey asserts, urbanisation is the primary means of both fixing and circulating capital.[28] Harvey surmises that "capital is always in motion and much of that motion is spatial: commodity exchange always entails change of location and spatial movement."[29] This is blatantly illustrated through an analysis of global real estate, which in 2016, made up $217 trillion U.S. dollars worth of total global financial assets a staggering fifty eight percent (Fig. 3).[30] The production of capital requires material commodification, with urbanisation the primary means with which to do this. As Harvey explains, the 'spatial fix' is how capitalism deals with its internal contradictions, in particular over accumulation.[31]

The wicked problem for architecture is that capitalism's need for material commodification and growth means there is always an inherent housing crisis and demand for new built capital.[32] If architecture cannot reorganise to operate with less financial and material resources, we risk further polarising the urban fabric between those who can afford to adapt and those who cannot. Like the Le's, people without the means will be left to fend for themselves more often than not. As cultural theorist Elke Krasny asserts, "architecture as a practical activity needs time, money and resources" and is therefore "always entangled with the ruling power and its specific economic system."[33] Because of this entanglement, any reorganisation will be difficult.

The goals of our economic system will always make practicing with less an unfathomably difficult task. However, the work of adaptation and repair will go on regardless, as can be seen with the Le's, simply because circumstances demand it.

Care-ethics

Degrowth is fundamentally about care and encompassing the feminist critique of growth, which argues that capitalist economics ignores social reproductive work. According to Matthias Schmelzer et al.:

> *Reproductive or care work is understood to mean all those activities that directly serve the maintenance and well-being of people, ranging from accompanying children and the elderly to cooking, housework, caring activities, and, in some definitions, gardening or repair work for personal needs, caring for nature or subsistence farming.*[34]

As a practical activity, within this definition, architecture is fundamental to care and thus must perpetuate in some form.[35] However, it is clear that building is primarily about exchange-value under capitalism — yet, from a paradigm of care, use-value is the fundamental function. Furthermore, as can be seen with the Le's, care work is rarely glamorous and in many cases, physically dangerous. Media studies theorist Shannon Mattern asserts, "we can learn from feminist critiques of the politics of care" and "avoid romanticising maintenance and repair."[36] That is to say, care work is often invisible, underpaid and dangerous. Expertise, the type that architects can certainly provide, is essential to protect people like Tom from the dangers that sit alongside repair work. While at the same time, we must recognise his amateur expertise. That is, the type of expertise one acquires through gritty hands on experience driven by necessity and passion, not professionalisation. How, then, can architects engage with these issues? Particularly in a time of climate crisis, with a built environment not fit to face catastrophic events such as heat waves, flooding, rising sea levels and refugee influxes.[37] Elke Krasny, in an essay on architecture and care, states "extreme weather events, accelerated and massive bio-extinction and millions of people displaced, evicted, chained to debt or mortgaged, are a warning that the need for architecture as care is more urgent and more obvious, than ever."[38]

My discussion with people impacted by the Maribyrnong River floods reflects Krasny's statement; their houses were uninhabitable, they experienced unimaginable material losses and financial instability. Furthermore, their ability to care for themselves, their family and their community was severely impacted. Emma Power and Kathleen Mee assert that housing is an infrastructure of care which "dynamically structures the possibility of care giving and receiving from the individual to the household and social scale."[39] In Tom's case, caring for his family meant repairing their home above all else, no matter the cost. The Maribyrnong floods, seen as a problem of the polycrisis, are at the intersection between the system of care work outside the boundaries of capitalist economics and earth system breakdown. Insurance companies, a type of outsourced, financialised care, are 'canaries in the coal mine' for how we forge a path through problems. A review of submissions from insurance companies to the federal inquiry into insurers responses to 2022 major floods claims shows how the logics of capital have clearly been prioritised over care.[40] One insurance company writes in its submission:

> *Unfortunately, the floods came at a time when the external economic environment, both globally and in Australia, was especially challenging. Supply chain shortages, labour market disruptions and an overheated construction industry resulting from the pandemic and ensuing high inflationary environment, created a particularly difficult backdrop for insurers to respond to the scale of the floods.*[41]

This quote is representative of submissions from other insurers. The financial cost of climate change is worrying insurers and they are fighting to stay profitable.[42] In numerous instances, insurance companies have denied claims and forced residents to take them to The Australian Financial Complaints Authority (AFCA), settle with underpayments, or proceed with DIY repairs.[43] In Tom's case, his insurance company has denied his claim and he will need to go to AFCA to try to recuperate some of his financial losses. However, this will not cover the enduring stress his family has had to deal with. Moreover, in completing the works himself, Tom may have rendered his house uninsurable. Of the people I have met, there has been little access to professional advice from the architecture and construction industry outside of insurers. While many residents are keen to implement repair works that protect them from future flooding, this expertise is conspicuously absent. Meanwhile, insurance companies often refuse to entertain the idea of Lawyer Madeline Serle, president of the Maribyrnong Community Recovery Association and a local flood affected resident still 'camping' in the upstairs area of her damaged home, said to me "the thing that has struck me and astounded me and infuriated me, is that the whole premise of insurance is that you have to restore as is. So you have to put back materials that are not resilient and completely ignore the opportunity to basically redesign your house if you wish. If you want to do anything that's any sort of material variation, you have to cash out. And that's absolutely disgraceful. It is basically setting up the community to be ready for another flood and to go through exactly the same waste and materials." Serle asserted that what is needed is “good domestic architecture, good social spaces and good built landscape” to “recreate the sense of place.” However, she says there is “systemic repugnance to thoughtful reconstruction.”

Insurance companies and the response to these floods are indicative of how all corporations will respond to the polycrisis — corporations are, after all, technological artefacts of capitalism.[44] Corporations are highly optimised and thus very successful at their job: profit and growth for shareholders. What we care for matters and corporations care for profits. The corporation, coincidentally, has evolved with the same objectivist philosophy as the famous fictional architect Howard Roark, created by Ayn Rand.[45] The corporation (a legal person) and its shareholders, are guided by rational egoism (self-interest) in order to "maximise wealth."[46] Insurance companies are corporations and following the logics of capital, optimise for profit. Benjamin Sovacool, a professor of energy and science policy at the University of Sussex, argues that “the corporation fails society by exacerbating financial inequality, socialising risk, commodifying human relationships and destroying the natural environment."[47] That is to say, where ecological and human care-ethics are concerned, corporations will always fail.

The individuals involved, such as claims assessors, are not necessarily bad people, but simply form part of a machine designed for profit. This is why insurance companies have evolved to deal with claims from a distance. Capitalist technologies confine the possibility space to the logic's of capital and thus direct productive forces, innovation and solutions toward profit. Explaining this phenomenon, Marxist and degrowth scholar Kohei Saito writes that technology mystifies and obscures problems, suppressing "the possibilities of imagining a completely different lifestyle and a safe and just society."[48] In this, Saito shows how the entanglement of social values with ideas of progress and technology disguise the true nature of the problems at hand and prevent envisioning solutions outside of normative capitalist realism.

The Possibility Space

Like the corporation, the global architecture industry works more like a technological artefact of capitalism than a system of design thinking aimed at solving issues of care. This is no more evident than in the post Hurricane Katrina clean up, where oversized egos destroyed any possibility of a caring architecture contributing to a positive outcome following a national disaster.[49] We must remember to engage all communities with humility and respect, acknowledging that we are not always the experts, we just have an additional and sometimes useful skill set. The challenge now is for individual architects and small businesses alike, to reorient their practices to help navigate the polycrisis with care. Political scientist Joan Tronto, writing on caring architecture, states:

> *Buildings protect people from the elements. But by themselves, they do not provide care; what happens within the buildings, how the building fits within its location and context, how it was built, who it will house or displace, all of these aspects vitally affect the nature of the caring that the building does.*[50]

Architects usually have strong imaginations, though often they are confined by the logic's of capital, because, as Mark Fisher has written, "capitalism seamlessly occupies the horizons of the thinkable."[51] In mapping out a careful path through the polycrisis, architecture needs to help open up a possibility space that allows design thinking to reimagine how we live on this planet. In 2019, the curators of the Oslo Architecture Triennial on degrowth drew on Henri Lefebvre’s ‘experimental utopias’ as an essential part of the exhibition’s theme.[52] That is to say, the imagination needs to be deployed to create a built environment not based on current forms or feasibility, but in the places of opportunity created in the voids between the social orders, hierarchies and systems.[53] To do this, architecture must be better oriented to care for and with existing materials and social ecologies as a path toward regenerating a built environment centred on use-value rather than exchange-value.

In doing this, our creativity can be deployed in a way that opens up the possibility of regenerating architecture for care. Architecture and the material and capital metabolism that surrounds it, needs to shift toward retrofitting, adapting and rebuilding for ‘passive resilience’ in the geographical locations, both globally and locally, most in need. These areas are, of course, those less serviced, or never serviced, by architects. At the same time, architecture needs to learn from people like Tom, who are already getting on with the job.

01 Note that 'Le family' and 'Tom Le' is a pseudonym used throughout this article.

02 Lance H Gunderson,Craig R. Allen, and Ahjond S. Garmestani, "Applied Panarchy: Applications and Diffusion across Disciplines," *Washington: Island Press,* 2022; B. H Walker, and David Salt, "Resilience Practice: Building Capacity to Absorb Disturbance and Maintain Function," *Washington: Island Press,* 2012;---, *Resilience Thinking: Sustaining Ecosystems and People in a Changing World* (Washington: Island Press, 2006).

03 GT Pagone et al., *Maribyrnong River Flood Review Independent Panel Report,* Melbourne, August 2023. https://www.melbournewater.com.au/media/22491/download.

04 Conrad Wasko et al., "A Systematic Review of Climate Change Science Relevant to Australian Design Flood Estimation," *Hydrology and Earth System Sciences* 28, no. 5, March 15, 2024: 1251-85. doi:10.5194/hess-28-1251-2024.

05 Geoff Crapper, "Submission 732.1 to the Inquiry into the 2022 Flood Event in Victoria," P*arliament of Victoria*: June 5, 2023; *GenWest. Our Community Our Voice: Lessons from the 2022 Maribyrnong Flood.* GenWest, 2024. https://dzulqse4m1jxi.cloudfront.net/media/documents/Our_Community_Our_Voice_ENG_WEB.pdf; Inquiry into Insurers' Responses to 2022 Major Floods Claims (Maidstone Community Centre: Parliament of Australia, April 17, 2024). https://www.aph.gov.au/floodinsurance; Ron Sutherland, Submission 558 to the Inquiry into the 2022 Flood Event in Victoria. (Parliament of Victoria: Melbourne, June 3, 2023). https://www.parliament.vic.gov.au/49489e/contentassets/c02a7264fb8947e49224d31946ae0914/submission-documents/558.-ron-sutherland_redacted.pdf.

06 Climate Council. *The Great Deluge: Australia's New Era of Unnatural Disasters.* Sydney, Australia: Climate Council of Australia, 2022. https://www.climatecouncil.org.au/wp-content/uploads/2022/11/CC_MVSA0330-CC-Report-The-Great-Deluge_V7-FA-Screen-Single.pdf; OpenStreetMap contributors. OpenStreetMap database. OpenStreetMap Foundation: Cambridge, UK; 2024.

07 Stéphane Hallegatte et al, "From Poverty to Disaster and Back: A Review of the Literature." *Economics of Disasters and Climate Change 4,* no. 1, April 1, 2020: 223-47. doi:10.1007/s41885-020-00060-5.

08 Sandra Banholzer, James Kossin, and Simon Donner. *The Impact of Climate Change on Natural Disasters. In Reducing Disaster: Early Warning Systems For Climate Change,* edited by Ashbindu Singh and Zinta Zommers, 21-49. Dordrecht: Springer Netherlands, 2014. doi:10.1007/978-94-017-8598-3_2.

09 Adam Hinge. *Resilience Issues in Building Energy Codes.* Edited by IEA. (Pacific Northwest National Laboratory, August 2023).

10 Jacobs, 2024 *Maribyrnong River Flood Model Report* Melbourne: Melbourne Water Corporation, 2024, https://letstalk.melbournewater.com.au/maribyrnong-river-flood-model/maribyrnong-river-flood-model-maps; Land Use Victoria, Brunswick, 1:30000, Vicmap Topographic (Melbourne: vicmap, 2023).

11 David Holmgren, "Permaculture: Principles and Pathways beyond Sustainability." *Hepburn, Victoria: Holmgren Design Services,* 2002;---. RetroSuburbia: The Downshifter's Guide to a Resilient Future. *Hepburn Springs: Melliodora Publishing,* 2018; Lilian Ricaud. "Permaculture Patterning, a Design Framework for Systemic Transformation." *Spanda Journal VI,* July 1, 2015: 195-203; Christopher Alexander, Sara Ishikawa and Murray Silverstein. *A Pattern Language.* (New York: Oxford University Press, 1977).

12 Alejandro de Castro and Marcelo López-Dinardi. Degrowth, Sufficiency, or Radical Environmentalism *ARQ Santiago,* no. 111, August 2022: 14-23. doi:10.4067/S0717-69962022000200014, P. 19.

13 Michael Lawrence, Scott Janzwood and Thomas Homer-Dixon. *What Is a Global Polycrisis?* Cascade Institute, September 2022. https://cascadeinstitute.org/technical-paper/what-is-a-global- polycrisis/.

14 Giacomo D'Alisa, Federico Demaria, and Giorgos Kallis, "Degrowth: A Vocabulary for a New Era" *London: Taylor & Francis Group,* 2014. http://ebookcentral.proquest.com/lib/unimelb/detail.action?docID=1843450; Jason Hickel. *Less Is More,* London: William Heinmann, 2020; Vincent Liegey and Anitra Nelson, *Exploring Degrowth,* Pluto Press, 2020; Matthias Schmelzer, Aaron Vansintjan, and Andrea Vetter, *The Future Is Degrowth,* London: Verso, 2022.

15 Jason Hickel and Giorgos Kallis, "Is Green Growth Possible?" *New Political Economy* 25 (4): 469-86, 2020). https://doi.org/10.1080/13563467.2019.1598964; Timothy Parrique, et al. *Decoupling Debunked,* "European Environmental Bureau," 2019. https://eeb.org/library/decoupling-debunked/; IPCC. IPCC 6 WG III. (Cambridge: Cambridge University Press, 2022). Pages 242-244. https://doi.org/10.1017/9781009157926; Jeim Vogel and Jason Hickel, "Is Green Growth Happening?" *The Lancet Planetary Health* 7 (9): e759-69, 2023. https://doi.org/10.1016/S2542-5196(23)00174-2; James D. Ward et al. Is Decoupling GDP Growth from Environmental Impact Possible? (PLOS ONE 11 (10): e0164733). https://doi.org/10.1371/journal.pone.0164733;

16 Brett Christophers. *The Price Is Wrong.* (London: Verso, 2024).

17 "Precautionary Principle - an Overview ScienceDirect Topics." (Accessed March 22, 2024). https://www.sciencedirect.com/topics/earth-and-planetary-sciences/precautionary-principle.

18 Donella H. Meadows et al. *The Limits to Growth.* (New York: Universe Books, 1972). https://bac-lac.on.worldcat.org/oclc/299359279.

19 Dennis Meadows, Jorgen Randers, and Donella Meadows, "The Limits to Growth: The 30-Year Update." (*White River Junction*: Chelsea Green Publishing, 2004).

20 Graham Turner. *Is Global Collapse Imminent?* (MSSI Research Paper 4, 2014: 21).

21 Arjuna Nebel, "Recalibration of Limits to Growth," *Journal of Industrial Ecology 28,* no. 1, 2024: 87-99. doi:10.1111/jiec.13442.

22 D'Alisa, Demaria, and Kallis, "Degrowth; Hickel," *Less Is More; Liegey and Nelson. Exploring Degrowth;* Schmelzer, Vansintjan, and Vetter. The Future Is Degrowth.

23 Richard Heinberg and Asher Miller, 'Welcome to the Great Unravelling: Navigating the Polycrisis of Environmental and Social Breakdown," *Corvallis: Post*

Carbon Institute, 2023. https://www.postcarbon.org/publications/welcome-to-the-great-unraveling/; Lawrence Janzwood and Homer-Dixon. What Is a Global Polycrisis; Adam Tooze. Welcome to the World of the Polycrisis, *Financial Times*: 28 October 2022. https://www.ft.com/content/498398e7-11b1-494b-9cd3-6d669dc3de33.

24 Michael J. Albert, "Navigating the Polycrisis: Mapping the Futures of Capitalism and the Earth," *The MIT Press:* Cambridge, 2024. doi:10.7551/mitpress/15041.001.0001.

25 Ibid. 89.

26 IPCC. 2022. IPCC 6 WG III. Chapter 8. doi:10.1017/9781009157926

27 Maria João Ribeirinho et al, "The next Normal in Construction," *McKinsey & Company,* 2020. https://www.mckinsey.com/~/media/McKinsey/Industries/Capital%20Projects%20and%20Infrastructure/Our%20Insights/The%20next%20normal%20in%20construction/The-next-normal-in-construction.pdf.

28 David Harvey, "The Limits to Capital," *London: Verso,* 2018.

29 *Globalization and the 'Spatial Fix.'* Geographische Revue: Zeitschrift Für Literatur Und Diskussion 3, no. 2, 2001: 23-30. Page 29.

30 Yolande Barnes, "Around the World in Dollars and Cents," *Savills,* 2016. https://pdf.euro.savills.co.uk/global-research/around-the-world-in-dollars-and-cents-2016.pdf.

31 Harvey, *Globalization and the 'Spatial Fix.'*;—. The Limits to Capital.

32 Manuel B. Aalbers, "The Financialization of Housing," London*: Routledge,* 2016. doi:10.4324/9781315668666; Peter Marcuse and David Madden, "In Defense of Housing: The Politics of Crisis," London: *Verso,* 2016. http://ebookcentral.proquest.com/lib/unimelb/detail.action?docID=5177364.

33 Angelika Fitz and Elke Krasny, "Introduction. In Critical Care," edited by Angelika Fitz and Elke Krasny, 33-41, Cambridge: *The MIT Press,* 2019. Page 14.

34 Matthias Schmelzer and Tonny Nowshin. "Ecological Reparations and Degrowth.*" Development 66,* no. 1, June 1, 2023: 15-22. doi:10.1057/s41301-023-00360-9, Page. 133.

35 Elke Krasny, Sophie Ling, and Lena Fritsch, "An Introduction. In Radicalizing Care," edited by Elke Krasny et al. 10-25, *Sternberg Press,* 2021. doi:10.21937/9783956795909; Elke Krasny. Architecture and Care. In Critical Care, 33-41.

36 Shannon Mattern, "Maintenance and Care," *Places Journal:* 2018. doi:10.22269/181120.

37 Hinge. *Resilience Issues in Building Energy Codes.*

38 Krasny. *Architecture and Care.*

39 Emma R Power and Kathleen J. Mee, "Housing: An Infrastructure of Care," *Housing Studies* 35, no. 3, March 15, 2020: 484-505. doi:10.1080/02673037.2019.1612038, P. 485.

40 *Inquiry into Insurers' Responses to 2022 Major Floods Claims.*

41 Ibid. *Submission 17* from QBE Insurance Group.

42 Insurance Council of Australia, "Insurance Catastrophe Resilience Report 2022-23," *Insurance Council of Australia,* 2023. https://insurancecouncil.com.au/wp-content/uploads/2023/09/20897_ICA_Cat-Report_Print-2023_RGB_Final_Spreads.pdf.

43 Crapper. S*ubmission 732.1 to the Inquiry into the 2022 Flood Event in Victoria; GenWest. Our Community Our Voice; Inquiry into Insurers' Responses to 2022 Major Floods Claims; Sutherland.* Submission 558 to the Inquiry into the 2022 Flood Event in Victoria.

44 Christopher M Bruner, "The Corporation as Technology, In The Corporation as Technology," edited by Christopher M. Bruner. *Oxford University Press,* 2022. doi:10.1093/oso/9780197635179.003.0005; Jerry Mander, "The Capitalism Papers: Fatal Flaws of an Obsolete System," *Berkeley: Counter Point,* 2012; Louise Metcalf and Suzanne. Benn. The Corporation Is Ailing Social Technology. *Journal of Business Ethics* 111, no. 2 December 1, 2012: 195-210. doi:10.1007/s10551-012-1201-1; Benjamin K Sovacool, "Broken by Design: The Corporation as a Failed Technology," *Science, Technology and Society* 15, no. 1, March 1, 2010: 1-25. doi:10.1177/097172180901500101.

45 Ayn Rand. "The Fountainhead," *London: Penguin Books,* 2007.

46 Yaron Brook. *The Corporation.* Ayn Rand Institute, October 27, 2017. https://ari.aynrand.org/the-corporation/.

47 Sovacool, "Broken by Design," Page 2.

48 Khhei Saite, "Marx in the Anthropocene," *Cambridge: Cambridge University Press,* 2022.

49 Richard Campanella and Cassidy Rosen, "14 to 1: Post-Katrina Architecture by the Numbers," *Places Journal,* July 12, 2016. doi:10.22269/160712; Wilfred Chan. Mold, Leaks, "Rot: How Brad Pitt's Post-Katrina Housing Project Went Horribly Wrong," *The Guardian,* February 3, 2022. https://www.theguardian.com/us-news/2022/feb/03/brad-pitt-post-katrina-housing-project-went-horribly-wrong; Martin C Pedersen, "Lessons from Brad Pitt's Failed Architectural Experiment in New Orleans," *Architectural Record,* March 21, 2022. https://www.architecturalrecord.com/articles/15571-lessons-from-brad-pitts-failed-architectural-experiment-in-new-orleans.

50 Joan Tronto. *Caring Architecture.* In Critical Care, 26-32. Page. 27.

51 Mark Fisher,"Capitalist Realism: Is There No Alternative?" *Winchester: Zero Books,* 2009.

52 Oslo Architecture Triennale, *Oslo Architecture Triennale 2019: Enough. The Architecture of Degrowth.* Oslo Architecture Triennale. Accessed September 14, 2022. https://www.oslotriennale.no/archive/2019.

53 Henri Lefebvre,"The Right to the City. In Writings on Cities," 61-181. *Cambridge: Blackwell,* 1996.

ALASKA'S RIVERS ARE RUNNING BRIGHT ORANGE

REALISM, OPTIMISM, REGENERATION

Olivier Cotsaftis

In Alaska, once-pristine rivers now run bright orange, creating visually striking yet otherworldly landscapes. This dramatic transformation is driven by rising global temperatures, whereby thawing permafrost (frozen ground) releases toxic acids and metals like iron, zinc and copper into waterways. From one year to the next, an anecdotal study reports, two fish species disappeared from a local river, altering the ecosystem balance and complexity.[1] As our environments degrade before our eyes, albeit less visibly so in urban contexts, concepts like regeneration, regenerative development and regenerative design are gaining global renewed prominence.

In response, the City of Melbourne declared a climate and biodiversity emergency in 2019, aligning with over 2,300 jurisdictions across 40 countries. This declaration calls for a radical shift in how we plan, design and build our cities, mobilising society-wide resources to safeguard the livelihoods and existence of both human and nonhuman species.

History, Theory, Ideology

Drawing from ancient global knowledges, general systems theory, the 1970s US bioregionalism movement and others, regenerative thinking is now increasingly influential and has already been adopted in various fields of practice such as architecture and urban planning.[2] Amidst the whirlwind of diverging modern ideologies, it provides a balancing perspective against the techno-solutionist and elitist creations dominating contemporary culture.[3] Above all, it can contribute to climate adaptation and mitigation efforts, promote social innovation, support economic revitalisation, and facilitate the coexistence of living species with other living and nonliving things.[4]

Against this backdrop of expanding recognition in academic discourse and practice, the contemporary understanding of regenerative design as both a system-led and place-based approach to designing is heavily influenced by the work of American architect and author Bill Reed. In his 2007 paper, *Shifting from 'Sustainability' to Regeneration*, Reed contrasts regenerative design with conventional, green, sustainable, restorative and reconciliatory practices.[5] But while practitioners intuitively relate to the practical distinctions between these various stages (with circular design now considered a form of sustainable design in other frameworks), the nuances between restoration, reconciliation and regeneration are primarily theoretical and ontological.

Of course, regeneration is more than a framework, and a framework is merely a guide to a conversation. However, according to Reed, Restoration thinks about design in terms of "using the activities of design and building to restore the capability of local natural systems to a healthy state of self-organization;" Reconciliation is the belief that "humans are an integral part of nature and that human and natural systems are one;" and Regeneration is a goal that "focuses on the evolution of the whole of the system of which we are part."[6]

"Logically," continues Reed, "our place — community, watershed and bioregion — is the sphere in which we can participate. By engaging all the key stakeholders and processes of the place ... the (regenerative) design process builds the capability of people and the 'more than human' participants to engage in continuous and healthy relationship through co-evolution ... The only way to sustain sustainability."[7]

Opposite: An aerial view of the Kutuk River in the Arctic National Park in Alaska. Image courtesy of Kenneth Hill/National Park Service.

Urban Greening: A Case Study

Looking at Reed's framework, it is easy to imagine how Urban Greening, for example, can be viewed as either a Restorative (Humans doing things to Nature) or Regenerative practice (Humans participating as nature.) At its best, Urban Greening can mitigate the effect of urban heat islands, increase biodiversity and ecological value, protect against environmental impacts, improve air quality, and enhance both outdoor and indoor comfort as well as social and psychological wellbeing.[8]

Urban Greening, however, can easily fall into Reed's Green Design category (which focuses on reducing environmental impact without addressing systemic issues) when plants are not suited to their local context, or when infrastructures are not adequately supporting plant needs and lifecycles. In addition, maintenance costs and potential structural damages are often overlooked. To the point, Urban Greening is unlikely to provide long-term benefits without rethinking design, construction and manufacturing through the lens of regeneration — a fact highlighting a difference between restoration and regeneration.

Restoration versus Regeneration: Reconciliation and Human Exceptionalism

According to Reed and others, Restoration considers Nature as an outsider and focuses on its commercial exploitation or conservation. In contrast, Regeneration not only aims to restore ecological integrity but also contributes to the resistance (capacity to absorb shocks) and resilience (capacity to recover from shocks) of ecosystems; humans and nonhumans included. Regenerative thinking naturally extends beyond urban greening and can be applied to all fields of practice.

Worth noting here, contemporary ecological restoration — traditionally defined as the action of returning something to a former condition — is now counterintuitively looking forward, making it more akin to regeneration. Additionally, Reed capitalises the word 'Nature' in his description of Restorative practices, referring to the human concept of Nature; but uses lowercase 'nature' when describing Reconciliatory and Regenerative practices, emphasising the ecosystem of nature where humans are only a part of the whole.

Philosopher Timothy Morton, in *Voices (towards other institutions)*, argues: "It would be much better to drop the idea of Nature, once and for all. I always capitalize it, because I think it is important to show what an artificial construct Nature is. It's not trees and dolphins and coral. Nature is a human idea, made by humans for the sake of humans, and it doesn't work at all."[9]

Above: Temperatures have fallen by an average of 2 degrees celsius in Medellin's green corridors. Photograph courtesy of Creative Commons.

In other words, for regeneration to achieve its aims, human exceptionalism needs to be challenged, which is the reason why Reed included Reconciliation (Humans are an integral part of nature) as a stage between Restoration and Regeneration in his 2007 framework (earlier versions exist without it, personal communication). At its core, Reconciliation simply involves acknowledging a biological fact that in no way inhibits the pursuit of creative, cultural and even financially viable endeavours.

Realism, Optimism, Unlocking Potentials

As we translate theory into practice and navigate the evolving landscapes of Alaska and beyond, regenerative thinking challenges us to design beyond sustainability, circularity and restoration. In this regard, a recent breakthrough study commissioned by the Belgian Government, *Regenerative Development and Design: Its Origins, Essence, Practice, and Potential as a Meta-Technology to Elevate Governance, Innovation, and Planetary Health*, published in June 2024, serves as a powerful resource for those working on systemic change or developing policies aimed at achieving regenerative sustainability.[10] How will Australia and the Melbourne metropolitan area respond?

At the government and corporate level, this requires progressive policies, governance models and funding that support regenerative ambitions. At a practice level, however, and as exemplified by the wide range of undertakings currently underway in academic circles and industry, regeneration begins by considering how our food, materials, clothes, objects, homes, infrastructures, cities, environments, processes and technologies can contribute to, rather than hinder, planetary health and wellbeing.

In 2023, for example, I prototyped 3D-knitted, customisable hospital scrubs made from SeaCell™, a hypoallergenic and compostable algae-based clothing fibre.[11] These scrubs were tailored to fit a specific healthcare worker's body shape and size using 3D-scanning technologies, enhancing comfort and reducing manufacturing waste. They were also designed to be downcycled in a so-called 'anaerobic digester' after use to produce natural gas and fertiliser, leaving no environmental trace. Building on this example, how can architects and urban designers apply these principles to the built environment? Can buildings and cities not only minimise their socio-environmental impacts but actively contribute to ecosystem health and wellbeing? Can urban infrastructures purify air, generate clean energy and enhance biodiversity? And how can we design with materials that grow and adapt over time? Considering regeneration should be seen as a systemic evolutionary goal rather than a design output, the question is not whether this is feasible, but how quickly we can innovate and implement these ideas at scale.

To make things tangible, we can look at projects like the *Bishan-Ang Mo Kio Park* in Singapore, which exemplifies how regenerative principles can transform urban infrastructure into thriving ecosystems that benefit both human and non-human inhabitants.[12] Briefly, *Bishan-Ang Mo Kio Park* is an intervention that transformed a 2.7 kilometre concrete drainage channel into a 3.2 kilometre naturalised river, integrating flood management with public space and ecosystem regeneration. The design incorporates bioengineered riverbanks, floodplains that double as recreational areas, and diverse habitats including wetlands and rain gardens. The impact has been significant: flood capacity increased, biodiversity soared, and water quality improved through natural filtration. The resulting 62-hectare park enhances community wellbeing while demonstrating how urban infrastructure can be reimagined to provide multiple benefits, including improved ecological function and climate resilience.[13]

In 1970s' Australia, permaculture design emerged as a holistic approach to regenerative living. Founded by Bill Mollison and David Holmgren, it integrated ecological principles, traditional knowledge and modern science to create resilient and self-sustaining ecosystems. Fast-forward 50 years and regenerative thinking is re-emerging once more. And while grappling with the realities of environmental degradation, optimism can be found in the potential for innovative, place-based, and culturally relevant futures for all.

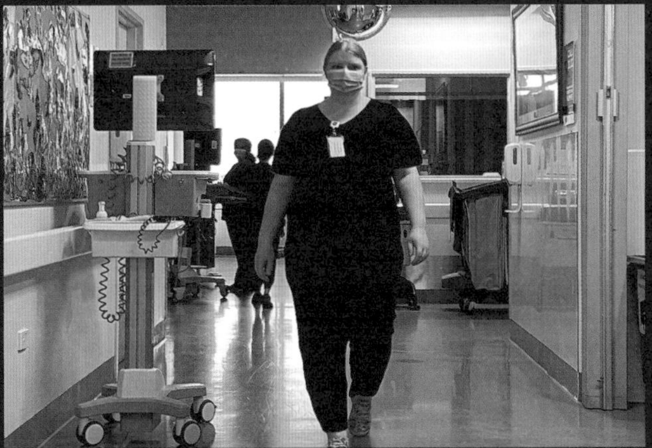

Above: A nurse from Peninsula Health wears a functional prototype of 3D-knitted, customisable scrubs made from SeaCell™. These scrubs were designed and prototyped for *Safety Sensescaping*, a multiphase project within the Thriving in Health program of work, a consortium approach to staff mental wellbeing led by Victorian healthcare provider Peninsula Health and supported by WorkSafe's WorkWell Mental Health Improvement Fund. Photography courtesy of author.

01 Jonathan A. O'Donnell et al., "Metal mobilization from thawing permafrost to aquatic ecosystems is driving rusting of Arctic streams," *Communications Earth & Environment* 5, Article number 268 (May 2024), https://doi.org/10.1038/s43247-024-01446-z.

02 Bill Reed, "Shifting from 'sustainability' to regeneration," *Building Research & Information* 35, no. 6 (September 2007): 674-80, https://doi.org/10.1080/09613210701475753.
Giles Thomson, and Peter Newman, "Cities and the Anthropocene: Urban governance for the new era of regenerative cities," *Urban Studies* 57, no. 7 (May 2020): 1502-19, https://doi.org/10.1177/0042098018779769.
"Regenerative Design Primer," UK Architects Declare Climate and Biodiversity Emergency, accessed July 1, 2024, https://www.architectsdeclare.com/uploads/AD-Regenerative-Design-Primer-March-2024.pdf.
"Arup Explores Regenerative Design: Towards living in harmony with nature," *Arup*, accessed July 1, 2024, https://indd.adobe.com/view/058d0389-e0a8-4462-8f8e-d49532d68181.

03 Laura Forlano, "The future is not a solution," *Public Books*, September 18, 2021, https://www.publicbooks.org/the-future-is-not-a-solution.
Hanna Kuusela, and Anu Kantola, "Unpolitical solutionism: Wealth elite sentiments against democracy and politics," *The British Journal of Sociology* 74, no. 4 (June 2023): 566-80, https://doi.org/10.1111/1468-4446.13043.
Henrik Skaug Sætra, *Technology and Sustainable Development: The Promise and Pitfalls of Techno-Solutionism* (Routledge, 2023), 286.

04 Peter W. Newton, Peter W. G. Newman, Stephen Glackin, and Giles Thomson Newton, "Climate Resilience and Regeneration: How Precincts Can Adapt to and Mitigate Climate Change," in *Greening the Greyfields: New Models for Regenerating the Middle Suburbs of Low-Density Cities* (Palgrave Macmillan, 2022), 105-20.
Abid Mehmood, Terry Marsden, Alice Taherzadeh, Lorena F. Axinte, and Cátia Rebelo, "Transformative roles of people and places: learning, experiencing, and regenerative action through social innovation," *Sustainability Science* 15 (March 2020): 455-66, https://doi.org/10.1007/s11625-019-00740-6.
Geordan Shannon, Rita Issa, Chloe Wood, and Ilan Kelman, "Regenerative economics for planetary health: A scoping review," *International Health Trends and Perspectives* 2, no. 3 (December 2022): 81-105, https://doi.org/10.32920/ihtp.v2i3.1704.
Olivier Cotsaftis, Nina Williams, Gyungju Chyon, John Sadar, Daphne Mohajer Va Pesaran, Samuel Wines, and Sarah Naarden, "Designing Conditions for Coexistence," *Design Studies* 87 (July 2023): 101199, https://doi.org/10.1016/j.destud.2023.101199.

05 Reed, "Shifting," 674-80.

06 Ibid. 677.

07 Ibid.

08 Matheus Gouvea de Andrade, "How Medellin is beating the heat with green corridors," *BBC*, September 23, 2023, https://www.bbc.com/future/article/20230922-how-medellin-is-beating-the-heat-with-green-corridors.

09 Timothy Morton, "Say "Nature" One More Time," in *Voices (Towards Other Institutions)*, ed. 2050.plus / Ippolito Pestellini Laparelli, and Erica Petrillo (Lenz Press, 2021): 208.

10 Leen Gorissen, Karla Bonaldi, Piet Haerens, and Lénia Rato, "Regenerative Development and Design: Its Origins, Essence, Practice, and Potential as a Meta-Technology to Elevate Governance, Innovation, and Planetary Health," Belgian Federal Public Service for Health, Food Chain Safety and Environment, accessed July 1, 2024, https://www.health.belgium.be/sites/default/files/uploads/fields/fpshealth_theme_file/study_regnerativedevelopment.pdf.

11 Shu Shu Zheng, "3D digital technologies tackling mental injury prevention in health care," *RMIT News*, July 18, 2023, https://www.rmit.edu.au/news/all-news/2023/jul/safety-sensescaping.

12 Herbert Dreiseitl, and Bettina Wanschura, "Bishan-Ang Mo Kio Park, Singapore," in Strengthening blue-green infrastructure in our cities: Enhancing blue-green infrastructure & social performance in high density urban environments, Ramboll, accessed July 9, 2024, https://static1.squarespace.com/static/Blue-Green+Infrastructure.pdf.

13 "Singapore: Bio-Engineering Works at Bishan-Ang Mo Kio Park to Prevent Urban Flooding," C40 Cities, accessed July 9, 2024, https://www.c40.org/case-studies/singapore-bio-engineering-works-at-bishan-ang-mo-kio-park-to-prevent-urban-flooding/.

DISCONTINUITY AGAIN

DISCONTINUITY, THE MINOTAUR AND THE RE-INDIVIDUATION OF ARCHITECTURE

Matthew Mindrup

Fig. 1: Pablo Picasso. *Bull's Head*. Paris, 1942. © The Museum of Modern Art.

> *Guess how I made the bull's head? One day, in a pile of objects all jumbled up together, I found an old bicycle seat right next to a rusty set of handlebars. In a flash, they joined together in my head. The idea of the Bull's Head came to me before I had a chance to think. All I did was weld them together... [but] if you were only to see the bull's head and not the bicycle seat and handlebars that form it, the sculpture would lose some of its impact.*[1]

In the above cited quote from Pablo Picasso, he recounts how he found inspiration for his 1942 completed sculpture *Bull's Head* in a discarded bicycle seat and handlebars (Fig. 1). The reuse of objects that were found having been made for other purposes as material for constructing art or architecture has a long history and was always practiced wherever there were some good stones, beams, metals, foundations, or partially ruined edifices that had exhausted their intended use values. Then, the assemblage of found materials became a popular approach to making art at the beginning of the twentieth century. Inspired by Picasso, who began to assemble found objects into art during 1912, Dada and later Surrealist artists adopted the use of found objects to create art as a method for challenging the dictates of utility, logic, academic art and mindless economic determination preoccupying post-World art society.[2] In its various guises, the bull and the Cretan Minotaur became popular tropes used by Picasso and his Surrealist peers to describe their art, its making and the experience of it. For these individuals, the bull and minotaur were associated with the subconscious, desire, creative instinct, and discontinuity.

Over the past forty years, the reuse of found objects in the form of building materials and entire edifices has received significant attention in architectural discourse. Amidst the rapidly rising energy costs and effects of global cooling during the mid-1970s, architects promoted the reuse of pre-existing old buildings and building materials as an achievable, economic alternative to building anew. Indeed, it was in this context that the term 'adaptive reuse' first entered the English language to describe such transformations in architecture, industrial design and even art.[3] In these discussions the reuse of a structure is viewed as an economic alternative to new construction, a viable method for reducing the energy consumption affecting global warming and above all as an approach to retaining the heritage value of a place.[4] However, to give new purpose to the forms, spaces and materials of existing structures requires designers to shift from a consideration of the historical background to speculative questions of their potentiality. In the interplay between history and memory, the latter is regarded as the hero and forgetting is the villain.[5] Yet as Paul Ricoeur has argued in his study *Memory, History and Forgetting,* memory and forgetting are two sides of one process which give shape to in our experience, thought and imagination in terms of past, present and future.[6] That is to say if Picasso kept looking at the bicycle handlebars as handlebars, he would only reuse them as handlebars and never see the bull's horn. The original identity of the bicycle parts as such never completely disappears but, as the French philosopher Paul Valery argues, in the making of art, such acts of exploration are a kind of sight, in which "seeing is forgetting the name of the thing one sees."[7]

An alternative to an emphasis upon the conservation of memory and identity in adaptive reuse is an approach to the regeneration of buildings and materials made for other purposes that discontinue their intended meanings in pursuit of new ones. This approach is exemplified by Picasso's *Bull's Head* sculpture and finds its contemporary application in architecture through the reuse of buildings and building materials. For those employing this approach, the first step in this process is an act of forgetting whereby the identity associated with an existing place or found object is disrupted, as it is ascribed with a new one in a new context as architecture. This is not to say that the identity of the former place is no longer present. Taking inspiration from the early twentieth century myth of the minotaur in the labyrinth, this paper aims to explore a much-overlooked view of adaptive reuse in the regeneration of the built environment that has forgetting as its cause. Through acts of assemblage, architects are shown to employ an approach to adaptive reuse that challenges an emphasis upon the conservation of memory and demonstrates the fecundity of discontinuity in forgetting.

The Bull and the Minotaur

During the first half of the twentieth century the bull, and its variant in the form of a half-man half-bull called a minotaur, became a popular trope in the work of several artists, writers and intellectuals within and surrounding the Paris Surrealists. The minotaur was an important mythological figure in Mediterranean culture that had been experiencing a renewed interest amongst Surrealists and intellectuals due to Sir Arthur Evans' archaeological rediscovery of the hybrid creature's mythical home, the Palace at Knossos on the island of Crete in 1900.[8]

The myth of the minotaur is an ancient tale of lust and betrayal but also a description of ideas about becoming, sacrifice and discontinuity.[9] In the Greek story, when King Minos wanted to change his waning power in the region, he asked the god Poseidon for help, who sent Minos a white bull to sacrifice. Minos, much taken with his prize, decided to keep the white bull for himself and sacrificed another in its place, thereby outraging Poseidon. To punish Minos, the god had his Queen Pasiphae develop a consuming passion for the animal. Pasiphae in turn asked the palace architect, Daedalus, to fashion a model of a cow within which she could reside to satisfy her erotic desire for the bull. Out of this unnatural union the minotaur was born with the head of a bull and the body of a human. Daedalus, it is said, built a complex labyrinthine structure beneath the palace as a home to hide the monster from the world. According to the legend, Athens, which was then a tributary of Crete, had to send seven youths and seven maidens every year into the labyrinth to satisfy the appetite of the beast. This pattern was ended when Theseus, the son of the King of Athens, volunteered to go to Crete, enter the labyrinth and kill the monster. After slaying the beast, Theseus found his way out of the labyrinth with the aid of a ball of yarn given to him by Ariadne, the daughter of Minos. [10]

The sacrifice and symbolism of the bull is deeply rooted in Mediterranean culture and is linked to ideas of transformation and discontinuity. The practice of offering up sacrifices to a divinity like Poseidon, is based upon a need to invoke the support of powers greater than oneself to receive some boon or change in a current state of affairs.[11] In the economics of communities based on agriculture, herds of cattle were counted amongst the society's capital resources and an animal was considered a suitable gift of sacrifice which symbolised fertility, discontinuity and the posterity of the community. Poseidon was one of the divinities associated with bulls, particularly in connection with their rather strange involvement with subterranean caverns and catastrophic phenomena such as landslip.[12] By sacrificing the bull, Minos sought to discontinue his waning influence and the resulting minotaur represented his renewed dominance in the region.

Amongst artists in the twentieth century, the symbolism of the bull and minotaur had different meanings for different people. For the surrealists, the minotaur was a symbol of the irrational, primal and instinctual forces that dwell within the depths of the human psyche that they sought to evoke in their use of found materials to make art. Picasso admitted that his own obsession with the minotaur emerged during this time and was fostered by his encounters with the Surrealists.[13] For Picasso, the minotaur represented power, virility and the primal instinct, and was a metaphor for the creative process.[14] After a succession of surrealist journals between 1924-1933 that called for a social revolution from the dictates of utility, logic and mindless economic determination, the Swiss art dealer Albert Skira founded a journal named *Minotaure* after the mythical beast.[15] The publication counted André Breton, the co-founder and foremost advocate of Surrealism, and writer Pierre Mabille among its editors.[16]

Minotaure was not only an advocate of Surrealist art and poetry but also a venue for important essays, writings on philosophy and art, and almost every issue featured a drawing or painting of a bull or minotaur from an artist. Picasso provided the first cover image with an assemblage entitled *Minotaure*, which included a drawing of a minotaur on a cut piece of paper amassed with other various bits of cardboard, ribbons, metal tacks and foil on a wooden board (Fig. 2). A 1932 article by Breton was almost entirely preoccupied with the status of the found object and Picasso's studio environment, reflecting on their states of becoming.[17] In particular, Breton echoes Louis Aragon's observation from a few years earlier that Picasso's materials were not beautiful or charming but waste products of utilitarian objects lying around his studio that the artist picks up and assembles into something new; a work of art.[18]

The second issue of *Minotaure* linked the preoccupations of the Surrealists with found objects to the bull sacrifice and minotaur when the ethnographer Michel Leiris published an account of a bull sacrifice in Africa, like that of Mediterranean culture mentioned previously.[19] This remnant of ritual magic harks back to Minos' bull sacrifice and the birth of the minotaur in the Greek story. The killing of the minotaur in the labyrinth is related to ideas about becoming and discontinuity that are essential to Picasso's *Bull's Head* sculpture and the adaptive reuse of objects and buildings in general.

Fig. 2 (Top Left): Pablo Picasso, Maquette for the cover of the journal Minotaure, 1933. © 2024 Estate of Pablo Picaso / Artists Right Society (ARS) New York.

Fig. 3 (Below): Ancient Greek coin from Knossos, 350-220 BCE. Courtesy of IRIS.

Fig. 4 (Above): Kurt Schwitters, Mz 601, 1923. © 2011 Artists Rights Society (ARS) New York / VG Bild-Kunst, Bonn.

The Labyrinth and Discontinuity

In depictions of the tale of the Cretan minotaur, the hybrid beast is often situated at the centre of a labyrinth that demonstrates the ideas of journey, sacrifice and discontinuity. In coins minted at Knossos from the fifth century BCE, this labyrinth is represented by a squarish plan diagram of a structure made up of only a single wall, like the line of a thread that defines a single path leading to its centre (Fig. 3). The plan does not represent a maze where, at every moment, the risk of getting lost is very great, but a path upon which the traveller cannot possibly get lost. The labyrinth has a single entry that is also its only exit. Therefore, Theseus needs only to follow the path like the unravelling of a thread given to Theseus by Ariande. The minotaur, by residing at the centre of the labyrinth, is both the aim of Theseus' journey but also an obstruction that must be overcome to change his own fate and the Athenian tribute of the fourteen youths.

The path of the Cretan labyrinth presents itself as a continuous journey along which there is not an end but a change in direction. Over the millennia different cultures have used the image of the labyrinth as a metaphor for the journey of life, spiritual transformation and artistic inspiration. In all these comparisons is the idea of an ending that is a beginning. It is a moment in the journey where an event, discovery or obstruction disrupts someone's path, and a change is created. Such moments of discontinuity are deeply rooted in early Greek thought through the concept of *panta rhei* (everything flows/changes).

The phrase *panta rhei* is attributed to Heraclitus by Plato in the *Cratylus* during the sixth century BCE. Plato claims that Heraclitus wrote that we cannot step into the same river twice, deducing that Heraclitus believed that all things are constantly becoming.[20] For Heraclitus the wooden bed upon which we rest, was a fully grown tree that was felled and cut into the boards a carpenter used to create the bed, which may one day become trash. A state of becoming can refer to the repeated occurrence of the same event, such as the slaughter of fourteen Athenian youths. The labyrinth represents continuity with the Minotaur as its guardian. Slaying the Minotaur is necessary to bring about change in Athens' cycle of tributes and punishments.

Picasso's *Bull's Head* sculpture conflates the ideas of becoming and discontinuity in the life cycle of everyday objects with the minotaur and labyrinth. The bicycle parts were following a typical path of production, use and abandonment. They were

at one time ore mined from a mountain that was smelted into iron and refined into steel tubes when a bicycle maker bent and hammered it into handlebars and a seat. Picasso disrupts this process of becoming trash and welds the bicycle parts together into a bull's head with horns. In the context of Picasso's and his peers the reuse of found materials, his assemblage of them into the appearance of a bull signifies discontinuity in its making.

Adaptive Reuse and the Discontinuity of Identity

Central to the reuse of found objects and building materials is the intricate connection between composition and identity. This relationship has been a longstanding topic of ancient philosophical discourse. Early philosophers recognised that the material and its forming were constituent elements that gave a thing its identity or substance. According to Aristotle, a table can be described as having four essential causes to be what it is including the material cause, a formal cause attributed to its arrangement or shape that gives a thing its specific form or essence, the agent or process that brings something into existence and the purpose or final cause for which something is intended.[21] For the French philosopher Gilbert Simondon, the substance of a thing was not an immutable fixed essence underlying reality but undergoing continuous processes of individuation.[22] Because the clay and forming of, for example, a mud brick is not the same from brick to brick, it is an individual. Against the form-receiving passivity of matter posited by Aristotle, Simondon takes the substance of matter to lie in the form-taking activity. As with Heraclitus, the making of a thing, like the clay formed in a mould, is not static, but undergoes a continuous modulation of its identity through the form-taking activity as a brick, wall, arch, ledge, walkway, table or dust.[23] This is particularly clear in Picasso's reuse of found objects and is reliant upon an ability to forget the identity of a thing to consider its application in other contexts for other purposes.

During the early twentieth century, a handful of German artists and architects began to experiment with and develop theories to explain their use of found natural or manufactured objects to create art or architecture. One of the earliest of these is the artist and amateur architect Kurt Schwitters, who began to assemble found materials in two and three dimensions as collages, sculpture and architecture during 1919 that he called Merz (Fig. 4). The foundational idea of his Merz oeuvre was that all physical things had an

Fig. 5: Rural Studio, *The Glass Chapel* car window facade, Alabama, USA, 2000. Photograph © Timothy Hursley.

Fig. 6: Luigi & Raffaello Rosselli, *The Beehive Office* facade, Surry Hills, NSW 2017. Photograph © Ben Hosking.

Eigengift (own poison) or identity that must be *Entmaterialisiert* (dematerialised) in the imagination of their user so that they may be employed as material for making art or architecture.[24] This dematerialisation is comparable to the German philosopher Edmund Husserl's concept of *Einklammerung* (bracketing), which enables one to bracket out, that is to wilfully hold in suspension the identities and meaning attributed to things such as a river, tree or even bicycle seat to consider them as they are given to consciousness.[25] An architect exploring the reuse of an existing building or building material similarly forgets the meanings attributed to them and considers how their formal and material characteristics can be altered or combined with others to satisfy a new use. For Schwitters this new use was in the service of creating purposeless architectural environments. In contemporary architectural practice such acts of discontinuity can be recombined in novel or unexpected arrangements for new practical uses.

For whatever reason, it is difficult to find examples of buildings constructed with materials that were made for other purposes until the turn of the twenty-first century. There are certainly examples like Herman Hetzberger's reorientation of concrete building blocks in the outdoor play area of his Montessori School and Willemspark School, Amsterdam, 1980-1983, or the reuse of tires and glass bottles to construct walls in the Earthships of New Mexico from the 1970s till the present. However, the found objects reused in these projects tend to retain their original identities as recycled materials. Conversely, one project that stands out as the poster child for the imaginative adaptation of found materials to new uses is the Auburn University's Rural Studio Community Center (Chapel) at Mason's Bend, Alabama from 2000, and its use of car windows (Fig. 5). This diminutive construction was built as part of a four-person team's design-build studio project. The structure consists of a rammed earth foundation supporting a timber structure and barn-like roof that is broken into two parts: a thin aluminium shed, and a glass façade comprised of curved sheets of automotive glass salvaged from a Chicago scrap yard. The idea of using the car windows and arranging them like the scales of a fish evolved through a process of constructing several mock-ups to test different fastening techniques and armatures.

Examples of novel new uses for found materials in the construction of buildings have increased exponentially over the past two decades, such as Encore Heureux Architectes' reuse of doors to create the façade of their Circular Pavilion in Paris from 2015 or CHYBIK+KRISTOF 2016 reuse of plastic chair seats to create the façade of Gallery of Furniture Brno-Vinohrady in the Czech Republic. In these instances, the object is intended to retain much of its original identity as a demonstration for the reuse of the found objects in the circular economy of architecture or as a kind of 'signage' for a furniture gallery. Such examples demonstrate the potentiality of the imagination to find new purposes for existing objects of production in what Simondon refers to as re-individuation.

For Simondon, re-individuation is the dynamic process through which buildings, building materials or found objects can come together to form a new entity or system such as a work of art or architecture.[26] Each natural and man-made thing brings to any process of fabrication its own history, properties and affordances, and through their arrangement and interaction they undergo a process of re-individuation as they form a new collective entity. In other words, against the Aristotelian notion of hylomorphism, and the Hegelian dialectic, transduction serves as the process by which individuated forms of being emerge. So, it is neither form being applied to matter, nor matter becoming a certain form, but a process that creates form through a propagation of structure and assemblage that actualises its potentiality. In the reassembly of materials and edifices made for other purposes, this process of re-individuation requires an act of forgetting the former identity so that a new one can be ascribed to it in a new context as architecture.

Simondon's concept of re-individuation finds resonance in contemporary architectural examples for the reuse of materials made for other purposes. For example, in Australian architect Luigi Rosselli's approach to the construction of his 2017 completed office facade in Surry Hills, NSW, where recycled roofing tiles are ingeniously repurposed to create a light-screening façade (Fig. 6). In this architectural endeavour, the process of re-individuation is evident as the discarded tiles, originally part of a different individuated structure, undergo a transformative journey. Rosselli's intervention allows these tiles to transcend their previous identity, forming a new, collective whole as a screening facade. The former identity of the thin, flat, hard, earthen forms as roof tiles are not completely forgotten, but acquire new function, meaning and aesthetic qualities within the architectural composition as a light-filtering system. Another worthy example is a pavilion created by the Berlin-based architecture collective Raumlabor in Tel-Aviv, Israel during 2019 (Fig. 7). To fabricate their pavilion the architects sewed together and suspended on poles air cushions normally used as dunnage bags for securing loads in shipping containers, in order to create a light-filtering pavilion for the Grand Opening of the Liebling Haus - The White City Center. Such works, however temporal, embody

Simondon's notion of re-individuation, illustrating how the uses for materials and elements can be discontinued by dynamically recontextualising them into novel configurations to satisfy new purposes.

Conclusion

While it may appear unconventional to begin a paper about the reuse of found objects in architecture with Picasso's *Bull's Head* sculpture and the myth of the minotaur, this association has sought to unveil profound insights into the nature of adaptive reuse in art and architecture as an exercise in discontinuity and forgetting. The symbolism embedded within the myth of the minotaur preoccupied early twentieth century artists about the creative process. For early Surrealist and Dada artists, the use of found objects as an important medium for creating their own work that aimed to challenge traditional notions of artistic material and meaning. The challenge of using found materials to create art or architecture is to overcome the identities already ascribed to such things and open oneself to considering the opportunities their material and spatial characteristics affords to new uses. Perhaps it is for this reason that Picasso would often wear the mask of a bull to portray himself as a minotaur, a metaphor for the struggle against his own limitations and entrenched artistic conventions.

Fig 7: Raumlabor, *Dialogue as Form,* Tel-Aviv, Israel, 2019. Photograph by raumlaborberlin.

Opposite: Raumlabor, *Dialogue as Form* (close up of dunnage bass). Photograph by raumlaborberlin.

Just as Picasso confronted his own creative obstacles by working with found materials, so too must architects confront the challenges inherent in revitalizing the built environment. Embracing the metaphorical imperative to 'take the bull by its horns,' designers are called upon to confront and transcend the inherent constraints of materials and spatial configurations in the adaptive reuse of existing buildings that have exhausted their use values. In this process of regeneration, it becomes essential to heed Schwitters' admonition to set aside the habitual influences of tradition and preconception, allowing one to perceive the intrinsic qualities and potentialities of materials and spaces anew. By doing so, we unlock the potential for innovation and transformation, harnessing the inherent affordances of architectural elements to serve novel purposes and adapt to evolving needs.

In essence, the journey from Picasso's *Bull's Head* to the realm of architectural design is one of creative metamorphosis, wherein myth, symbolism and identity converge to inspire new modes of thinking and practice. By embracing the challenge of navigating obstacles head-on, architects can harness the power of imagination and ingenuity to shape a built environment that transcends the constraints of the past and embodies the aspirations of the future.

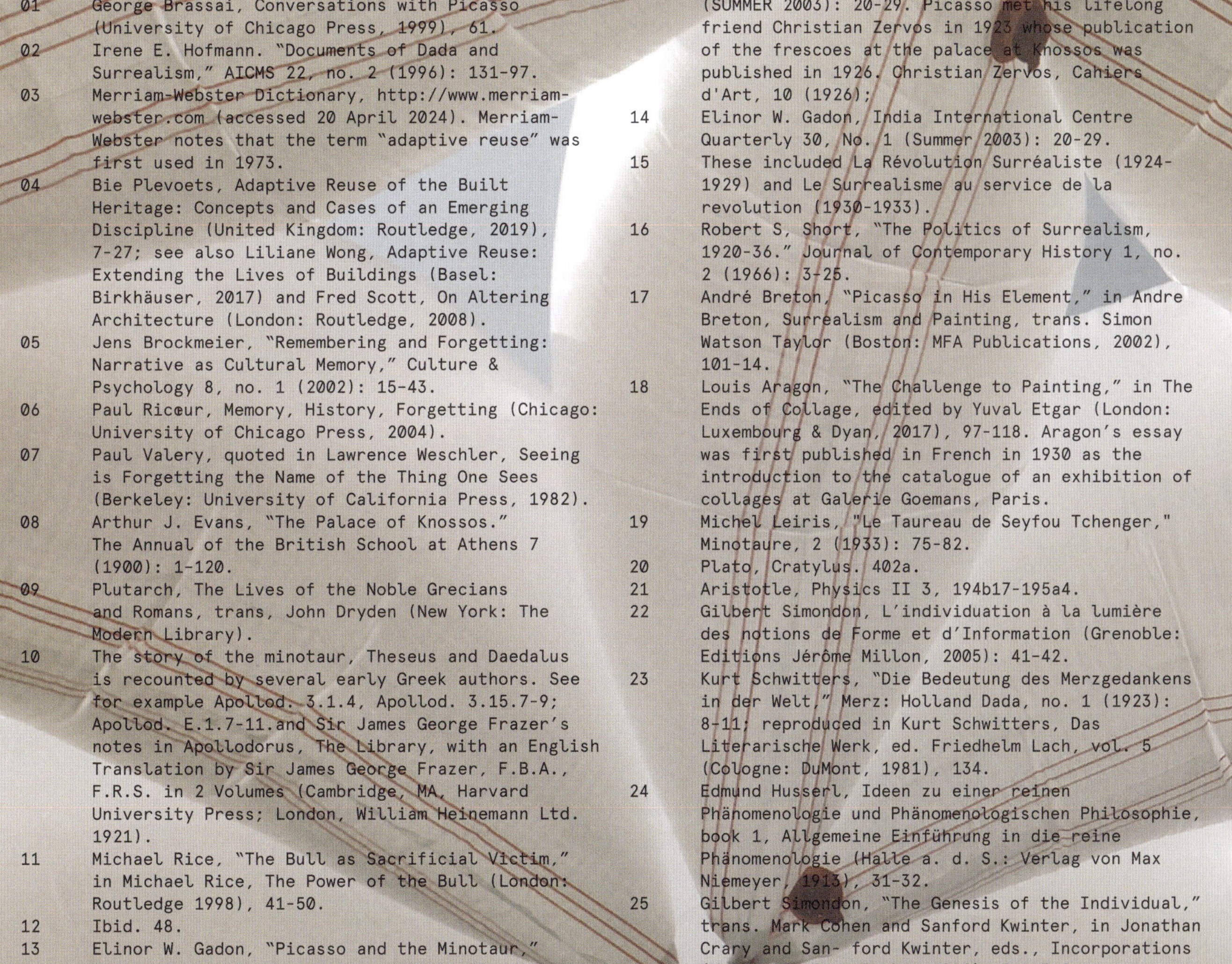

01 George Brassai, Conversations with Picasso (University of Chicago Press, 1999), 61.

02 Irene E. Hofmann. "Documents of Dada and Surrealism," AICMS 22, no. 2 (1996): 131-97.

03 Merriam-Webster Dictionary, http://www.merriam-webster.com (accessed 20 April 2024). Merriam-Webster notes that the term "adaptive reuse" was first used in 1973.

04 Bie Plevoets, Adaptive Reuse of the Built Heritage: Concepts and Cases of an Emerging Discipline (United Kingdom: Routledge, 2019), 7-27; see also Liliane Wong, Adaptive Reuse: Extending the Lives of Buildings (Basel: Birkhäuser, 2017) and Fred Scott, On Altering Architecture (London: Routledge, 2008).

05 Jens Brockmeier, "Remembering and Forgetting: Narrative as Cultural Memory," Culture & Psychology 8, no. 1 (2002): 15-43.

06 Paul Ricœur, Memory, History, Forgetting (Chicago: University of Chicago Press, 2004).

07 Paul Valery, quoted in Lawrence Weschler, Seeing is Forgetting the Name of the Thing One Sees (Berkeley: University of California Press, 1982).

08 Arthur J. Evans, "The Palace of Knossos." The Annual of the British School at Athens 7 (1900): 1-120.

09 Plutarch, The Lives of the Noble Grecians and Romans, trans, John Dryden (New York: The Modern Library).

10 The story of the minotaur, Theseus and Daedalus is recounted by several early Greek authors. See for example Apollod. 3.1.4, Apollod. 3.15.7-9; Apollod. E.1.7-11.and Sir James George Frazer's notes in Apollodorus, The Library, with an English Translation by Sir James George Frazer, F.B.A., F.R.S. in 2 Volumes (Cambridge, MA, Harvard University Press; London, William Heinemann Ltd. 1921).

11 Michael Rice, "The Bull as Sacrificial Victim," in Michael Rice, The Power of the Bull (London: Routledge 1998), 41-50.

12 Ibid. 48.

13 Elinor W. Gadon, "Picasso and the Minotaur," India International Centre Quarterly 30, no. 1 (SUMMER 2003): 20-29. Picasso met his lifelong friend Christian Zervos in 1923 whose publication of the frescoes at the palace at Knossos was published in 1926. Christian Zervos, Cahiers d'Art, 10 (1926);

14 Elinor W. Gadon, India International Centre Quarterly 30, No. 1 (Summer 2003): 20-29.

15 These included La Révolution Surréaliste (1924-1929) and Le Surrealisme au service de la revolution (1930-1933).

16 Robert S, Short, "The Politics of Surrealism, 1920-36." Journal of Contemporary History 1, no. 2 (1966): 3-25.

17 André Breton, "Picasso in His Element," in Andre Breton, Surrealism and Painting, trans. Simon Watson Taylor (Boston: MFA Publications, 2002), 101-14.

18 Louis Aragon, "The Challenge to Painting," in The Ends of Collage, edited by Yuval Etgar (London: Luxembourg & Dyan, 2017), 97-118. Aragon's essay was first published in French in 1930 as the introduction to the catalogue of an exhibition of collages at Galerie Goemans, Paris.

19 Michel Leiris, "Le Taureau de Seyfou Tchenger," Minotaure, 2 (1933): 75-82.

20 Plato, Cratylus. 402a.

21 Aristotle, Physics II 3, 194b17-195a4.

22 Gilbert Simondon, L'individuation à la lumière des notions de Forme et d'Information (Grenoble: Editions Jérôme Millon, 2005): 41-42.

23 Kurt Schwitters, "Die Bedeutung des Merzgedankens in der Welt," Merz: Holland Dada, no. 1 (1923): 8-11; reproduced in Kurt Schwitters, Das Literarische Werk, ed. Friedhelm Lach, vol. 5 (Cologne: DuMont, 1981), 134.

24 Edmund Husserl, Ideen zu einer reinen Phänomenologie und Phänomenologischen Philosophie, book 1, Allgemeine Einführung in die reine Phänomenologie (Halle a. d. S.: Verlag von Max Niemeyer, 1913), 31-32.

25 Gilbert Simondon, "The Genesis of the Individual," trans. Mark Cohen and Sanford Kwinter, in Jonathan Crary and San- ford Kwinter, eds., Incorporations (New York: Zone Books, 1992), 311-312.

THE AYLESBURY FRAGMENTS

Harriet Mena Hill and Theo Beck

Harriet Mena Hill is an artist who has lived and worked in Walworth, South-London since 1984. Since 2018, she has been documenting the redevelopment of the Aylesbury Estate in South East London and the effect of on-site regeneration on the community who remain in situ as the estate is demolished and rebuilt around them.

The Aylesbury Estate

Designed by Hans Peter 'Felix' Trenton, construction of the Aylesbury Estate started in 1963 and was completed in 1977. Built using large slab concrete panels, the Estate, comprising 2700 dwellings, was, at the time of completion, one of the largest social housing projects in Europe. During the period of post-war reconstruction between 1945 and 1950, the UK government built around 1.2 million council houses in the UK. Bomb-damaged buildings and Victorian slums were cleared and rebuilt so that poor communities, essential workers and veterans were able to rent high quality housing from their local authority.

As part of her push to divest local governments of the responsibility of the provision of social housing, Conservative Prime Minister Margaret Thatcher introduced laws allowing for the sale of government owned social housing to its tenants in 1980. Subsequent Government investment in social housing has been minimal, and many estates have been allowed to fall into decay. In the mid-2000s, with their proximity to central London and abundance of neglected social housing stock, the Aylesbury and her sister estate, the Haygate were prime candidates for aggressive developer-led gentrification. Phased demolition of the estate began in 2009 and is ongoing.

Above: A sketch of The Chiltern House on the first piece of salvaged concrete. All pieces by and images courtesy of the author.

Left, counter-clockwise from top: 02 'Wendover Stairwell,' 20x20cm, mixed media on salvaged concrete, 2021.

34 'Walkway,' 23x13cm, acrylic on salvaged concrete, 2021.

40c 'Long Shadows,' 23x15cm, mixed media on salvaged concrete, 2022.

46 'Elegy,' 19.5x14cm, mixed media on salvaged concrete, 2022.

The Aylesbury Fragments

I am an inveterate collector of things which have been thrown away, gathering objects which are ingrained with an unknowable history. Working on found surfaces has been part of my painting practice since the mid-1980s. *The Aylesbury Fragments* series is in keeping with this except for one factor. All the concrete substrate in this series has been salvaged from a demolition site I know very well.

I have worked with members of the Aylesbury resident community since 2018 when I was invited to run an open air sculpture project as part of the summer outreach program. The estate has a notorious reputation, locally and nationally — it was the poster child for all that was deemed to have failed in postwar social housing but what I encountered from my first contact there was totally contrary to its reputation. I have worked on the estate ever since delivering numerous workshops with younger and older residents, collaborating, hearing life stories and joining in community celebrations — all against the backdrop of a regeneration which is gradually removing the homes of the community, replacing them with a significantly higher density build, the majority of which are privately owned, many of which will be sold overseas.

For the first time in my working career, the Aylesbury Fragments fuses my community engagement work with the content of my studio practice.

In the early weeks of the UK Covid lockdown (April 2020) I was cycling through the estate on my way to the studio. This took me via demolition works of the First Development Site (FDS); Chiltern House, a large housing block comprising several hundred flats and formerly home to many of the young people I work with.

Small pieces of concrete waste had fallen onto the pavement, overspill from the demolition. I did not have a preconceived project in mind, it was more an instinctive act of retrieval. The experience of handling the fabric of these former homes created an extremely powerful connection to the community and the physical reality of their circumstance and vulnerability. It spoke too of a deep sense of impending loss. For the preceding six months, every evening, on my journey from the studio, I had seen Chiltern House being stripped out, progressively skeletonised against the sky. What I ended up holding in my hands were fragments of the homes of the young people and families I had been working with.

In the studio I began to draw directly onto the surface of the first salvaged fragment. What emerged was a recreated section of the demolished Chiltern block. In the first iteration of *The Aylesbury Fragments* all the concrete was salvaged from FDS. These works incorporated the original paint surface, many with the ubiquitous pale turquoise, prevalent across the whole estate.

In the second series, concrete was sourced from Ellison House Probation Hostel. This building was the last remaining structure on the plot for many months while the new hostel was completed. It was a very bleak site prior to its demolition, rubbish strewn and dilapidated. Contemplation of this new batch of concrete raised questions around how the estate provides safe shelter beyond the formal housing contracts issued by the local council. During the pandemic the estate stairwells and empty flats had become home to an increasing number of homeless people, many experiencing challenging drug dependence and/or mental health issues for which there was very limited access to support. Many of the young people I was working with remotely during lockdown (via zoom) were having to negotiate these shared spaces on a daily basis. The paintings in this series depict shared interior transit spaces, landings and corridors; simultaneously gloriously illuminated and occasionally very edgy.

The third and current phase of the artwork titled 'The Ground Beneath Your Feet' utilises paving slabs as the painting substrate to depict the Wendover Building and its surrounding blocks. Wendover is currently in the midst of a planning dispute, with remaining residents living in semi derelict, rat infested blocks, in immediate proximity to ongoing ground clearance.

The project raises a myriad of questions; what do we lose and what do we gain through this kind of 'regeneration'? Who are the beneficiaries? What are the actual costs? Financial? Ecological? Societal? The forecast end of the regeneration is now sometime in the 2030s.

Opposite Left: 08 'Stairwell,' 21x15cm, mixed media on salvaged concrete, 2020.

Opposite Right: 41b 'Blue Tiles,' 22x22.5cm, mixed media on salvaged concrete, 2022.

Top Left: 38c 'No Parking!' 36x22cm, mixed media on salvaged concrete, 2022.

Top Right: 32a 'Reflections and Washing,' 20x21cm, mixed media on salvaged concrete, 2021.

RE(GENTRIFICATION)

OBSERVATORY TOWER AND SIRIUS

Jack Rogers

The year is 1996. Observatory Tower, a new luxury housing development by Crone Architects primely located towards the northern tip of Sydney's CBD, has just opened its doors. Architecturally, it is imbued with a sense of sophistication worthy of the residents who would now call it home. Dark-green colour, slick glass balustrades and a golden box sitting on its roof to complete the picture; a crown resting atop regal real estate. The building is starkly different to what had stood on the site for nearly forty years prior: the decisively modernist IBM Building.

Now, nearly thirty years later, balancing on the edge of the escarpment overlooking the Opera House on one side and the Harbour Bridge on the other, the infamous Sirius is on the precipice of completing its own transformation into similarly exclusive housing. The narrative of the acquisition, eviction and conversion of each of its seventy-nine units from social housing to luxury apartments has been heavily documented over the last decade. The metallic-clad additions forming the majority of the renewal stand as testament to this narrative, boldly separating themselves from their older counterparts.

While each of the pair draws on their predecessors as the basis for their transformations, their respective architectural qualities are vastly different. Observatory Tower wraps around the envelope of what was once the IBM Building. The structural skeleton of columns and slabs have largely been retained in the redevelopment, now reskinned and disguised to hide like ghosts in the hallways of the apartment block. The exterior, once characterised by white concrete fins which gave the building its iconic pagoda-like form, now only hints at the old through subtle tells like differentiations in window sizing in its elevations. Sirius' renewal, meanwhile, is clearly demarcated from its original extents. The new modular boxes are added to the former like stacking new bricks on an old wall, paying a kind of warped homage to Tao Gofers' original design.[1]

This veil of regeneration, though, belies their true faces. Renewal, in this sense, is used as a disguise for their true functions, in which each finds common ground. Their individual architectures only reveal part of their greater stories, and only when understood through their shared context can a holistic story be realised. The pair are ultimately conjoined in a tale much larger than themselves, a tale at the heart of which lies the transformation of the very notion of housing itself.

The locale encompassing Miller's Point, Dawes Point and the Rocks, where both Observatory Tower and Sirius find themselves, is one of the oldest developed areas in colonial

Above: Observatory Tower among its neighbours.
All photography by author.

Opposite: Sirius at sunset.

Australia. It had once been home to an intrinsically working class population, most of whom were employed at the working docks on the waterfront nearby. This demographic informed the high concentration of public housing which lined the streets, and families would likely spend their entire lives in the area due to the close link between community and employment opportunities.[2]

In its urban environment, Observatory Tower was embedded in a community that was still characterised by this history. Indeed, at the time of the IBM Building's rebirth into Observatory Tower, the neighbourhood was largely functioning as it had been for over a century: residents lived in a strongly-tied community bound by common blue-collar employment and social housing tenancy just as their parents, grandparents and so on had done before them.

When the IBM Building was being reshaped as Observatory Tower, it was poised to stand in socioeconomic opposition to the nature of its context. Prospective residents were white-collar workers likely capitalising on the trend towards inner-city living for the wealthier class. The urban informed the architectural, with Observatory Tower's design turning the building inward both to reflect and to exacerbate the alienation of its residents from their surroundings. In other words, the architecture was used as a tool to conceal the building from its context because the speculative value of the apartments within was tied to a sense of perceived separation from the distinct character of the neighbourhood.

In the years that followed Observatory Tower's opening, the community underwent radical and irreversible change. While much of the dock-work that had characterised the area had already moved away by the time the building was completed, the social fabric of the neighbourhood had remained strong. However, once the foreshore completed its transformation from working docks to service hub, that same fabric fell too. Factories became offices, and the already-limited employment opportunities available to the existing community faded away. The state government gradually sold the publicly-owned housing to private investors, finally forcing any remaining residents from the area in which they had lived for generations.

Sirius was often lamented as the last bastion of the old community, and its conversion into luxury housing signalled the completion of the fiscal takeover of the area.[3] If Observatory Tower represents the dawn of the financial conquest of the areas of Miller's Point, Dawes Point and The Rocks, then Sirius is symbolic of its conclusion. Sirius' design, just like Observatory Tower's before it, can be seen as a reflection of its urban setting. The decision to gradually sell

social housing in the area from the state government, while often scathed at as myopic or impetuous, can be viewed as a microcosm for the larger shifts to a privatised economy that occurred in the years between the completion of Observatory Tower and the sale of Sirius. With employment opportunities limited and public housing supply essentially exhausted, the working-class community dissolved and was replaced by a mix of wealthier households and professional offices. Sirius, sitting at the edge of The Rocks, bore witness to this transition for years. By the time it was finally sold to private investment, it had fallen victim to near-constant scathing from populist opinion which rendered the sale as an unspoken victory for the masses. Now, fitting aptly into its context as a symbol of housing status, it turns outward to embrace its surroundings and sits proudly in its site. It has become a proverbial monument to the slow process of regeneration that has taken shape over the last three decades.

The greater narrative of the renewal of the neighbourhood of Miller's Point, Dawes Point and The Rocks binds the individual regenerations of Observatory Tower and Sirius. Their individual selves are informed by the wider changes of their urban context, each being informed by a setting that is geographically the same, and yet socially and economically disparate. Analysing their differing designs offers a view into how this narrative unfolded.

The architecture of Observatory Tower turns the building inward, concealing and, more aptly, protecting it from the city in which it sits. Coming from the North along the Harbour Bridge, the road points one's eye directly toward the building. Despite this, it hardly jumps to attention; in fact, it is almost camouflaged against the others adjacent. This effect is created primarily by two elements: the building's colour and its envelope. The distinct metallic-green paint covering most of Observatory Tower blends against the steely blues and greys of the office towers behind and around it. Its comparatively modest height is not large enough to stand out amongst the taller buildings in its surrounds nor is it small enough to appear dramatically out of place — it hovers in a blind spot, so to speak. Compare the building with the former IBM Building: the stark white concrete of the IBM Building and its unmatched height at the end of the city rendered it nearly instantaneously recognisable across all of the harbour.

Approaching Observatory Tower on foot is, of course, a vastly different experience than in a vehicle, yet hints of its inward turn are clear all the same. The building creates a hard border in

Top: The entry to Observatory Tower.

Middle: Sirius behind old housing in The Rocks.

Bottom: The reflectivity of Sirius from behind the Harbour Bridge.

its ground plane, a border which is pierced sparingly in carefully chosen moments. Glazing on the ground floor is sparse; most of the street-face is characterised by heavy walls which anchor the building. The commercial tenancies to the South provide exception to this, yet this is momentary. The hard border is punched only by slender recesses, providing no clues as to what remains in the belly of the plan. In this way, the 'true' ground floor remains purposefully hidden, revealed only by passing through the residential entry. Paramount to the inward turn, the entry is a semi-circular enclave demarcated through a break in the street-face and a shading structure overhead. The hard wall continues round the circular side, and in the gap left in the plan's straight edge lies a line of iron bars quite literally like those found in prisons. The wall in the enclave is broken in two places. The first is the mail chute, a shining steel hinged-door that maintains the anonymity of the interior by permitting entry only to the packages destined for residents. The second break is via the front doors, which act as the final piece to the armour that enwraps the ground plane. Two tall metal faces tower over potential visitors, whose sheer physical heaviness and sense of imposition banish any notion of entry for those not part of the building's community. With the swipe of a keycard for those who are in this select few, the doors swing open quietly and smoothly. Providing only a glimpse of the inside before quickly swinging shut, the doors complete the ground plane's turn inward to secure the building from prying eyes.

If one does manage to navigate past the obtrusions and step inside Observatory Tower, they will first enter the lobby. Watching carefully is the concierge, positioned conspicuously just out of view until that first step into the lobby is made, acting like a guard as one last measure of maintaining sanctity within. The lobby itself gives an immediate impression of prestige and exclusivity. Glossy parquet floors, chandeliers, golden-crested mirrors; even the structural columns that once laid bare in the IBM Building are dressed up with marbled cladding. Along with resident parking, the next few floors above form the podium and house the communal amenities: a pool, gym and,curiously, a library. Each space has a propensity to exude its own air of luxury which leaves it clearly distinct from the others. The same IBM-era columns that were adorned with marble in the lobby are clad in sandstone pieces sculpted with fluid shapes and forms in the pool, the floor of the gym is a carpet coloured too closely to the green of a golf course to be coincidence, and in the library sit busts of philosophers and grand cushioned armchairs. There is, however, an overt sense of the inward turn amongst all this. The pool is entirely indoors, not necessarily unusual in an apartment building, save for the umbrella and table sitting inside to provide shade from the simulated sunlight of the overhead lights dotted along the ceiling. The equipment in the gym covers each wall almost completely and each piece faces the bare middle of the room, thereby forcing users' gaze toward its interior. The busts and armchairs of the library, meanwhile, are accompanied by red-velvet walls which do the desired work of creating a quiet atmosphere through sound absorption, but seem to serve a different purpose when the library itself has only a handful of books on display.

Beyond the podium and its amenities, the typical plans continue to unveil clues about the intention of the architecture of Observatory Tower. The structural columns of the IBM Building that were decorated below are now hidden behind parti walls framing the apartments, further obscuring the building's past from its present inhabitants. Meanwhile, the details within the balconies illustrate a carefully orchestrated relationship between maximising views outwards for those within and minimising views inward for those not. While the IBM building framed the site's views of the harbour behind a concrete shading system, Observatory Tower's apartments embrace these same views with fully glazed doors which slide open onto large balconies. The glazing type deployed in both the sliding doors used to access the outdoor spaces and in the glass balustrades which run along their outer edges is notably of high reflectivity. Reading from the outside, the dual layer of reflective glass, added to by the depth of the balcony itself, creates a sense of visual separation from inside and outside. This is compounded by the depths of the balconies themselves, altogether obscuring any views inward. While this does of course serve to maintain resident privacy, it also amplifies the isolation from the building's context seen in the ground plane, thereby continuing to turn the building inward.

At the peak of Observatory Tower, just above the top-floor apartments, lies its proverbial crown. In truth, this is nothing more than a box of cladding on the lift overrun and the other risers which terminate at the roof. However, the particulars of its design provide a final notion of the inward turn. Breezeblock-like panels are stacked on each of the four sides of the box, capped by an angled-steel awning and a spire which reaches another storey upwards. These panels, unlike most of the building in its muted green, are coated with an eye-catching gold paint. At night, lights reflect off the awning and onto the box such that it shimmers like a beacon. Where the rest of Observatory Tower does its best to remain secluded, this desperately wants to be noticed. Herein, though, lies the trick. Its function is merely to mark the building as distinguishable from others in the city from afar. It is in the most inaccessible part of the building, and thereby is protected by the many fortifications that the architecture has provided. As one approaches, the rest of Observatory Tower gradually obfuscates the view to the box until it has completely vanished. Like a case around a precious artifact in a museum, Observatory Tower protects the box from all but fleeting glances. This encompasses the entirety of what the architecture of the building affords to those outside its walls; a passing moment to stop and notice taken only from a comfortable distance. The box, like the rest of the building, turns away from all who draw too close.

Standing between a pair of icons in the Harbour Bridge and Opera House, the Sirius Building seems comparatively insignificant when overlooked from the heights of Observatory Tower. For those on the ground, though, Sirius is anything but. In many ways, it is the stark opposite of Observatory Tower. Sirius' story has lived in headlines for generations, from its inception amidst the Green Bans movement to its slow dereliction from years of neglect and finally to its ongoing rebirth rife with controversy. Its redevelopment has seen it move from social housing estate to luxury apartment complex, drawing the eyes of the city as it nears closer each day to completion. Its architecture, as the antithesis of Observatory Tower, embraces its prominence. Thus, its narrative is read under the lens of the outward turn.

Sirius was designed by the then-Government Architect Tao Gofers in 1979. Responding both to the opposing forces of the NSW Government demanding new social housing in the Miller's Point area and the Green Bans movement advocating for an architecture sensitive to its prospective historic context, Gofers proposed a modular system of stacked concrete pods forming a shell in which apartments would interlace in multiple combinations of one, two, three and four-bedroom units. The building became an infamous point of discussion surrounding urban development in Sydney; it was deemed by many as an eyesore and unworthy of its unrivalled position overlooking Circular Quay and the Opera House, whilst others vehemently defended its importance as both a Brutalist icon and a symbol of social equity.[4] Sirius was sold in 2016 by the NSW Government to private investors, who then began to undertake the renovation of the building to luxury apartments. It is important to understand this context because it has informed the outward turn the building has undergone in its regeneration.

Sirius' redevelopment has been overseen by architects BVN, whose design has taken a vastly different approach to that of Observatory Tower. The modules that Tao Gofers drew up for Sirius have been reimagined in the rebuild and stitched onto the original building. While taking nods from the original proportions and shape of the Gofers' design, these modules stretch and grow to take on a life of their own and are critical to forming the outward turn. Clad in a coppery finish, they sit mostly atop the building but are also dotted intermittently along the original extent of the façade, indicating a clear distinction between new and old. Sirius' original height peaked just over the road of the Harbour Bridge, but the new modules sit atop the original roofline and thus assert themselves directly into view for those crossing the bridge in vehicles and on foot. Meanwhile, from the Opera House, they cleverly occupy a space beyond the height of the Cahill Expressway, therefore contrasting against the empty sky behind them and further accentuating their presence. The textural quality of the metal punctuates this effect, too. Where the concrete of the original modules has a subdued matte finish, the new modules catch the sunlight on a bright day and glisten like the waters of the harbour below. The metal wraps around the modules to create the appearance of a largely solid metallic face in both north and south elevation, taking advantage of the natural sunlight in one direction and the artificial city-light respectively to enhance the reflective effect. The new Sirius thus commands attention from all sides, stamping its place amongst its eminent neighbours. Modifications made to the ground plane of Sirius turn the building outward. Like Observatory Tower's ground plane, Sirius' functioned to accentuate the sense of separation between its interior and the city. Where the concrete modules met the ground in each arm of the building, they were shielded from the street by private courtyards and landscaping. The break in the modules in the heart of the plan, the communal Phillip Room, was hidden from the street by the building's façade and secluded entry. While the Phillip Room did open outward with large glazing to the East, this too was cleverly separated from the outside as Gloucester Walk, the ground plane to this side, dropped to a level lower than it did on the street-facing side. The renewed Sirius, on the other hand, explicitly opens to the public life of the city. Public visitation and thoroughfare are catalysts in design; visitors are now greeted at Cumberland Street with a commercial tenancy and a large forecourt. The building opens to this forecourt, lifting itself up to carve a new pathway directly through its centre to create a new access-way. Thus, the two main facades of Sirius, its Cumberland Street-east and Gloucester Walk-west, are now directly connected by Sirius itself. The ground plane invites the city in, turning outward to encourage exploration and discovery.

The final turn outwards that the architecture of the redeveloped Sirius makes is in treatment of its prospective residents. The details of the apartments themselves turn the private life of residents' outwards to the city. The East and West faces of the new modules are punched through with glazing that stretches out wall-to-wall and floor-to-ceiling, dually increasing visual access both in and out of the units. That is, while residents' unmatched views of the city from their apartments are celebrated and maximised, the city's views into residents' apartments are also simultaneously optimised. The glazing itself magnifies this phenomenon. In the original design it was

Opposite: Observatory Tower's southern facade.

prescribed that units facing the Harbour Bridge, those with most exposure to inward gazes, have tinted windows to alleviate the obvious concerns over resident privacy. This tint is absent in the new Sirius, where windows are almost perfectly clear and life inside the units is left bare to see. The modules, lined side-by-side and stacked bottom-to-top, create an overall effect in elevation like a voyeuristic art gallery; a Sirius menagerie. The public display of resident lifestyle is clear in the planning of the building's amenities. Almost typical of a modularly stacked apartment building, Sirius' units have always been arranged such the roof of one apartment may be used as a terrace for the apartment above. Gofers' original terraces were home only to modest rooftop gardens, and while these gardens have been retained and extended, purveying a certain visual archetype of verdant greenery spilling freely over balconies and hanging in the breeze, they have been paired with the addition of infinity pools. The pools are positioned to rise to the same level as the parapets of the modules. The gardens, unlike the pools, were always sunken comfortably beneath this line and therefore afforded some degree of privacy for those standing in them. The luxuriant ritual of bathing in a private pool; the unfurling of a bathrobe, the dive into the water and the splash that follows, becomes a focal point of observation. Likewise, it is easy to imagine gazing up at Sirius on a hot day while the sun bakes the pavement of the ground and seeing the sunbakers on their terraces out in force.

In the near quarter-century between the openings of Observatory Tower and Sirius, an unparalleled shift in the function of housing occurred; the transformation of housing as a right, to housing as a speculative investment. This shift catalysed remarkable changes within the urban sphere. The changes have been as gradual as they have been indiscriminate, moving slowly through the fabric of inner-cities and beyond into the suburbs. It has been extensively documented and debated, and today finds itself at the heart of a devastating housing crisis impacting massive swathes of Australian society. Despite their extensive differences, Observatory Tower and Sirius are intrinsically linked through this shift.

Housing speculation in this context refers to the flow of the real estate market based on the expected growth or fall in property value predicated on financially based assessments; what a property *could* be worth drives what it *is* worth. The factors impacting this flow are often contrived as complex and rather esoteric, but crucially at their core are strictly intangible. In this sense, architecture can be decoupled from its physical qualities and instead be used as a vessel through which to extract value: design becomes to housing as a pickaxe is to a mine. In Australia, speculative investment has been fuelled by a myriad of factors. The introduction of the discount on Capital-Gains Tax in 1999 and subsequent rise in the practice of negative-gearing, although typically misunderstood to be the sole causes of the rise of the view of housing as investment, has undoubtedly acted as one of the greatest forces driving speculation.[5] It can be argued, then, that the financialisation of housing in this country was only in its nascent form when Observatory Tower opened three years earlier in 1996. Over nearly thirty years, housing speculation has evolved and entrenched itself in the core ideas of housing itself, where Sirius' renewal has been realised.

The once working-class community of the Miller's Point area has transformed into a mix of wealthier households and professional offices. Sirius now sits comfortably in its environment and turns outward to highlight this, whilst Observatory Tower stands silently and remains inwardly-focused as it always has, away from a demographic that has since disappeared.

01 TKD Architects, Modern Movement Architecture in Central Sydney: Heritage Study Review (Sydney: City of Sydney, 2019), 37-38, https://www.cityofsydney.nsw.gov.au/-/media/corporate/files/2020-07-migrated/files_m/modern-movement-architecture-in-central-sydney-heritage-study.pdf.

02 Cameron Byrne, Uneven Development: an opportunity or threat to working class neighbourhoods? (Ph.D., UNSW, 2007), 14-17, https://www.be.unsw.edu.au/sites/default/files/upload/pdf/schools_and_engagement/resources/_notes/5A3_10.pdf.

03 Tao Gofers, "I designed the Sirius building but I wish the government had knocked it down," *Sydney Morning Herald*, June 23, 2021, 5.30am AEST, https://www.smh.com.au/politics/nsw/i-designed-the-sirius-building-but-i-wish-the-government-had-knocked-it-down-20210620-p582n2.html.

04 Dominic Perrottet, "Sirius building in The Rocks is 'as sexy as a car park'," *Sydney Morning Herald*, August 10, 2016, 4.58pm AEST, https://www.smh.com.au/opinion/sirius-building-in-the-rocks-is-as-sexy-as-a-car-park-says-nsw-minister-dominic-perrottet-20160810-gqp31n.html. Michael Bleby, "Tao Gofers, the closet showman behind Sydney's Sirius building," *Australian Financial Review*, November 11, 2016, 9.00pm AEST, https://www.afr.com/work-and-careers/management/tao-gofers-the-closet-showman-behind-sydneys-sirius-building-20161007-grx54i#:~:text=Tao%20Gofers%20was%20the%20architect%20behind%20the%20Sirius.

05 Australian Council of Social Service, Fuel on the fire: negative gearing, capital gains tax and housing affordability (Sydney: ACOSS, 2015), 10-12, https://www.acoss.org.au/wp-content/uploads/2016/04/Fuel_on_the_fire_ACOSS.pdf.

HOTELES
PLAZAELBOSQUE

NOMADIC DOME (RE)ASSEMBLE

LIFECYCLE OF ARCHITECTURE PAVILIONS

Ephemeral Research[1] and Jun Sato Laboratory[2]

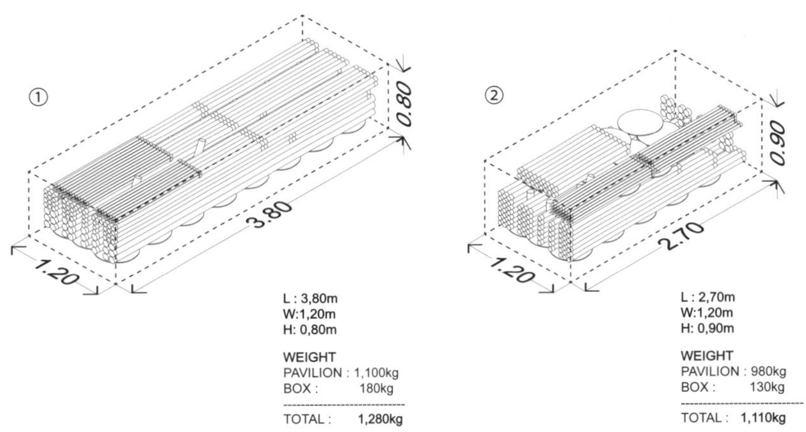

In the face of the rapidly worsening climate crisis, the architectural community is under urgent pressure to act, necessitating a profound shift towards adopting circular construction methods. But how do Architectural pavilions adapt in this context? Ephemeral Research, a committed collective, delves into design for disassembly solutions through collaborative processes, exploring potential pathways forward for architects and stakeholders alike. This text delves into the lessons learned in the construction process of a workshop, examining the intricate challenges and complexities of implementing circular techniques while offering innovative solutions, tangible examples, and adaptations to local methods and available resources.

This abstract serves as a call to the architectural community for strategic foresight and sustained collaboration. It's a call to action in pursuing circular construction methods and a reminder for architects to transcend the confines of conventional practice, embracing a holistic approach that acknowledges the interconnectedness of environmental, social, and economic considerations. This is not just a theoretical concept but a practical necessity for the built environment to shift towards a new architectural discourse and practice era. A temporary installation can explore these new challenges and take a more strategic, holistic approach to respond to these industry challenges to minimise the environmental footprint of our designs. The Nomadic dome (re)construction is a prototype that results from an integrated design process that involves extensive collaboration with stakeholders, students, and experts at all stages.

The pavilion's design focused on creating a dismantlable structure using standard materials. Initially, the team wanted to explore options for relocation, but the constraints of reality, costs, liabilities, and transport proved this to be a challenging endeavour. The pavilion was first assembled in Santiago, Chile (2017), and after seven years, it was relocated for reassembly in Lake Yamanakako, Japan (2024). The following are four main lessons learned from this process and modifications that led to its successful implementation in a different location.

Above: The Pavilion Box: Assessing the transport feasibility and design. Image by the author.

Opposite: Nomadic Dome, Santiago, Chile , 2017. Photography by Benjamín Matte.

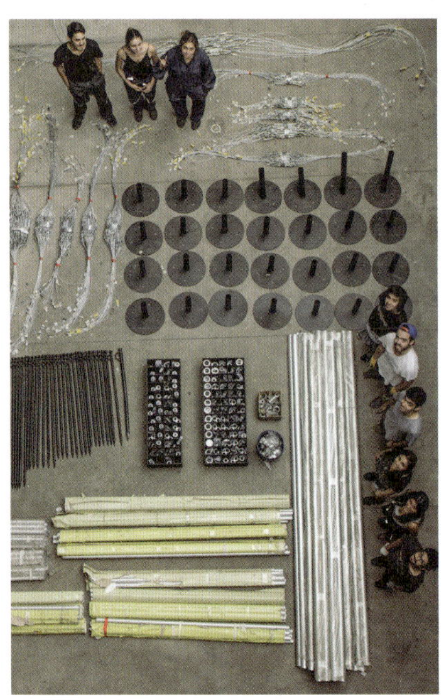

Circular Design Agencies are imperative

Many questions arise in the early stages of relocation of a structure: Who bears the liabilities? Who manages the logistics? Is it the client? How long is its tenure? In our attempts to find solutions to the questions above, we had a few attempts with different institutions: Yokohama Museum (Attempt 1), the Ishinomaki Council (Attempt 2), and the third attempt involved exploring donation options. Through social networks, colleagues in the Chilean government's flagship projects department expressed interest in repurposing it as an aviary in a park adjacent to the Mapocho River. Additionally, we received various requests to utilise it for events and parties. They all seemed feasible at first, but they did not go through when it came to logistics, legal matters, costs, and other things. This experience underscores the necessity for Circular Design Agencies. Such agencies would facilitate the repurposing and reutilization of structures and streamline the logistical challenges involved. By centralising expertise and resources, Circular Design Agencies can effectively address the complexities of sustainable design practices, furthering the advancement of environmentally conscious architecture.

Implementation of Design for Disassembly (DFD)

By focusing on the importance of components rather than viewing structures as indivisible wholes, we unlock significant potential for sustainability. This approach emphasises the need for detailed design considerations throughout the manufacturing process. It prompts us to reflect on the various barriers and challenges in construction and the design process that may impede practical disassembly and material reuse. Moreover, relocating the structure to Japan involved refining existing connective pieces to meet new location conditions, such as temperature change and permanence onsite, ensuring that structures remain easily maintainable in the long term. This approach is crucial for fostering material reuse, which promotes environmental conservation by minimising waste and contributes to the efficiency and resilience of our built environment.

Collective Construction and Rethinking Experiential Learning

Academic workshops act as dynamic educational centres, fostering collaboration among students of diverse backgrounds, professionals, and local communities. Workshops were part of the dome's construction process. This time, approximately 60 students participated. Through an open digital call, Ephemeral Research formed partnerships with over 10 Japanese universities, orchestrating engaging workshop sessions for the students.

They provided a platform for collaboration and idea exchange among students, professionals, and communities, contributing to the ongoing construction activities and practical design implementation. The collective knowledge

from the workshops informed the construction process by integrating diverse perspectives and expertise from various fields, such as architecture, engineering, and the arts. This collaboration likely led to innovative and practical solutions during construction, ensuring the design was effectively realised and adapted to real-world conditions.

The workshops facilitated learning that would not have been possible without the collective knowledge of participants from diverse backgrounds. For instance, integrating architectural aesthetics with engineering practicality and artistic creativity led to unique construction solutions, such as connection details, structural tension adjustments, shading tests, and risk mitigation at the pedestrian level. Without this collective input, the construction might have lacked the adaptability and multifaceted approach necessary for practically realising the design.

Using models as communication tools served as a common language among disciplines, essential for explaining the operation of a complex structure like a tensegrity of this scale to a travelling group of students from diverse backgrounds, disciplines (architects, engineers, and artists), and academic levels required varied modes of interdisciplinary communication. This involved utilising hand-drawn sketches, small on-site models, language translators, sign language, and body movements. Additionally, discussions encompassed reflections on construction and on-site challenges when transferring the accurate digital model into reality. Ultimately, it became evident that the best model was experienced directly in the field.

Top Left: Ephemeral Research & Jun Sato Laboratory, Components, Santiago, Chile , 2017. Photography by Esteban Arteaga.

Top Right: Ephemeral Research & Jun Sato Laboratory, YAP Constructo 7 - Nomadic Dome, Santiago, Chile , 2017. Photography by Gonzalo Zuñiga.

Opposite (Top Left): Ephemeral Research & Jun Sato Laboratory, Yamanaka Terrace Workshop, Yamanakako, Japan, 2024. Photography by Claudio Torres.

Opposite (Top Right): Ephemeral Research & Jun Sato Laboratory, Yamanaka Terrace Workshop, Yamanakako, Japan, 2024. Photography by Yuji Harada.

Working with Relocation Challenges

Relocating pavilions globally presents a significant design challenge. Although these temporary structures are often intended for potential relocation, their designs typically overlook practical aspects that could transform this challenge into an opportunity. Considerations such as transport size, the number of people required for reassembly, and the potential to relocate and reuse portions of the building are often neglected. As the site changes, these considerations provide opportunities to optimise and enhance the efficiency of such structures, like the optimisation efforts applied to permanent buildings.

In 2017, we designed this pavilion to fit into a box measuring 1.2 meters by 3.8 meters by 0.8 meters, with a total weight of around 1,100 kg. Given the various attempts previously explained, we began considering different ways of partially relocating the pavilion depending on the distance of its final relocation. The distance from Santiago, Chile, to Lake Yamanakako, Japan, in a straight line is approximately 17,000 kilometres. Budget and environmental considerations restricted our options for sending the parts. Therefore, we decided to minimise the volume of the pavilion by donating the pipes to a local builder in Santiago for reuse in new construction and relocating only the head connectors. This allowed us to fit all the pieces into five large suitcases weighing 23 kg. Once in Japan, the remaining pieces were standard and easily found in local warehouses.

However, not everything revolves around the structure; context, location, events, and activation are essential for keeping these experimental spaces vibrant. In addition to the experience of assembling the structure, we managed to create a workshop for building tables and chairs adapted to Enzo Mari's design, which exercised ideas of design for disassembly on a different scale. We focused on enhancing the site by incorporating vegetal pavements, gathering fallen leaves from the surrounding forest and installing them as textures on the ground.

It has become clear that while design intentions are essential, they are insufficient to propel sustainable development forward. Thus, we must advocate for cultivating enduring relationships between design agencies and clients, rooted in a shared commitment to prioritising life cycle considerations over the transient allure of temporary endeavours. The need for long-term engagement and strategic collaboration underscores the indispensable role of architects in effecting lasting change.

As we stand at the precipice of a new era in architectural discourse, the implications of this research reverberate far beyond the confines of academia, permeating the very fabric of architectural practice. The Nomadic Dome project stands as a manifesto for the transformative power of circular construction methods, serving as a signal of hope in a world challenged by environmental uncertainty. We can redefine tomorrow's architecture through collaboration, innovation, and unwavering commitment, forging a path toward a more sustainable and resilient built environment.

Technical Specifications

Project Name: YAP Constructo 7 - Nomadic Dome (2017-24)
Authors: Ephemeral Research + Jun Sato Laboratory
Architects: Ephemeral Research. Clara Reutter , Yuji Harada, Emile Straub and Claudio Torres.
Engineers: Jun Sato Laboratory, University of Tokyo + Jun Sato Structural Engineers: Jun Sato, Shohei Furuichi and Midori Tsuzuki.
Location: Parque Araucano, Santiago, Chile (2017) and Yamanaka Terrace, Lake Yamanakako, Japan (2024)
Client: YAP Constructo (2017) and Yamanaka Terrace (2024)
Custom Manufacturing and Engineering Solutions: Julio Brito & Enercom S.A.

01 Ephemeral Research is a collective of architects of Clara Reutter, Yuji Harada, Emile Straub, and Claudio Torres based in Australia, Japan, and Chile. They specialize in design-build lightweight structures, collaborating with community members, academics, and stakeholders. Their notable project, "Nomadic Dome," was featured in YAP Constructo 2017 and showcased in exhibitions across Japan, Australia, and Chile. The collective was nominated for the MCHAP 2018 Emerging Architecture Award, was a finalist at the Tallinn Biennale in 2019, and participated in one of the finalist curatorial groups for the architecture exhibition at the Japanese Pavilion for the Venice Biennale 2025. Currently, they focus on workshops that design and build prototypes exploring circular design and building lifecycles.

02 Jun Sato is a structural engineer at the University of Tokyo, where he leads the Jun Sato Laboratory on the Kashiwa Campus. He focuses on advancing structural design and lightweight structures through innovative methodologies. His laboratory combines theoretical research with practical applications to enhance structural integrity and efficiency. He has collaborated with notable architects, including Junya Ishigami, Erika Nakagawa, Kengo Kuma, and Sou Fujimoto.

Opposite: Ephemeral Research & Jun Sato Laboratory, YAP Constructo 7 - Nomadic Dome, Yamanakako, Japan , 2024. Photography by Yuji Harada.

ENTITLEMENT

Architect Brew Koch

The settlement and cultivation of land on a vast scale required surveying and parcelling. To make the measured and subdivided land productive, not just for subsistence but for profit, required intensive labour. For this reason, the English made the virtues of cultivating and thus 'improving' land the main ideological basis for the exclusionary right to own property ... English colonisation was motivated explicitly by the idea of settling a territory by improving its productivity.[1]

entitlement

This house is on a property that is a remnant of a parcel of land that was first settled in 1850. The original land title was one square mile, one of the nearly 60,000 mile squares in a Cartesian grid that extended across the state. The location of this square is the Country of the Watherwurang people. Entitlement and dispossession are not different ideas, they are the same concept. Property titles entitle or permit a set of behaviours and exclude others. These were granted in the first instance as an exchange by the Crown for 'improvement' in time. This meant evidence of labour on the land, which could be in the form of built fences, removed trees, cultivated fields, the keeping of domestic animals or the constructing of buildings provided they can be shown to contribute to productivity, in effect the supply of commodities into the market. The State's claim to the appropriation of the land was that its status at that time was Terra Nullius, that is to say it was wasted or non-productive. We find this formulation in the treatise by John Locke in 1690.[2]

If the 'title' was once thought of as an 'entitlement,' a privilege that permits the productive use of the land, it was also an obligation to do the same. If the lawful (productive) use of the land was the mechanism by which the colonial project was enacted, then the tariffs raised on commodities produced by those granted use of the land and exchanged in markets was how the State was funded. Entitlement continues to be an instrument for the realisation of the social and political ideology of the State.

That same title has come to us today, albeit altered. We can see it on numerous additions and subtractions; easements have been imposed for passage and use, parts of the land have been re-appropriated by the State, sand has been mined by local authorities for their roads and, for the duration of the Second World War, it was requisitioned by the Commonwealth and occupied as part of a distributed storage facility for ammunition. More recently portions of the site have been fenced off and placed under covenants as part of biodiversity offset agreements that allow further development of other sites in the region.

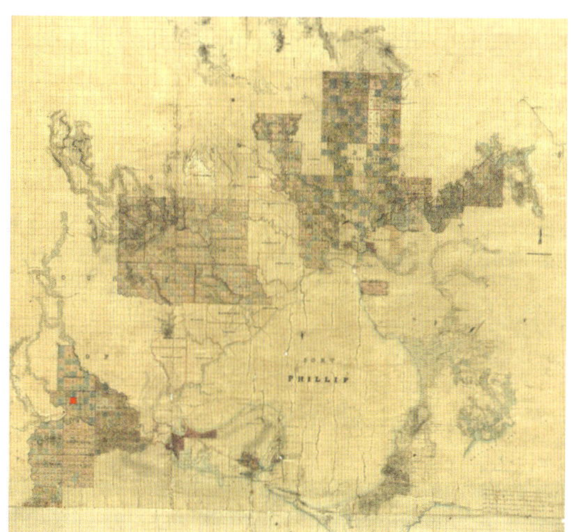

02

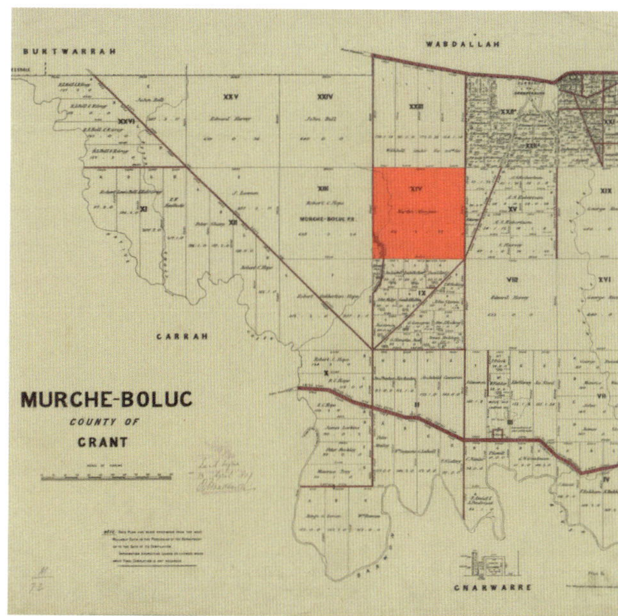

03

About half the land in the title is now recognised and protected as significant remnant ecologies; old trees and open grassland have been funded to remove them from earlier models of production. The title which once was a simple page is now a small volume, a palimpsest that like repeated folds in a page determines its form but shapes its next fold. This sees our removal of grazing, fences and improvements from the land as being a new form of production. We might think about this as unsettling.

The law of property as it applies to land is fundamentally the same as that which applies to other things. It is no coincidence then that land appropriated by the granting of a title is registered by the State with the same law, or at least the same idea of the law, to that which is used to entitle and then register certain occupations; apiarists, dairy farmers, plumbers as well as professionals, in our case architects. Though here 'property' does not take the form of a specific parcel of land so much as a 'domain' architecture. Like registered landholders, architects are the agents by which State ideology is enacted. Architects are street-level bureaucrats who ensure the final steps of laws and policies of the State are carried out. Professionals are registered and constrained to enact the will of the sovereign. Architects generally do not admit to this, even to themselves, they do so anyway, just as the useful idiots had progressed the Soviet agenda during the depths of the Cold War. As the many registered landholders champion the opinion that 'entitlement' grants them liberty, proclaiming: "This is my land and I can do anything that I want on it," they fail to complete the thought: "as long as that is the will of the State." Similarly, architects mistake the limited autonomy granted to them for the purpose of the State's bidding as a licence for self-expression. Perhaps they never heard of the Clash song *Know Your Rights,* where Joe Strummer proclaims: "You have the right to free speech, as long as you're not dumb enough to actually try it."

The real architecture of today appears only by accident. An accident like the diabolical effects of colonisation when seen by the colonialists amongst us. Along with these effects of colonisation of the country, its people and its ecology, other accidents might include the redistribution and appropriation of wealth from the people to the oligarchs, all forms of housing inequality and homelessness. Once we learn to see architecture in this way, it becomes apparent that accidents are in fact the design features of architecture, then building failures, flammable cladding, financial collapse and market failure are its monumental design achievements. Rather than by accident, our project has to been to design with intention, thereby accepting our situation as real and using the instruments available to us to affect the subject, that is to affect Architecture. We act as professionals, not artists.

04

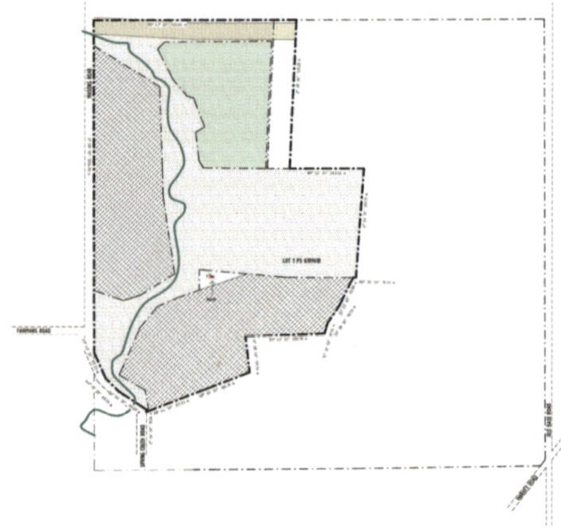

05

obligation

We required a small Class 1 building on this remnant sheep farm in the Western District. To expedite the project, we set out to design a building that strictly adhered to the provisions of the State, The Architects Act and Building Act, the local Planning Scheme and the National Construction Code. There were few briefed requirements other than the need for adequate daylight from which to read a book, and that the house would be 'off-grid' so to speak (grid referring to State infrastructure provision).

In the Planning Scheme, it is a Rural Zone which allows for productive farming, a house on this land is permitted only insofar as it contributes to that purpose. Under the designation Rural Zone (RZ) in the Golden Plains Shire, land greater in area than 100ha is granted an as-of-right use of a dwelling, assuming it meets with the provisions included in the zone. The dwelling must be built in accordance with the National Construction Code and Victorian Building Act to the satisfaction of a building surveyor licenced by the State. The Planning Scheme identifies significant vegetation and areas of cultural significance as Overlays that would require an application to be made to the Local Authority.

Otherwise, the building surveyor has delegated power to authorise any building works providing they meet general Clauses, in this instance set back distances from food-producing fields and natural watercourses, and have approval from the Environment and Fire Authorities. Confirmation of soil compression and absorption tests, vehicular access conditions, designated water storage and requirements and proof of the provision of uninterrupted power.

The house sits towards the centre of the property, as far north as we could build without triggering an additional approval process due to a covenant on the title over the native landscape. To the south are cultivated fields, and it is sited the minimum required distance from these. To the west is a natural watercourse and wooded area, which have spatial requirements for septic fields and fire hazards. To the east, the house paddock tapers with the setback on the other three sides. Each orientation then aligns with a different landscape and a different idea of land. The house as it faces the cultivated fields appears as a shed; as it faces the grassland to the north, a worker's cottage, its scale diminished.

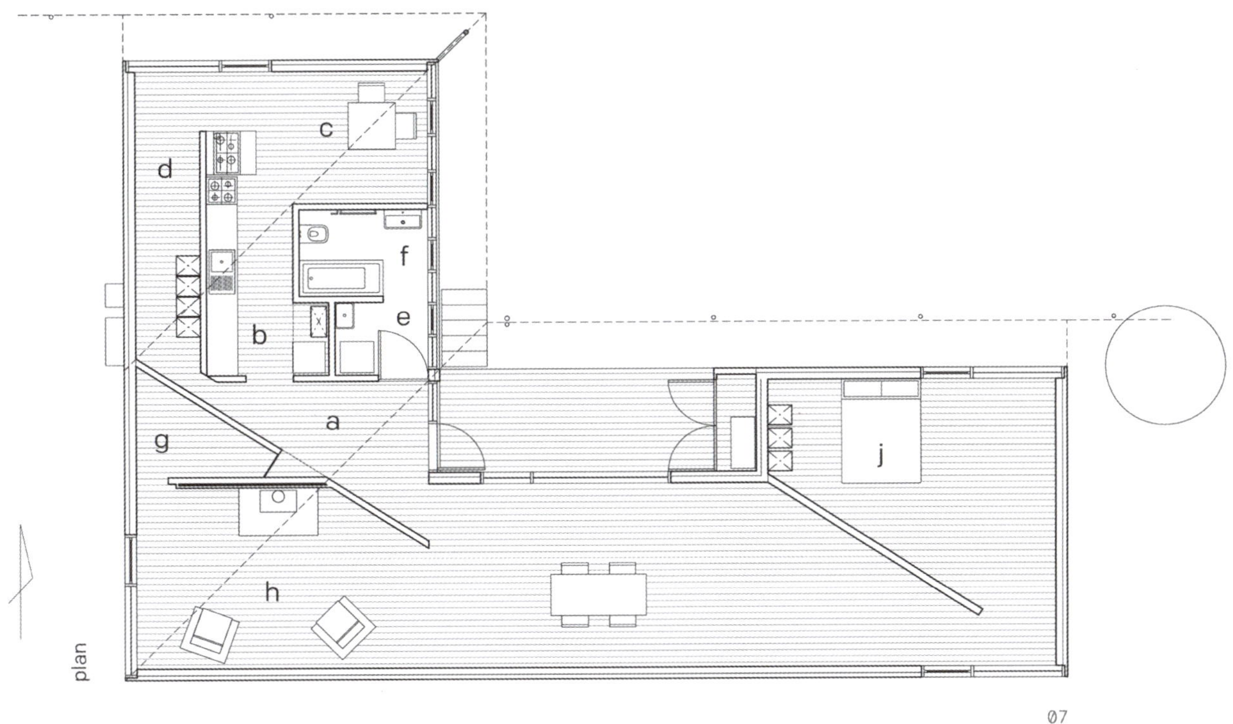

07

a	enter	f	bathe
b	cook	g	read
c	eat	h	lounge
d	store	i	dine
e	launder	j	sleep

06

Rainwater is captured on the roof, sloped at the angle and orientation required for solar panels, with a single gutter extending to the water tank to avoid an additional downpipe. The plan is L-shaped, made from four six-metre squares. The roof form comprises a valley and half a hip to the shorter arm, intended to reduce as far as possible the volume of that portion of the house. This contains a small kitchen and lunch table, allowing for rapid heating or ventilation depending on the season. The remaining house is permitted a larger volume for the stratification of air in summer. Domestic details are stripped from the exterior. Walls, windows and vents are clad in metal to refuse both weather and fire. Service appendages appear as necessary on the roof and the west wall.

As per the NCC, with a rule little different to one Christopher Wren added to the London Building Code in 1667, the area of window in each habitable room is equal to 10% of the floor plan, while the area of openable ventilation in those rooms is 5%. The deck is not more than 1000mm above the ground, the length of the gutter to a downpipe is 12m, there are three sinks, and the stairs are even. This of course is true for all

08

09

Class 1 buildings, though not all Class 1 buildings in RZ zones produce the same building. What differentiates one house from another then is a combination of professional judgment as to the application of the rules by the architect/building surveyor and the circumstances of each situation.

The interior of the house follows from the schema of its form, in no small part due to the need for a window on each wall to meet the sole briefed requirement of the occupant to be able to read in natural light. To this end, in each orientation, one of the four identical windows was placed (an additional two windows and the sun-room casements for amenities were required to meet the State legislated requirements).

Something is lacking here though: joinery that determines the use of each room, doors that define spaces, a finish to the wall and ceiling surfaces, a sense of luxury that unites the elements, an excess. The house is not a place of leisure. It speaks of the necessity of use and demands an engagement with its place. The stove requires fallen wood to be cut for heating and cooking, the garden requires tending for the provision of food. The landscape beyond demands perpetual care.

The internal walls, unfolding from their container, hold the situations of our days spent maintaining, repairing and cultivating the land, providing refuge and relief from its conditions. And a place to read. The fluidity of the plan hints that our situations are not distinct.

The house in its place gives appearance to the reality of our existence. We discover truths that are embedded in the very title created to erase complexities but that now obligate the care of this place. If we set out to give expression to the default condition of architecture, we might have demonstrated something more about our obligation as a profession to the places we inhabit and those that we work. The house gives us access to the idea of care. In a way that is not a pledge or commitment but a binding and enforceable obligation. Our interest in this work is restricted to the extent to which our reality is made accessible through it.

01 Gary Fields, Enclosure: *Palestinian Landscapes in a Historical Mirror* (Oakland: University of California Press,2017) 143 as cited by Pier Vittorio Aureli, *Architecture and Abstraction* (Cambridge, Massachusetts, The MIT Press, 2023), 106.

02 John Locke, *The Second Treatise of Government*, 1690.

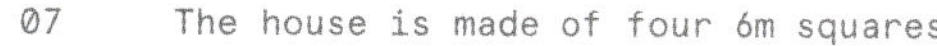

01 Farming Zone the dwelling is set back to avoid being adversely affected by agricultural activities on adjacent land due to dust, noise, odor, use of chemicals and farm machinery, traffic and hours of operation.

02 Cartesian grid extended across the state as a means of dispossession.

03 The settlement of Murghe-Boluc on Watherwurang land.

04 The gutter is continuous from the overflow to the west to the rainwater tank to the east.

05 The title cut from the original mile has a palimpsest of easements and covenants, the dwelling site cut from the food-producing paddock avoids disturbance of the native landscape.

06 The deck is 1m above the ground and the steps are equal.

07 The house is made of four 6m squares.

08 The remaining volumes are as tall as possible for stratified air in summer.

09 The fireplace hearth extends to the front and sides and is 150mm above the timber floor – the mantle extends 600mm above the top of the fireplace.

10 As it faces the grassland to the north, a worker's cottage, its scale diminished.

11 Something is lacking here: a finish to the wall and ceiling surfaces, a sense of luxury that unites the elements, an excess.

12 The ceiling springs from 2.1m along the cooking, lunching and bathing walls, and in the sleeping room.

13 The house in its place gives appearance to the reality of our existence.

10

12

11

13

EMOTIONAL HERITAGE

REFLECTIONS ON ADAPTIVE REUSE

Ricardo Flores and Eva Prats
Flores & Prats Architects

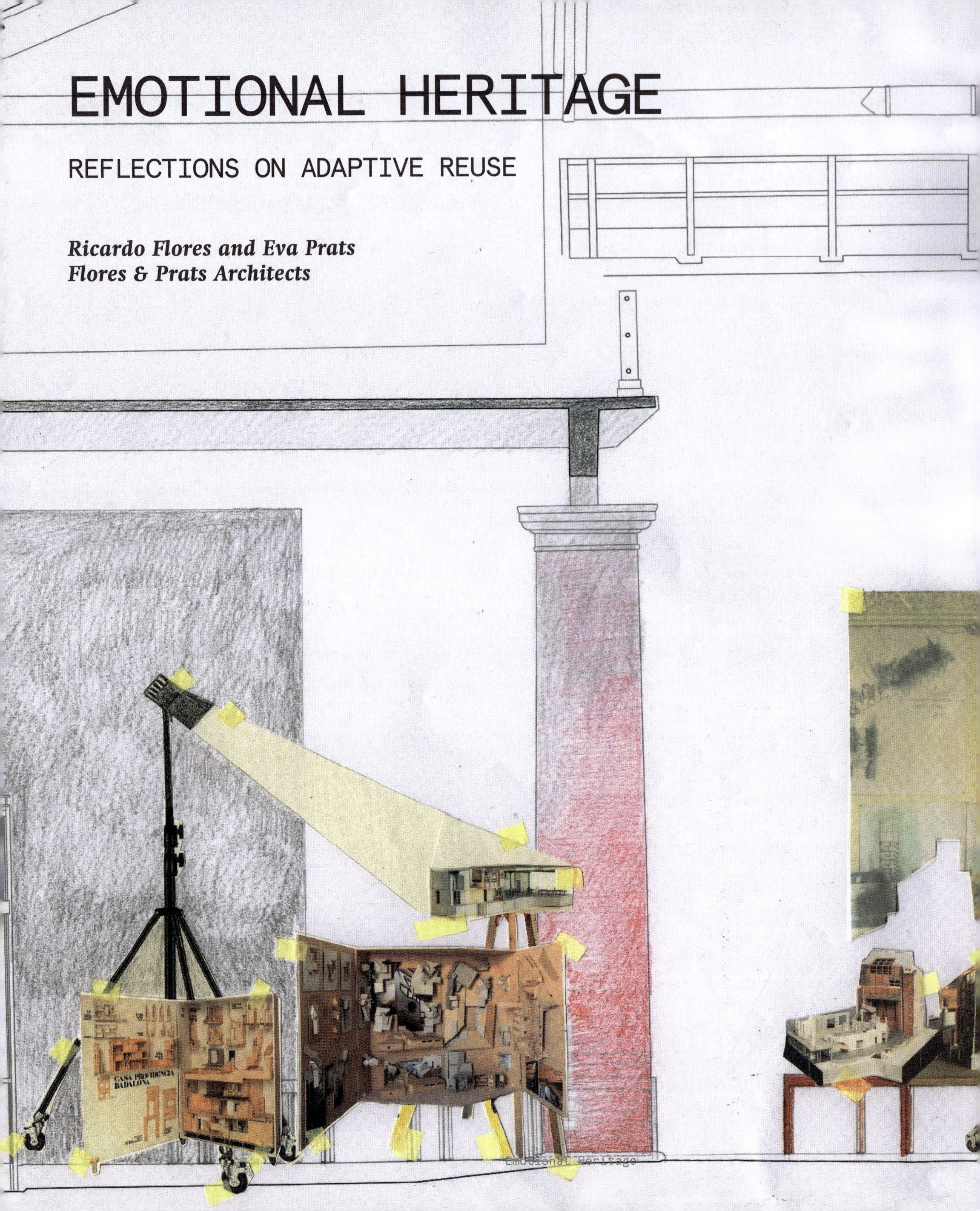

It is not only people that contain the memory of a place — buildings too are loaded with memories of the uses and lives that occupy them. The built fabric reflects social behaviour. It speaks of a way of using the ground and the sky, of a way of inhabiting. As an architect, to read the memories held in buildings and in people is to think about a future that counts on that past. When a building is closed and abandoned, it remains alive in the memories of those near it. The abandoned building carries the civic and moral values embedded through use and over time. The building contains the stories of the people who experienced the place over the years. This creates an invisible constellation of social relationships that expand the influence of this construction to a universe around it, including to those that may form future associations with the building's materiality and story.

When architect Lesley Lokko, upon inviting us to the Venice Architecture Biennale 2023 (*Laboratory of the Future*), asked us to respond to the question of how we can face the problem of decarbonisation in the world today, our thoughts were to bring to Venice and put on the table a discussion on how to re-use all that we inherit, everything that has come to us and is adapted to new programmes. So we named our exhibition *Emotional Heritage*, reflecting our wish to debate the importance of reusing and recuperating not just our physical inheritance, but also our emotional inheritance.

To invite reflection on this theme, we thought of bringing process material to Le Corderie; tests on six different projects that would be placed on large tables. Some of these were built projects from the first years of our studio, others were still in development, but they were all works on adaptive reuse, and the documents that went to Venice made visible the different research and interests that have been appearing whilst working on them over the years.

The Workshop

When Lokko mentioned that we were going to exhibit in an area of the Arsenale that she called the 'Workshop,' we immediately thought that it was important to transfer the experimental atmosphere of our studio to Venice, its immersive character, full of materials that create reflections around them. We thought that we must count on our studio tables to convey this atmosphere; the places where we draw and reflect on the projects everyday and that are able to hold on their surface all the thoughts and the doubts, the models and the drawings, books and papers and the lamps that focus our attention. Those horizontal surfaces contain all the research that takes place in the studio; the uncertainties, the questions that the projects raise, and the creative process.

Many times, when working on a project, we build legs for our models, so that they can stand alone by themselves, like in a parade, and once the project is finished, we also build containers to keep all the models and documents that narrate the story of each project, holding their time and their memory, their physical and emotional remains. The models kept inside the containers are fragmentary pieces, working material used during the design process to test proportions and to help the conversations with the clients and builders, and now also with the visitors to the Biennale. These containers are carefully thought through, specifically for each project, taking the shape and the size that responds to the world they contain, allowing us to question the themes that the project opens up through the way we decide to archive it. As they have wheels, they become portable memories that can be transported and opened where needed, to display what is kept inside. So, we thought these would be interesting luggage to bring to Venice.

Everything that came from the studio was there: inside containers, hanging from the walls, films projected on the models, models on top of high legs, drawings suspended from the balconies, on top of the tables... a universe of material from different times and with different formats, as if one was entering into the architect's mind. Because of their unfinished, open character, these models and drawings would act as objects that bridge between visitors to La Biennale, helping to create exchange on the themes that these documents proposed.

Our proposal was to occupy all the space given by the curator at the Arsenale from side to side, from wall to wall, not leaving any corridors to cross it, with the material expanding and filling in all the section, all the available space. But, to help navigate the exhibition we divided it into five groups, whose titles referred to a theme or interest in the field of *Adaptive Reuse: Drawing with Time, The Right to Inherit, The Open Condition of the Ruin, The Value of Use* and *Emotional Heritage*. Each of these groups related to one of the huge pillars of Le Corderie, which acted as magnets to tables and all the materials.

Drawing with Time

When visiting the exhibition, one of the first tables one would find was dedicated to *Drawing with Time*, a title that referred to documents that have such an intensity that are able to contain and hold together the different layers and moments through which a building has passed. The advantage of working with

Frontispiece: Le Corderie as a stage, collage proposal of drawings, models, photos, containers and films.

Above: An immersive experience. Photo by Adrià Goula.

Bottom Left: Models on legs. Photo by Adrià Goula.

Bottom Right: Scenography taking over the studio, Photo by Judith Casas.

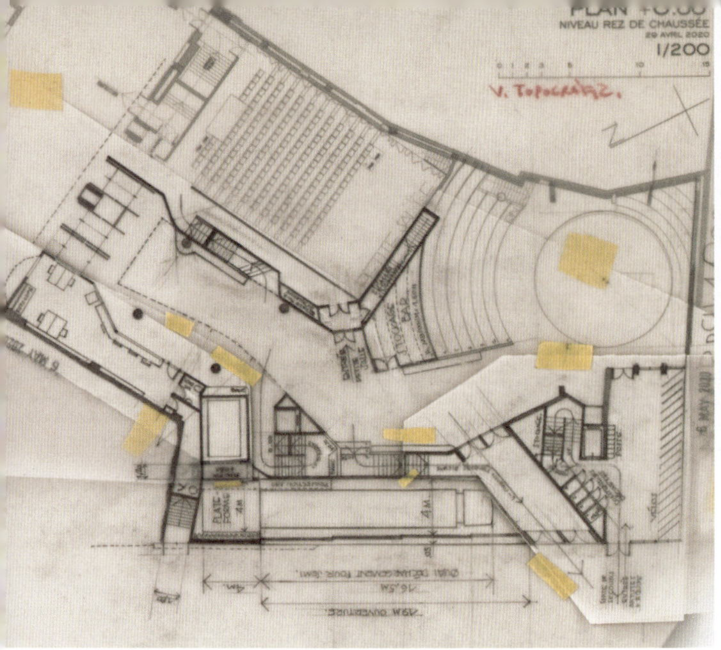

existing buildings, in places where you have not taken part in their creation, is that you can play the role of an observer. You begin by observing ... things made by others, things that you discover as a visitor. In our case, we observe by drawing and recording everything, including what we value and what we do not, until it becomes our own drawing, our own project, which we then begin to modify, adapting the existing to fit the new brief. We are interested in drawing with time, without the need to erase or prioritise one era over another, incorporating the temporal dimension of buildings, not from nostalgia but from memory. Drawing the existing to get to know it is, at the same time, an exercise in making it one's own. In that drawing, the different generations that built it are all expressed at once, and then one realises that drawing, in adaptive reuse, is a collaboration with time.

To discuss this subject, we brought to Venice the Mills Museum of Mallorca, a project where we worked to heighten the existing qualities and geometries of the original building, amplifying them through excavation and the introduction of natural light, to the point that their influence on the whole space was multiplied. The project was born from an old flour mill in Palma, which was later occupied by various Romani families who subdivided it to live in it, opening new doors and windows to the initial ones. The museum adds to all the different lives of the building and does not erase them, leaving the different traces of occupations in sight, and incorporating them into its final state. The drawings of this project contain the original state of the flour mill, the old entrances and exits that we found in the competition process, and the final state of the new mill's museum.

Top Left: *The Open Condition of the Ruin*, Variétés Laboratoire d'Expressions Culturelles, process drawing.

Top Right: Sala Beckett pop-up animated theatre. Photo by Adrià Goula.

The Right to Inherit

Near to the Mills Museum were the tables dedicated to *The Right to Inherit*. If one accepts that each generation has the right to work with what it inherits from those who came before, adapting that legacy to the conditions of current times, then we should accept that the materiality and the history of this legacy — the physical and emotional weight of what is inherited — has the strength to resist design decisions. This forces us to work critically with the conditions we have found, and to understand them and incorporate them until we reach a balance wherein the design actions are not new, but rather the next evolution of what has been found. To discuss this subject, one of the projects we presented was the Casal Balaguer Cultural Centre in Mallorca, developed with Duch-Pizà Arquitectes, a project for a palace with origins in the 14th-century, renovated in the 16th and extended in the 18th, which had to change from a family home to a public building open to the city. Here we worked again with natural light combined with the need to restructure the circulation in a building which had turned into a confusing labyrinth from successive additions, the result of the many generations that had occupied the site. For this new public programme, it was necessary to access previously closed areas, activate abandoned rooms and design an intuitive circulation that would facilitate the understanding of such a complex geometry. We united light and circulation, allowing natural light to guide the route while avoiding the loss of that mystery and spatial complexity that had accompanied the growth of the house. Our approach to the project was accepting the amalgamation of epochs which

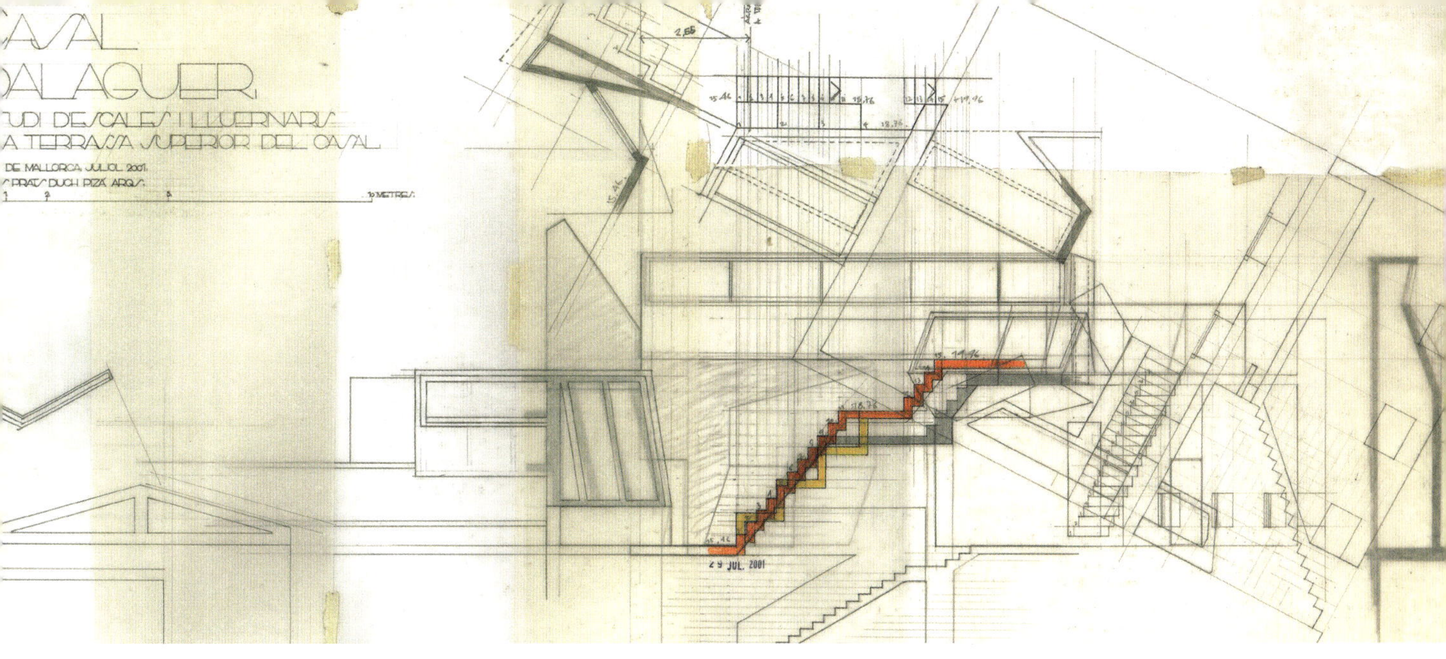

we found in the building as something not to be returned to its original condition. On the contrary, what already existed was drawn on as a starting point for progressing the evolution of the building and its spaces, slowly distorting some things into others, accepting the metamorphosis of certain elements that are transformed as new parts of the programme are added to them.

The Open Condition of the Ruin

The next table at La Biennale contained a project in Brussels which helped us to talk about *The Open Condition of the Ruin.* How much we enjoy the discreet and calm whole of the ruin when we are inside and it presents itself as such, waiting patiently in silence for our evaluation. That ruin, which describes the passage of time in the marks left upon it, does not separate out its different periods; instead, they are joined together, and the building becomes a palimpsest. This timeless character of the ruin opens it to interpretation, allowing us to find that precise moment when we feel an affinity between our own memories and the memories of the place. In the Variétés Cultural Laboratory in Brussels, developed alongside Ouest Architecture, we worked on giving a new use to a 1930s Theatre, a building that has been abandoned for decades. When we first visited it, we all had in mind the programme requested in the brief: two concert halls and a 'forum'—an area where everyone could enter for free, like a covered public square. Seeing the dimensions of the abandoned stage of the original theatre we thought that if we could maintain it intact while introducing the rest of the programme, this space could be the forum. So, the smaller concert hall (for 450 people standing) became the ground of this public space, and the larger one (for 1000 people standing) floating above it.

The Value of Use

For us, the idea of heritage has nothing to do with what is monetarily valuable or monumental, but arises from time and experience, and from what is radically collective. This condition is present in ordinary architecture, accumulated in an infinite number of layers, latent in every detail, ready to reawaken in shared memory. One must keep an attitude of openness and curiosity towards the 'ordinary.' The elements that one could find in an abandoned building; doors, windows, claddings, glazing, cement tiles, and plaster decoration, are often worthless in terms of trade value, but very precious from the perspective of their use-value. To draw these elements and catalogue them is to recognise and learn from their building culture.

One of two projects exhibited to represent this theme was The Sala Beckett / Theatre and Drama Centre, a project in Barcelona where a great effort was made to reuse materials such as doors, windows, tiles, lamps, and everything found at the site, all organised in a large inventory prepared after winning this design competition. The story of Sala Beckett starts with the former workers Cooperative Pau i Justicia that once occupied the site. The most fascinating condition of the original state of this building was the generous scale of its spaces, with almost no columns interrupting them, a quality that worked very well for theatre activity. The applied decoration of mouldings, tiles, glass, roses, mosaics, windows and doors interested us, since they reflected the cultural and social moment in which that building had been created, and had turned these large volumes into a place to enjoy and celebrate free time.

Above: *The Right to Inherit,* Casal Balaguer Cultural Centre, process drawing.

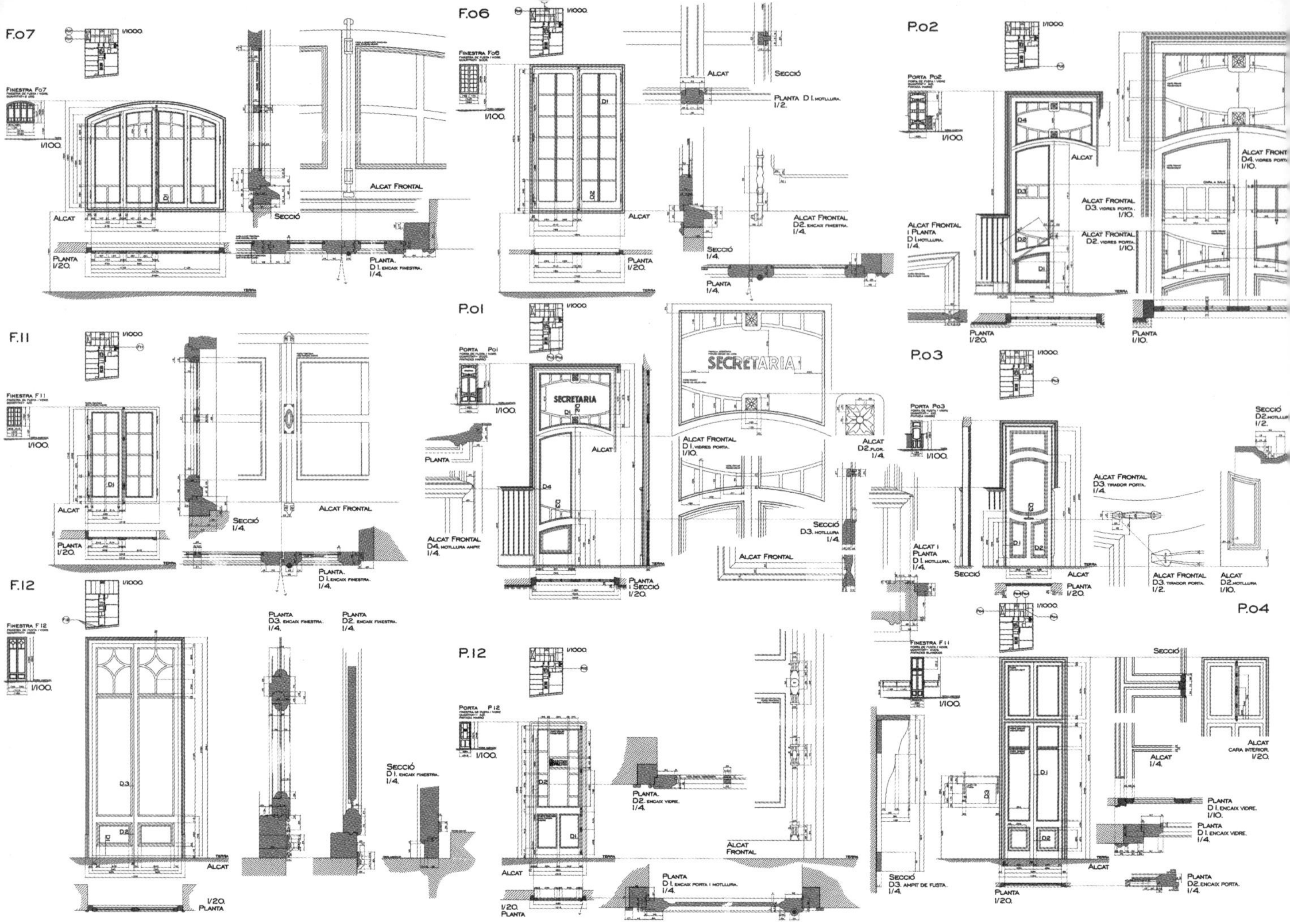

The Cooperative building had no heritage protection. There was no obligation to preserve it, so in the competition designers had to decide whether to keep it or demolish it. This is a design decision of the greatest ideological importance; it is actually the beginning of the project. The building, abandoned for more than twenty years, was still very present in the memory of the neighbours living around it, so this project became about the recovery of social heritage as well as physical heritage. We found a building whose walls and ceilings were full of stories and emotions, scattered with the lives of those who had occupied it for so many years. Those traces and scars on the surfaces of all the spaces formed the atmosphere we wanted for the new drama centre, and became a way to ensure that it would function in a place with accumulated time, already in use before arriving. All the stages through which this construction had passed interested us equally, without hierarchies, and without deciding that one stage was more important than the others: its beginning in 1924, its reform in the 50s, its abandonment in the 80s and 90s, the rain entering through the broken roofs, the pigeons, squatters, the builder's own actions when making the new project. The final result captures the time of the Cooperative, the time of abandonment, and the time of the new Sala Beckett.

Above: *The Value of Use,* The Sala Beckett - Theatre and Drama Centre, inventory of existing carpentry.

Emotional Heritage

The Biennale is a moment of exchange, to learn from the experience and the many reactions from an international community of architects and other visitors. Lesley Lokko's *Laboratory of the Future* reinforced the idea that our imagination is the main tool needed to build a better world, through architecture. The *Emotional Heritage* contribution and its themes were presented at the Biennale with a focus on the craft of making architecture, yet, rather than presenting the projects as closed chapters, they lie open as a process, as an imaginative instrument that uses drawings, models, films... a condition which awakened the curiosity of friends, critics and other visitors to Venice to interrogate and debate. This installation caused pause for thought on the value brought by the "extraordinary slowness" of process as a critical element of these themes and projects, the need for time and space to have the freedom to interpret radical possibilities of appropriation of what we inherit, or, as the architect Cherubino Gambardella noticed, to be able to take risks and not be afraid "to make mistakes."[1]

The representational documents of our studio continue to evolve whether a project is finished or not, to guide this research and continue to engage different audiences in the discussion, to spark free and varied interpretations of the same theme, to create a 'workshop' to debate complex conditions: *Emotional Heritage* tests how to work with what we inherit, with the physical and the emotional heritage of what has reached us, giving space to both the material and immaterial, the personal and social, the past and future.

Top: *The Value of Use*, The Sala Beckett - Theatre and Drama Centre and Yutes Warehouse, documents on the table. Photo by Adrià Goula.

Middle: *The Value of Use*, The Sala Beckett - Theatre and Drama Centre, layers of use in the found condition. Photo by Adrià Goula.

Bottom: Flores & Prats at Le Corderie, *The Laboratory of the Future*, Venice Architecture Biennale 2023. Photo by Adrià Goula.

All drawings and images courtesy of Flores & Prats.

01 Arda Inceoglu, "Biennial Impressions - We're closing in on ourselves," *BI ÖZET*, June 23rd 2023, Turkey; Cherubino Gambardella, "Il futuro dell'architettura. Riflessioni sulla Biennale di Venezia 2023," *EXIBART*, May 27th 2023.

To purchase this and other copies of *Inflection*, please go to Melbourne Books at https://www.melbournebooks.com.au/